BENDING YOUR EAR
a collection of essays on the issues of our times

"There are many things that have occurred and are still occurring in our lives. We view them all through the belief systems we grew up with. Life is about the choices we make and the consequences, good or bad, we encounter. It is seldom when you have someone lay out the case in a way you can understand it. In *Bending Your Ear-a Collection of Essays on the Issues of Our Times*, Drew Nickell lays out many of these events that have occurred, and are occurring in our lives, and shares his belief system on why and how they happen. The practical insights in his messages will give you a commonsense approach so you can make the best choices for you and your life."

—**Dave Sanderson**, Managing Partner, Dave Sanderson Speaks Enterprises, former sales manager with Oracle USA Corporation, author of *Moments Matter* and contributing author of *Brace for Impact*.

"No, you're not crazy, a prude or living in the dark ages if you've reached the point of disillusionment in America. The country was once a child to behold but, as the young nation reaches early adulthood in the eyes of the world, it is eroding with a smart-alecky arrogance, inherited from and enabled by its so-called 'leaders' of late. In his book, *Bending Your Ear-a Collection of Essays on the Issues of Our Times*, Drew Nickell will bend your ear as he unabashedly speaks for the minds of intelligent and principled Americans with a truth and eloquence you may want to emulate the next time you're surrounded by whiny socialists and other opponents of individual freedom, liberty and the true American spirit."

—**Nora Firestone**, author of *The $10,000 Apostrophe*, journalist, and talk-radio host of the *Nora Firestone Show*

"Drew's book, *Bending Your Ear-a Collection of Essays on the Issues of Our Times*, is a thought provoking "must read" before the Presidential election of 2016. Drew's sense of humor and deep insight are brilliant. He masterfully articulates what we should all know...Enjoyable and educational!"

—Bill and Sue Federer, Former US Congressional candidate, Best-selling author of over 20 books, including *What Every American Needs to Know about the Qur'an- A History of Islam & the United States*, host of the *Faith in History* television series, and his inspiration- his wife, Sue Federer, who authored *Miracles in American History*.

"Drew Nickell's new book, *Bending Your Ear-a Collection of Essays on the Issues of Our Times*, is a collection of commentary gleaned from the current news and events of our time. His essays are clear and thought provoking."

—Sgt. Robin Comfort (Retired), U.S. Air Force Tactical Air Command, F-15 Avionics Technician, 1st CRS.

"Drew Nickell is a compelling, thoughtful and prolific writer. Whenever he releases one of his articles, I always take the time to read what he has to say. Drew looks at this troubled world through a different prism and I have come to appreciate his 'take' on life today. You will enjoy this new book, *Bending Your Ear-a Collection of Essays on the Issues of Our Times*. Drew has always been a good and supportive friend, and we both also just happen to be fellow graduates of the greatest high school in Virginia- Douglas Southall Freeman High School in Henrico County!"

—Kathleen Willey, former White House aide (during the Clinton administration), and author of *Target: Caught in the Crosshairs of Bill and Hillary Clinton*.

"I was very impressed with *Bending Your Ear-a Collection of Essays on the Issues of Our Times*. Many times, when I read a book, I'll skip the introduction and go right to the first chapter. Do not skip Drew Nickell's introduction. In it, Drew explains briefly how the advances in technology since the 1970s have resulted in a world with no direction, which leads us to be destructively consumed with denial of what surrounds us. In the collection of essays that makes up *Bending Your Ear*, the book contains beautiful and appropriate references to our history and our Constitution while covering a series of topics such as cultural decline, foreign policy, monsters like President Obama and the United States Congress and political correctness. *Bending Your Ear* concludes with a very appropriate description of the murky future that we all face. *Bending Your Ear* isn't just a book worth reading . . . it is a book that should be used by colleges and universities as a textbook in classes concerning today's political culture."

—**Pat Cardwell**, attorney-at-law specializing in small business, former candidate for Congress in Virginia's 2nd Congressional District, and general counsel of Zippy Shell, Inc.

"In his book, *Bending Your Ear-a Collection of Essays on the Issues of Our Times*, Drew Nickell has his finger in the air and has correctly gauged the winds of our time."

—**Bruce Goodson**, former Chairman of the James City County Board of Supervisors and Delegate to the Republican National Convention in Cleveland.

"Change is definitely inevitable. Throughout his book, *Bending Your Ear- A Collection of Essays on the Issues of Our Times*, Drew Nickell offers specific examples of what is changing in our lives as we used to know it. No matter your political or religious beliefs, this book is beyond enlightening. If you've ever said to yourself, 'What is happening to this world?' then this is something you must read. Such an eye-opening read!!"

—Danny Hewitt, best-selling author of *This is How We HEWITT*, and co-founder of Liberty Tax and Franchise Enterprise

"*Bending Your Ear-a Collection of Essays on the Issues of Our Times* by Drew Nickell proves to be a refreshing take on various political and social issues facing our country today. So often our media sources and written sources come from the left of center, it is refreshing to read the commentary from a centered author. His profound common sense and clear understanding of our current events unfolding in real time lets the reader gain a down-to-earth perspective on both politics and society. He clearly demonstrates his gift of critical thinking in his essays. Both perspectives are displayed in a way that cannot be ignored by the reader, leaving us to draw our own conclusions based on the wealth of information he has provided on both fronts. For these reasons, I highly endorse this book. Readers stand to benefit greatly from reading his very profound and thought-provoking commentary on our world today. I thoroughly enjoy and look forward to his essays regularly. This book is a winner . . . without question!"

—Anita Farries Kessler, former deputy sheriff, City of Norfolk, Va., currently college instructor and Department Head, Constitutional Law & Psychology, Centura College-Chesapeake (VA) Campus

All that Rendered Trump
and what led up to his election

a reprint of

Bending Your Ear:
A Collection of Essays on the Issues of our Times

by Drew Nickell

ISBN: 978-1-953278-05-0 Soft Back
ISBN: 978-1-953278-06-7 E-Book

Published by

 IndignorHouse

Chesapeake, VA 23322
www.indignorhouse.com

All that Rendered Trump

and what led up to his election

Drew Nickell

CHESAPEAKE, VA

For Mary Ella,
who encouraged me from the very start

Table of Contents

Introduction

All That Rendered Trump (and what led up to his election) was originally published in the summer of 2016, as Bending Your Ear—a Collection of Essays on the Issues of Our Times, and was comprised of essays written in the years 2010 to early 2016—before Donald Trump won the Republican nomination and, ultimately, the presidency, later that fall. What was then considered to be "contemporary commentary" has become since, a point-in-time retrospective look into the personalities, political and cultural upheavals taking place- forces which set the stage for Donald Trump's election, and why his election was the direct result of these same forces. Therefore, what follows must be viewed in the context of the times in which it was written. As such, there may be a few instances where certain passages have since been proved otherwise. As in all things, the passage of time can allow us to see things more clearly than before. So, take a moment to time travel back to a period of time before there even was a President Donald Trump... and maybe, just maybe, you will see that his election seems almost pre-ordained...

...and just to let you know. a follow-up to this volume, which discusses his election and his presidency, right up through the 2020 re-election campaign, will be coming out soon, so please be on the lookout for What Trump Hath Wrought (since his uncanny election), due for release in early 2021.

(original introduction to Bending Your Ear- a Collection of Essays on the Issues of Our Times)

SITTING IN MISS JORDAN'S first period Senior Government class in the spring of 1977, I knew that in a few months, I would leave Douglas Southall Freeman High School forever. My naïve and inexperienced eyes looked toward a murky and distant future, with absolutely no idea as to whether I would live to be fifty (seems I passed that one) or how my life, our lives, would forever change. It was an awkward time to grow up, in the grand scheme of things, and I thought then, as I do now, that ours would be the generation struggling for identity. After all, it was our parents who had survived the Great Depression and a World War that spanned the entire globe and defeated the Axis forces bent on world domination. It was our older siblings that ushered in the era of rock and roll, civil rights, assassination, the Cold War, Vietnam and campus unrest. Compared to these generations, ours seemed filled with a very real sense of denouement. To what would we lay claim? Watergate? Carter? Tylenol tampering? Son of Sam? *Disco*? Give me a break! It's pretty lame stuff by comparison, wouldn't you say? Back then, our biggest concern was that our moms might find our baggies and flush the stuff down the toilet, or our dads would ask us what the hell we were doing with rolling papers and roach clips. Our hair was bigger, our clothes were smaller, our music was better, and our cars were worse . . . but we had no way of knowing any of this back then.

Now, forty odd years hence, we have been "internet-ed," "cell-phoned," "cable-visioned," "Clinton-ed," "Bush-ed," "Obama-ed," "terrorist-ed," and spied upon by our neighbors, our own cars (for cryin' out loud), our employers, and our government ad nauseam, and what do we have to show for it? Shrinking retirement accounts, devaluation of our homes (if we have managed to hang on to them), waylaid careers, and, aside from the virtual connections of Facebook and twitter (whatever the hell that is), the absence of any real sense of interpersonal connection in ways we used to understand this concept. Our kids grew up with video games and virtual reality, knowing nothing of hopscotch, kick-the-can, or German dodgeball. They never learned how to play army, or cowboys and Indians (or "doctor" LOL), because these pretend games became politically incorrect. Never mind the fact they can indulge themselves in the bloodlust-filled games of "Warcraft" and "Grand Theft Auto" . . . go figure. They have traded our peashooters, our squirt guns, our water balloons and our slingshots for their assault weapons . . . so much for not allowing them to have cap guns when they were young.

Today, those of us who grew up in the '70s are now entering the "autumn of the years," as Sinatra used to sing, having no idea (still) of where we are headed. We have a firm sense of our innate goodness, still have a very good sense of right and wrong, and we all have the shared desire for the prosperity of our offspring. Yet in a very real sense, the passage of these last decades has clouded our vision, figuratively and literally, and filled us with much angst about a collective future that we either get destructively consumed with or outright dismiss in naïve attempts of denial. Ask me not the answer, my friends, for it's tough enough for me to know even the questions anymore.

What follows is a collection of essays which provide my commentary on the issues of our times, written during the course of five years and categorized by subject chapters appearing within. At the top of each essay will appear the dates in which they were written, and these will be sorted within each chapter in the chronological order they were written. So have a seat, get comfortable, and allow me to bend your ear, so to speak. I promise it will be one helluva ride.

Drew Nickell

Part I
Persistent Problems

Chapter 1

Cultural Decline

Ray Rice, a Sordid Example of Domestic Violence

8 September 2014

First, I offer a disclaimer. I am a lifelong Baltimore football fan, a fan of the Baltimore Colts from the time I was old enough to recognize a football through the 1983 season (their last in Baltimore), a fan of Baltimore's CFL Stallions in 1994-95, and a diehard fan of the Ravens since 1996. My loyalty to Baltimore football knows no bounds, as anyone who knows me can readily attest. In the autumn of each year, my blood turns purple and remains that way until the Ravens have played their final game of every season, and my mood on Mondays is almost solely dependent on how the Ravens have fared the Sunday before.

As a diehard Baltimore fan, I want to share my thoughts of the video showing Ray Rice punching his then-fiancé (they have since married) in an Atlantic City elevator, as well as the NFL's response to his specific offense, and their policy of treating similar offenses going forward. In a word, I am as disgusted with Ray Rice personally, as I am with the management of the Baltimore Ravens and the National Football League in how they dealt with this situation.

There is nothing new about male athletes treating women badly. All of us have memories of scholastic and collegiate "jocks" pressing their advantage with female coeds and the comparative lack of consequences vetted towards these miscreants. Every year we read about allegations of sexual and physical assaults perpetrated by athletes of every sport against women at all levels of athletic competition, and it seems that the more noteworthy the athletic prowess of the perpetrator, the more notorious the offense, and the more feckless the consequence.

Not that I would ever be able to dream of being a billionaire owner of a National Football League franchise, but I can tell you this without equivocation. Were I Steven Bisciotti, owner of the Baltimore Ravens, I would have summarily fired Ray Rice when the first video appeared showing him dragging his fiancé out of the elevator, regardless of whether the team went on to win another Super Bowl or finished the ensuing season 0-16, and I would have done so faster than the team mascot can utter a "caw-caw." Were I Roger Goodell, the Commissioner of the National Football League, I would have put into place a policy which banned for life any player, coach, or member of team management who perpetrated such an offense the FIRST time it occurred. Were I John Harbaugh, the head coach of the Ravens, I would have refused to allow Rice to take part in any practice or play in any game, even if it meant my job being lost as a result.

Until such time as we cease and desist, from mollycoddling these overpaid egomaniacs that play a child's game for salaries that have well passed the very point of being ludicrous, we will continue to see, year after year, similar occurrences as we have too often become too far accustomed to seeing. Until, at the scholastic levels, we see a wholesale change in the way high school athletes are allowed to cheat on exams, take advantage of their female classmates, and display violent and disruptive behavior without punishment, there will never be the reintroduction of good sportsmanship and character-building that athletic competition once instilled, and professional sports will ultimately suffer under the weight of its own excess, as a result of not taking a more strenuous stance on the behavior of athletes on the field, in the locker rooms, in the off-season, and in their very own homes, as well. In the meantime, Go Ravens!

Today's Youth, Tomorrow's Nightmare

21 May 2015

Last weekend while visiting Las Vegas to attend a niece's wedding, I managed to catch a glimpse of the twenty-somethings who will one day be running the remains of what used to be the country of our own youth. Needless to say, I came away less than encouraged by that which I saw.

Generational fears of generational progeny are nothing new. My grandparents doubtlessly shook their heads when watching their children jitterbug to the sounds of Tommy Dorsey. Then I watched as my father was convinced, on the night of February 9ʰ 1964, that the entire world was "going to hell" because of four "mop tops" clad in suits and ties, mind you, who were preforming on *The Ed Sullivan Show*. Later on, we shook our own heads when our own children began *Keeping up with the Kardashians*, and I thought to myself, "What the f---?" These are all cultural phenomena, stretched across four generations, but this is not what I am referring to when discussing what it is that I fear from these twenty-somethings today. No, not by a long shot.

I took the opportunity to go to breakfast at 5:00 a.m., PDT, largely because I was still operating on east coast time, we usually eat breakfast around 8:00 a.m., EDT, and hadn't made the adjustment. In the hotel's restaurant, a place called the "Hash House," I noticed bunches of twenty-somethings staggering in, some of whom (the girls) were dressed up like "hoes" and some of whom (the guys) were dressed up as "gangstas"—but, again, it wasn't their dress, nor their excessive use of cosmetics, nor their elongated beards, nor their baggy clothing that I found so disturbing—it was their behavior. They acted precisely the way they dressed: staggering into the restaurant, pouring liquor out of their own bottles into paper cups, dropping the "f-bombs" loudly and with such frequency as to outnumber all of the other words spoken in between, and falling out of their chairs where they sat, or attempted to sit.

Mind you, these were not the poor, unwashed unfortunates that one might find on city streets all over the country, but young adults staying at a pricey Las Vegas hotel, presumably on their parents' dime, celebrating the end of their spring semesters in college. Just listening to their conversations conveyed that these were not educated college students exploring the world of adulthood, but rather indoctrinated narcissists pushing the limits, as if doing so were the veritable ends in and of themselves. Many of these (forgive the term) kids sported a king's ransom in ink on their skin and a pharaoh's treasure of all sorts of implements piercing their faces, as one might pierce a pin cushion. The thought occurred to me that once out of school, these kids would stand about as much of a chance getting a decent job as I would in making the Baltimore Ravens' active roster in my mid-fifties.

These are the kids that have come of age believing they are entitled to all that life has to offer by sheer virtue of their having been born. They have cruised through schools without having learned. They have slid through college without having been tested, and they have done so as the result of student loans, for which they fully expect to be excused, and/or their parents' largesse for which they are unappreciative. Work? Hell, they have never done hard work and don't expect to either. Patriotism? That's an idea that is now out of date, politically incorrect, and something associated with white racists and senile old people of all races. Responsibility? Yeah, right. Respect? They call each other "niggah" and "bitch" with no regard to those who stand and sit in immediate proximity.

In other words, in their world, others do not matter, and when society has sunk to a place where others do not matter, then society has sunk to a point of no return, which is why I find trouble sleeping at night, for fear of all that tomorrow might well bring.

In short, we as a society are imperiled from our own excess and the lack of responsibility that all of us should have otherwise imparted onto the children we raised.

The Slippery Slope of Unintended Consequences

29 June 2015

"Congress shall make no law respecting an establishment of religion, or prohibiting the free exercise thereof; or abridging the freedom of speech, or of the press; or the right of the people peaceably to assemble, and to petition the Government for a redress of grievances."

—First Amendment to the Constitution of the United States, 1789

"The powers not delegated to the United States by the Constitution, nor prohibited by it to the States, are reserved to the States respectively, or to the people."
—Tenth Amendment to the Constitution of the United States, 1789

Anyone familiar with the Constitution of the United States is doubtlessly aware of the Bill of Rights, a set of ten amendments whose purpose was to limit the power of government as it relates to the lives of the people. The first of these amendments, as referenced above, in essence guarantees the freedom of thought as well as the freedom to express such thought. While we cannot delve into the mindset of the founding fathers who believed this first amendment to be of primary importance (those that followed were set down in the order of importance), it is noteworthy that the freedom *of* religion (*not* the freedom *from* religion as is often stated by contemporary "liberals," especially those opposed to organized religion) was and is listed first and foremost, before the freedoms of speech, press, assembly, and petition that follow.

Elsewhere in the Constitution lies the framework of our federal government, essentially a three-part institution, with a delicate balance of powers shared by the three branches: a legislative branch (i.e. the House and the Senate) which enacts laws, an administrative branch (i.e. the President and the Cabinet) that enforces laws, and a judiciary branch (i.e., the Supreme Court), which rules on the constitutionality of laws; at least, that's the way it's supposed to be.

With regards to the latter branch of government, specifically, it is the job of the Supreme Court to determine the constitutionality of laws, but not to violate the Constitution's delegated powers (Tenth Amendment) and enumerated powers (Article 1, Section 8) by writing laws that do not exist. Nor does the Constitution allow the Federal Government to enact laws reserved for the States. Yet when the judiciary takes on the trappings of the legislative, then justice is the first casualty in a democracy. The second casualty is the rule of law, and the third casualty is the will of the people.

Nowhere in the Constitution does it authorize the Supreme Court to change the meaning of specific laws as they are explicitly stated (i.e., the Affordable Care Act, which specifically refers to "exchanges established by the States," meaning the fifty states, and *not* the state, meaning a general reference to government). Nowhere in the Constitution does it authorize the federal government to determine what marriage is or what constitutes marriage and, alas, who may or may not marry. Such "delegated powers" are reserved to the States in accordance with the tenth amendment.

Last week, the Supreme Court effectively overturned the Tenth Amendment by usurping these powers away from the several States in its two rulings on ACA (Obamacare) and on gay marriage. Some of the States have set up exchanges, some others have not, and the Supreme Court has essentially said, "It doesn't matter; we will force this on all the states to operate as though the exchanges are set up."

Likewise, some of the States have enacted laws providing for legal marriage between members of the same sex, while other States have enacted laws saying that marriage is defined as one man, one woman (just as President Clinton's "Defense of Marriage Act" says). Last week, the Supreme Court effectively disintegrated the DOMA, while also taking the power away from the States (who by the way, issue marriage licenses) to make this determination, all without the constitutional authority to do so.

In the case of the latter ruling, those who support the Supreme Court's decision cite the Fourteenth Amendment, Section One, which states:

"All persons born or naturalized in the United States, and subject to the jurisdiction thereof, are citizens of the United States and of the State wherein they reside. No State shall make or enforce any law which shall abridge the privileges or immunities of citizens of the United States; nor shall any State deprive any person of life, liberty, or property, without due process of law; nor deny to any person within its jurisdiction the equal protection of the laws."

Such an argument is fallacious and specious, because marriage is not a right, but rather a licensed enterprise, like the license to drive or to own a pet, or to practice law or medicine, and the States hold the right to determine the requirements for licensure, not the federal government.

Worse, in doing this, the Supreme Court has now opened the door for those who wish to make these same claims, as have lesbians and homosexuals, to demand marital rights for bigamists or polygamists. We are already hearing calls to force churches and synagogues, under the threats of tax exemption revocation, to either permit gays to marry or to lose these financially imperative tax exemptions. Such moves will effectively destroy the first freedom in the First Amendment, the freedom of religion, which would be just fine with atheists and agnostics, but would trample upon the rights of believers to practice their religion as they deem fit.

This is the slippery slope of unintended consequences, which imperils all of us and lays credence to the belief that we have arrived upon the dreaded point in time where our most precious and sacred rights are under attack by the special interests of the few, who would gladly take these rights away from us and then laugh all of the way to the perdition they seek.

The Bitter Harvest (-ing)

30 July 2015

Perhaps the most difficult of lingering issues which politicians are loathed to discuss, due to the extremes of emotions associated with both sides of the debate, is the legacy of *Roe vs. Wade,* which bedevils all of us forty-two years hence. For Americans who argue either side of the issue, there is little room for equivocation because it is in the final analysis a life and death issue, not so much for the mother in most cases, but for that of the unborn child.

Those who favor unrestricted access to abortion can and do euphemistically dismiss their advocacy of abortion as "pro-choice," even though the most grievously affected person, whose very life is terminated, is denied such choice. Referring the unborn child as "a fetus," while clinically sound, is merely another way of objectifying a human being in an attempt to dismiss the central argument of life itself, an absolute right to life that is specifically listed in this country's founding document, the Declaration of Independence. Juvenile attempts to justify all instances of abortion, due to the comparatively rare cases of "rape and incest," are also a convenient dodge since such cases are merely a fraction of one percent of all abortions performed in the United States. Similar attempts at such justification, based on vague concepts of the mother's health, are merely rationalizations of the procedure, which are all too easily contrived by doctors performing the procedures, rather than empirical medical realities. An expectant mother whose life or health is *truly* endangered by her pregnancy is by far the rare exception, as opposed to the oft-cited frequency (still a vast minority) of instances so contrived by doctors who have a financial incentive to do so. In the end, it is an inescapable and undeniable conclusion that well over 95% of abortions are merely elective procedures, purely based upon convenience and economics, rather than medical realities. But don't tell this to a "pro-choicer," lest you be labeled as engaging in a war on women. Regardless of the position one takes on the issue of abortion, the recent videos of officials of Planned Parenthood dismissively discussing the marketing of organs harvested from aborted babies should make *everyone* step back from the central issue of abortion and consider the ghoulish implications associated with such callous dialogues. Planned Parenthood, taxpayer-funded to the tune of $500 million per year, is the largest provider of abortions in the United States, and despite what proponents say about the other services this organization provides, Planned Parenthood derives the lion's share of its revenue by performing abortions. The mere fact that taxpayers, the majority of whom are opposed to *unrestricted* abortion, pay to prop up this business is ludicrous enough, but the fact that such funds support an entity which would harvest infantile organs for resale on the open market is monstrous to an extent not seen in decades. Those doctors, one of whom is seen sipping wine and casually discussing such marketing, along with brainstorming ideas of how to make such procedures "less crunchy" so as to preserve the viability of such harvested organs, are nothing more than the modern day equivalent of Nazi Dr. Josef Mengele. Ironically, when President Obama recently praised such activities of Planned Parenthood as "performing God's work," it reminds us all that the Nazis once used those precise words to justify the slaughter of millions in concentration camps across eastern Europe.

Setting aside for the moment the primary issue of terminating lives of many millions of babies who are denied their right to live, do we really, as freedom-loving and life-respecting Americans, want to continue to support and abide the monstrous and bitter harvesting of body parts by any organization, particularly one so endowed with government largesse? For those of you who would say "yes" to this question, I challenge you to look at these videos and answer to yourself alone as to whether or not this is truly a good thing, regardless of whether or not you would say so publicly. While you are doing so, consider your own humanity and how precious you view your own life, and then decide for yourself if you or anyone else truly has the right to determine whether or not another person has the opportunity to live when such a person is not afforded to be party to such an existential decision.

When Too Far Is Too Far

25 August 2015

(Full disclosure- I was initiated into Sigma Nu Fraternity at Virginia Wesleyan College in February of 1978 and then affiliated with the Chapter at James Madison University in the Fall of 1979)

Most of us have seen the pictures of bed sheets hanging from the balcony of a Norfolk, Virginia Sigma Nu fraternity house. One says, "Rowdy and Fun, Hope Your Baby Girl is Ready for a Good Time", while another reads, "Freshman Daughter Drop-Off" with an arrow pointing to the house's front door, and the third reads, "Go Ahead and Drop Off Mom, Too."

In a word, lame.

When the world was young and I was both young and stupid, it was a tradition for college men to sit on a wall at Virginia Wesleyan College and watch the arrival of freshman coeds as they moved into campus dorms. Occasionally, a whistle was sounded, or a comment was made as to the co-ed's looks, but never anything "over the top," as has been expressed in these bed sheets. Sometimes, as a means to break the ice and draw some degree of favor from the young women, I and my frat brothers would offer to help carry in their belongings, which generally delighted their parents. In other words while, yes, what we did could be construed as "ogling" by today's politically correct mores, it really was an expression of curiosity, given the fact that Virginia Wesleyan College was a very small school back in the 1970s, and everyone on campus knew practically everyone else. Still, it could be argued that the college men were "checking out" the new arrivals.

So be it. I'll plead guilty.

The difference is that, back then, I knew where to draw the line . . .

Thirty-eight years later, I marvel at how times have changed and, in many ways, I fear for the worse. It is indeed ironic that in today's culture, where sexual harassment (that wasn't even a term in the mid-1970s) is constantly talked about, written about, "policy-ed" about, etc., etc., that some undergraduate men think that such over-the-top displays, as evidenced at Old Dominion University, are funny.

In a word, they're not.

The problem is maturity or, in reality, the lack of maturity on the part of the miscreants. Let's face it. Young college students caught in the cusp between adolescence and adulthood can and will do stupid things, like the time I kicked a football some thirty-five yards through a second story, plate glass window. I went straight to the building and grounds superintendent, told him of my "career placekick" and I was rewarded with a reprieve for being honest THAT time. (I never made a second attempt). Still, it was pretty stupid, to say the least.

While it can be argued that the sheets hung from the frat house balcony, in and of themselves, caused no harm per se, the fact that they were hung at all speaks volumes about a general lack of respect that these fraternity members showed toward the young women, their parents, their school, their fraternity, and, in truth, themselves. While suspending the fraternity chapter (as opposed to the actual guilty parties) may seem a bit draconian, the school's president and the national fraternity were correct in bringing swift action against the chapter, which has besmirched college fraternities in general and Sigma Nu in particular.

I would ask every young man entering college today that he be mindful of the way he treats the opposite sex, and that he would do well to remember his own sister, his mother, and looking ahead, his daughter as well, when expressing himself. Never would the "golden rule" have a more fitting place than in such a situation.

So, to our fraternity brothers, I'll simply say, "Grow up and act like men, REAL men. Otherwise, your alumni are going to have to pull out the proverbial paddle and tan your hides!"

The Slippery Slope of Cultural Decline

28 August 2015

Nobody wants to own up to it, much less discuss it. Yet, it seems so tangible that we can almost smell it in the air, taste it in our mouths, and feel it in our bones. It is the slippery slope of cultural decline that is painfully obvious, painful to the point of denial and obvious to the point of certainty.

Think about it.

Our culture, collectively speaking, that is, has gradually, yet undeniably been in decline for the last century, to the extent one could almost plot it on a graph. As time has passed, the culture in which we live has regressed to the point where we are close, very close, to hitting the skids.

Case in point: Times Square.

In 1900, a woman exposing her stockinged ankle, her ANKLE, mind you, could be arrested, as many were, for indecent exposure. Today, while we shake our heads at such draconian, such Victorian attitudes and standards of decency, in 2015 women are parading around the same Times Square baring their painted breasts and charging money for posed pictures, albeit without any censure or citation. In fact, Sunday, August 23rd was declared "National Go Topless Day," encouraging women all over the country to bare their breasts under the rationalization and contrived aegis of "equality." For those of us who came of age in the 1970s, such an initiative would not have been possible in our wildest and weirdest fantasies, and for our parents who disdained women trotting about in public *sans brassiere,* not even considered within the remotest realm of possibility.

Case in point: Popular Music and Dancing.

With the arrival of the "Jazz Age" in the 1920s, replete with flappers donning hemlines above the knees for the first time, much was made at the time about the perceived indecency of the music and new dances, such as "the Charleston." In the 1940s, men wearing oversized "zoot suits" jitterbugging to the tunes of Duke Ellington and Cab Calloway caused an actual and deadly riot in Los Angeles. In the 1950s, television cameras would not show images of Elvis Presley's hips due to the suggestive nature of his gyrations. In the 1960s, parents of baby boomers bemoaned the mop tops of the Beatles when they appeared on *The Ed Sullivan Show*, and this quartet was wearing dress suits! Go to a dance club today, and one can easily find young people "grinding" one another in a way their parents would describe "dry humping" in the back seat of an automobile a generation before. One only needs to compare the lyrics of Cole Porter to the lyrics often found in rap music to see a vast difference in what is seen as appropriate for public consumption.

These are but two examples of cultural decline. There are many more examples, enough to fill a book, but the point is sufficiently made, nevertheless.

It is indeed a vast dichotomy to consider that, given all of the technical, scientific, medical, and informational advances made since the turn of the century, our culture has taken an absolute nose dive into the abyss of what constitutes acceptable behavior, and this dive doesn't seem to be abating anytime soon. Just as the arrival of the internet promised to bring all of us closer together, it did the polar opposite as people today seem to be more isolated from one another than ever before. There are even cases of young people having "texting dates" where they sit across from one another, texting back and forth without a spoken word. Call us crazy, but if that had been the norm when we were dating back in the 1970s, there would have been no romantic progression past the first date, not to this writer, in anyevent.

History tells us that, time and time again, societies which have experienced extended periods of cultural decline have presaged their own eventual self-destruction, and anyone who believes that contemporary cultural decline will not repeat this eventuality knows neither their history nor their destiny. As William Shakespeare once wrote in act II, scene I of *The Tempest*, "what's past is prologue," and we are speedily sliding down the slippery slope of our own demise.

Chapter 2

Domestic Policy

Apathy and How It Will Destroy Us

17 June 2014

Prior to my current position supporting indirect agents selling wireline services for a major telecommunications carrier, I made my living as a sales representative for seventeen years. Having met in the tens of thousands of potential customers in those years, I came to understand that the most difficult prospects were the apathetic customers, the ones who just didn't care. I learned that it was far easier to overcome the objections of a hostile prospect, meeting his discrepancies head on, than it was dealing with a prospect who couldn't care less either way.

Whether politics is a microcosm of or an extension of life in general, it surely is bedeviled by the very same phenomena of apathy. All of us know countless others who say, "I'm just not interested in politics," or "I just don't know the issues," or "My vote doesn't matter," or "One's just as bad as the other, so why bother?"

Looking around the world, it has always irritated me immensely that in countries such as Iraq and Afghanistan, where voting is potentially and truly a life-threatening enterprise, voter turnout as a percentage of the enfranchised electorate is actually much higher than here in the United States, where, save for a precinct or two in Philadelphia, voters can cast their ballots without any harassment whatsoever. This is symptomatic of an electorate that just doesn't seem to care, and that, ladies and gentlemen, is the thing upon which our future as a free and independent nation lies in grave peril.

Save for a few momentary spikes, voter participation in the United States has been very much a declining enterprise over the past decades, which amazes me, given the struggles over the course of two centuries we encountered to bring suffrage to, in chronological order, first, white males who did not own land, then black and native American males, then women, then people who refused to pay a poll tax or could not pass a proficiency test, and finally, people between the ages of eighteen and twenty-one. For reasons I cannot begin to surmise, each and every time the United States expanded suffrage, the percentage of eligible voters actually voting has eventually declined.

Now, it is true that when a particular voting sector has an external stimulus to be so motivated, electoral outcomes can be affected, and the inevitable results often reflect this. The Great Depression of 1929 moved voters to elect Franklin Roosevelt in 1932, when millions of unemployed were motivated to make a change perceived to be in their favor. In 1960, a very handsome young Senator from Massachusetts motivated women to come out, as never before, and pull the lever for Jack Kennedy. With the first post-World War II baby boomer to lead a presidential ticket, baby boomers were motivated to pull the lever for Bill Clinton in 1992, in what turned out to be a battle of a younger generation opposing a candidate of their parents' generation. There is no question that the presence of the very first African American on a major party ticket motivated African Americans to come out to the polls in record numbers to elect Barack Obama president. Rest assured that it is entirely possible that the nomination of a woman to lead the ticket of a major party would motivate many women, who might not otherwise do so, to vote in 2016, or so Hillary hopes.

In other words, a motivated electorate can and will affect the outcome of an election even if, retrospectively, as with the case of our current president, the choice proves to be a bad one. That is the inherent problem of identity politics. For example, when a voter votes against someone solely because of their race, they are labeled "racist." Yet, when someone votes *for* someone solely because of their race, isn't that just as racist? And wouldn't the same be true when it comes to a candidate's sex? Throw in media manipulation and their inherent partisan bias, and that's where things can become truly murky. Say that Republicans were to nominate an African American woman, like Condoleezza Rice, to head the GOP ticket in 2016. I largely doubt that the media would advocate for her, as they did for Obama or potentially would for Hillary, despite the fact that Ms. Rice is vastly more qualified, more intelligent, and more independently accomplished than either Mr. Obama or Mrs. Clinton.

With all of these cross currents, it is no wonder that voters can and do become averse to participating in a broken political process. Yet it remains just as true that, given the wreckage America has suffered here at home, across our borders, and around the world, the election of 2016 is perhaps the most important election in the history of our country, because it will largely determine whether we reverse the failures of these last seven years or continue down the road to our own demise, and that is where apathy can and will destroy the nation as we know it.

Borders

9 July 2014

bor·der \'bȯr-dər\ n. 1. the part or edge of a surface or area that forms its outer boundary; 2. the line that separates one country, state, province, etc., from another; frontier line: i.e., One cannot cross the border without a visa; 3. the district or region that lies along the boundary line of another; 4. the frontier of civilization; 5. the border: i.e., the border between the U.S. and Mexico, especially along the Rio Grande (source dictionary.com)

It is often said that America is a nation of immigrants. Even Native Americans migrated from Asia to the land that eventually became the United States, centuries before Europeans first arrived. America has always been the place to which people come, and all for the same reason.

Exactly twenty years prior to the very day my mother was born, my grandfather arrived on Ellis Island in 1901, having immigrated to this country from a small village in Sicily, at the age of ten with exactly twenty-five cents in his pocket. He was accompanied only by his older brother (who was twelve years old), as an "installment." In those days, the father would come over with the eldest son, work here in America to save up enough money for the second installment of his family, and then the third, and so on, until at last my great-grandmother came with this youngest member of their family, a process that took eight years to complete. Their story was repeated millions of times during the years 1892-1954 by people from all parts of the world who came here in search of a better life than they had experienced in the places they left behind. They worked hard, learned to speak English, and assimilated into a new and emerging American culture, leaving the trappings of their old country behind. Every single individual who was admitted through this port of entry did so legally.

"Legally." *That* is the real issue of immigration. A country without borders is *not* a country, plain and simple, as the definition above clearly states. Politicizing the issue of immigration is nothing new. The "copperheads" of the 1850s did their level best to discourage Irish immigration (including my father's maternal grandparents). Then as my mother's father was immigrating, there were all types of concerns regarding immigrants from southern and eastern Europe. Politicians have also exploited the new arrivals, promising all sorts of jobs and benefits in exchange for votes which kept them in office (i.e., Tammany Hall). History substantiates the fact that such exploitation has been the exclusive purview of the Democratic Party going back well into the 19th Century.

Today, we have many politicians from the very same Democratic Party wishing to exploit immigrants from our southern borders, in the very same manner. "Come here, we'll take care of you, we'll give you low paying jobs and medical care and education for your children, all to a greater degree than you will get from your homes in Mexico and Central America" seems to be the mantra from far too many of these leftist opportunists who really don't give a damn about their country, but rather their precious office seats, instead. The difference nowadays is that these politicians couldn't care less whether these immigrants come here within or outside the law. They smugly know that somehow, these poor people will eventually become voters, citizenship not necessary, not really, not eventually; their precinct cronies will see to that. "If they bring communicable diseases, so what? We have got the Affordable Care Act (Obamacare). That'll handle it." Meanwhile, the humanitarian crisis taking place in California, Arizona, New Mexico, and Texas continues on at an accelerated place, "but don't blame Obama – it's George Bush's fault." George Bush's fault for signing legislation passed by both Houses of Congress (at the time, both houses in the control of Democrats) as a means to stop child sex trafficking. Never underestimate the power of liberals to play the part of that hockey goalie, which fends off every shot and blames it on the GOP.

And yet, while the problem festers in the real world, a world created by Barack Obama and his continued refusal to enforce immigration law, thus turning our U.S. Border Patrol into a vast day-care center, the President couldn't give enough of a damn to even visit the beleaguered border, opting instead to raise money for his party in Texas on this very day. He is exploiting this crisis, and the unfortunate children pouring across the border, in an effort to secure more money from Congress without bothering to include in his request funding necessary to better secure the border, all because he didn't get the "Dream Act" he wanted, and all because he hasn't gotten the immigration reforms that he wants, the kind of reforms that will only ensure more voter registrants to Democratic party, borders be damned. In essence, our borders will never be secure until such time as the "boarders" at 1600 Pennsylvania Avenue have relocated, thus ending another example of how President Barack Hussein Obama is in direct violation of his oath of office by refusing to uphold the Constitution, the laws of his country, and common decency.

The Coming Pandemic

2 August 2014

Pandemic—(n) an epidemic occurring on a scale which crosses international boundaries, usually affecting a large number of people. (Source: "Dictionary of Epidemiology," Oxford University Press, p. 179. Copyright 2012)

It is often said that what we don't know can be deadly, and while humanity is always under the threat of extinction, be it from an unthinkable nuclear war, the strike of a large meteor on the surface of the earth, a gamma ray burst, or the eruption of a caldera which would result in a years-long blockage of sunlight, it is the microscopic world of viruses that pose the biggest threat to humanity.

Pandemics are nothing new. In 430 BC, a pandemic of typhoid fever wiped out 25% of Athens. Smallpox took the lives of as many as ten million during two outbreaks in the second and third centuries AD. Beginning in 541 AD and lasting until 750 AD, the first pandemic of bubonic plague wiped out 25% of the known world population and resulted in a 50% decline of the population in Europe. More infamously, it was the second wave of bubonic plague that killed 75 million people, beginning in the fourteenth century. Known as the Black Death, as much as a third of the world's population was completely wiped out during a six-year period, 1348-54 AD, and repeated waves of this plague continued to eviscerate as much as 50% of the European populace, up until the Great Fire of London in 1666, which virtually eradicated the disease in that city. Another wave of the bubonic plague hit China in 1855, spread to India, and killed an additional 10 million. Bubonic plague even hit San Francisco in the six years leading up to that city's devastating earthquake in 1906, killing many thousands.

Smallpox, brought by Spanish conquistadores in the 1500s, virtually wiped out the native populations of Central America in the decades that followed, the same smallpox that killed off 90% of the Native Americans in the Massachusetts Bay Colony in the mid-1600s. Recurrences of smallpox, along with influenza and measles, ravaged the Plains Indian tribes in the mid-to-late 1800s and killed millions around the world, as well.

More recently, the Spanish flu pandemic of 1918-1919 infected 500 million people across the world in a brief eighteen-month period and killed some 50 million during a six-month period during the height of its devastation, more than were killed in the First World War that was just ending when this pandemic began.

Respectively, outbreaks of Asian flu in the late 1950s and Hong Kong flu in the late 1960s killed three million people worldwide, including over 100,000 in the United States alone.

Today, one third of the entire world's population has been infected with Mycobacterium tuberculosis; that's two and a half billion people around the world. Five to ten percent of these people will progress to having active tuberculosis; that's anywhere from one to two million people developing a disease which has a mortality rate in excess of 20%.

And then, there is Ebola. This excerpt is from a CDC report dated 29 July 2014:

> "Ebola hemorrhagic fever (Ebola HF) is one of numerous Viral Hemorrhagic Fevers. It is a severe, often fatal disease in humans and nonhuman primates (such as monkeys, gorillas, and chimpanzees). Ebola HF is caused by infection with a virus of the family Filoviridae, genus Ebola virus. When infection occurs, symptoms usually begin abruptly.
>
> The first Ebola virus species was discovered in 1976 in what is now the Democratic Republic of the Congo, near the Ebola River. Since then, outbreaks have appeared sporadically. The natural reservoir host of Ebola viruses remains unknown. However, on the basis of available evidence and the nature of similar viruses, researchers believe that the virus is zoonotic (animal-borne), with bats being the most likely reservoir. Four of the five subtypes occur in an animal host native to Africa."

The bad news is that Ebola hemorrhagic fever has an 80% mortality rate, and up to 100 health care workers who went to West Africa as part of a humanitarian effort to control the disease have become infected themselves *despite* the protective precautions these professionals have taken to prevent contracting the disease. Two of these professionals, Americans working for the Samaritan's Purse, are now en route to the United States, destined for Emory University's Center for Disease Control (CDC). This is a decision that boggles the mind when one considers the illnesses that are coming into this country by illegal aliens on our southern borders, 600 of whom have been placed in isolation for being infected with tuberculosis.

Whether these latest developments are due to gross incompetence, intentional disregard for public safety, or some kind of ulterior and nefarious intent by the Obama administration is yet to be known, but this much we do know. The introduction of Ebola hemorrhagic fever onto American soil is something we should all be attuned to and, combined with the health crises erupting from Obama's decision to relax the deportation of illegal aliens who are carrying virulent diseases, is something that should not be tolerated, regardless of one's political inclinations, moral philosophies, or humanitarian concerns. To do otherwise and abide in this onslaught is morally repugnant, intellectually degenerate, and pandemically suicidal.

Is Martial Law Coming to America?

6 May 2015

The temptation for the reader will doubtlessly be to assume that this writer is some kind of "conspiracy theory kook," or words to that effect, but this is being written based upon personal experience.

For the fifth consecutive year, training exercises are being held at Camp Pendleton in Virginia Beach, Virginia, as this is being written. Camp Pendleton, not to be confused with the U.S. Marines Corps Base in California, is a Virginia National Guard Training Base located about one mile south of the boardwalk in Virginia Beach, Virginia. It is also right across the street from where we live. For the past few years, it has also been used by the Joint Forces Command of the military and naval bases located nearby for what appears to be secret training operations, secret because there is absolutely no news about these exercises, none at all. Inquiries about what is going on are not answered, nor are these exercises being acknowledged that they are even taking place. Local news (newspaper/television) makes no mention of what is going on either, and there is nothing on the internet concerning this. And yet. . .

In the afternoons, in the early evenings, and late at night, large military helicopters approach from the southwest toward the base, flying very low over our house, no less, low enough to rattle the house and sway nearby trees. They come in groups of three or four, land in a field across from our driveway, remain running for several minutes, and take off again. These are the large helicopters that resemble the Black Hawk or HH-60G Pave Hawk type of helicopters that are used in tactical theaters overseas, and when they approach, they are extremely loud and quite alarming. These helicopters are not the type used by the National Guard in cases of emergency, but rather the type of helicopters utilized in combat operations. These exercises go on for several weeks at a time, on a nightly basis, and when the weather is commensurate to such operations—never in heavy rain, for instance, but when the weather is more enabling. These exercises occur about three times per year, and the scope of these exercises have been increasing since they began about five years ago or so.

The fact that they are taking place, especially late at night (i.e., 11:30 p.m. EST/EDT or later) and that there is absolutely no news about this nor even acknowledgement that they are even occurring, makes us wonder just what the hell is going on. We have been reading much about exercises in the western part of the US, such as Jade Helm 15, but there is no news about any of these exercises taking place, here. None.

This brings us to a conclusion that when these activities are taking place in secret, such as those which are occurring over our very heads, literally, perhaps there is something to these "crazy conspiracy theories" about the possibility of the military imposing martial law at the behest of the president. These exercises didn't occur during his predecessor's term in office, but nevertheless have been taking place during Barack Obama's term in office and have been increasing in both size and scope since his re-election in 2012.

The fact of the matter is that we don't know what is taking place, cannot know what is taking place, and not knowing and not being able to know is the most disconcerting and frightening thing of all.

Given this secrecy, is it so farfetched to wonder if indeed martial law is on the near horizon, here in the United States? Well, is it?

Looking Back in 2130

26 May 2015

Everyone who reads this today will be long gone in 2130, so to indulge this, please put on the "imagination cap" and pretend for a moment that you are your great-grandchild and the year is 2130. You are pondering events of the previous century.

"A century ago, Americans were deeply divided along racial, religious, and philosophical lines to an extent that they hadn't been in many decades. Fifty years after major civil rights legislation had been passed under the administration of Lyndon Johnson, Americans once again found themselves increasingly polarized on the issues of racial and ethnic coexistence.

"Having elected its first African-American president, largely because of his race, and its first woman president, largely because of her sex, Americans had then elected their first Hispanic president, largely because of his ethnicity, and then elected their first openly gay president, largely because of his sexual preference. Yet, because each of these "identity" presidents chose to place emphasis on their own identity group at the expense of the larger country as a whole, America slipped into a chain of events which figuratively and literally tore the country apart.

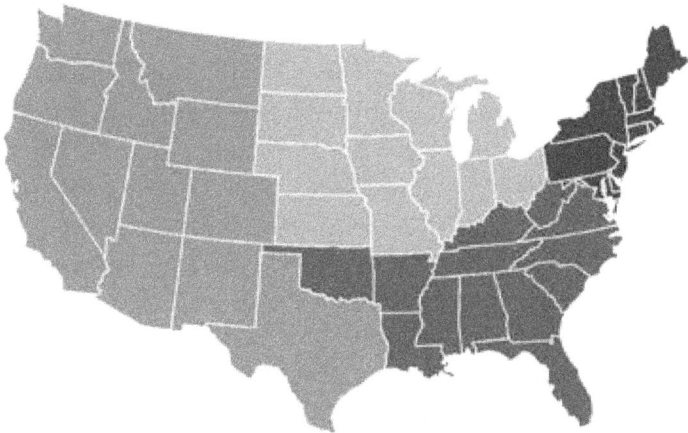

"Today, in 2130, what had been the United States of
America is now divided into four separate nations
following a second American Civil War, which tore the
country apart, those being the (northeastern) Socialist
Republic of America, the (western) Nacion' de America
Hispanica, the (southeastern) Federal Republic of
America, and the (central, upper midwestern) Islamic
State of America. Following the second American Civil
War, fought in the years 2036-2040, there occurred a
mass migration, largely upon ethnic and philosophical
lines . . .

"Encouraged by events taking place in Europe,
Asia, and the Middle East, radical Islamists migrated to
the central and upper Midwestern part of what once had
been the United States, established their capital in
Minneapolis and renamed it 'Obamastan' after the forty-
fourth president. They enacted Sharia Law, and virtually
all of the people in these regions are Muslims. Women
must cover their faces in public and are not afforded the
right to vote, nor leave their homes unescorted.

"Increasing immigration of Mexicans and Central
Americans to the southwestern and western portions
of what once had been the United States, Hispanics
voted in separate referenda to secede from the United
States and established their own capital in Los Angeles.
Spanish was declared the official language in these areas.

"Conservative and Christian Americans who were
facing increasing intolerance before and after the war
migrated to what had once been the southeastern United
States, setting up their government in Atlanta. Foreign-
born Christians, seeking asylum from Islamic
governments in Europe and Asia, were grudgingly
admitted into the ports of Miami, Hampton Roads, and
New Orleans, prompting a significant increase in
population in the southeast. There was also a notable
migration of Israelis, who had miraculously survived
their war with Iran, forced to leave what had been their
homeland in the Middle East.

"LGBT Americans, realizing that remaining in the

central and Midwestern regions would mean capital punishment, largely migrated east, along with many socialist and academic liberals (also not tolerated in the Islamic States), establishing a new, single-party government in what had been Washington, DC, and changed the name of this city to 'Alinskygrad', named after Saul Alinsky, the creator of community activism and author of *Rules for Radicals.* Christianity was outlawed in this area, as was gun ownership, and citizens remaining there were forced to sign an oath repudiating the Constitution of the United States, as well as all forms of conservativism.

"Each of these newly formed republics continue to struggle with interregional trade and commercial issues, but it appears that a trade agreement is currently in the works between the southeastern Federal Republic of the United States and the Nacion' de America Hispanica, since both tolerate religious freedom and have agreed to bilingual labeling of products going in and out of both nations."

* * *

Back to 2015. Think about the scenario described above and ask yourself whether such a scenario is good for America and how this might happen, assuming the world survives. If you take issue with this scenario, then challenge yourself to make sure that this does not happen, based on what you do today, tomorrow, and in the near future.

Religious Indoctrination in Our Public Schools

29 May 2015

It sounds so un-American, but it is happening in every state of the union, religious indoctrination being forced, yes forced, upon our children and grandchildren, in public schools across the country. Not since the landmark Supreme Court decisions in 1962 *Engel v. Vitale* and 1963 *Murray v. Curlett,* has religious proselytizing been officially permitted in public schools, when these cases brought an end to school prayer and Bible reading, respectively. Yet in the last decade, religious indoctrination has been taking place in public schools across the country.

The religion being force-fed upon our youth is not Catholicism (which isn't even "force fed," per se, in Catholic schools). Nor is it any form of Protestantism, nor any other form of Christianity, nor Judaism, nor even any form of Islam, Buddhism, Hinduism, nor even agnosticism nor atheism. None of these monotheistic, nor polytheistic, nor antitheistic religions is being taught in our public schools. None.

Nevertheless, a growing religious doctrine is not only being taught, but also being proselytized and forcibly being indoctrinated upon our youth today, and any heresy being spoken or written or even being otherwise mentioned is responded to with disciplinary action, censure, and even failing grades.

This is the religion of man-made climate change, formerly known as the religion of man-made global warming, most notably being advanced by former Vice President Al Gore and international so-called scientists who advance their dubious theories in a disingenuous effort to acquire government funding for their continued research and their insidious and clandestine efforts to destroy western capitalism as we know it.

The tenants of this religion, which are being force-fed as fact upon our youth, include dubious data about global warming (not proved), man-made climate change (unsubstantiated), and the proposition that the United States is the principal culprit, when it is clearly obvious that Russia, China, India, and other countries are far more polluting than the United States, where regulations concerning atmospheric output are far more stringent than the other countries listed. Once again, the loony liberal left is first to blame America and American capitalism, than pointing their fabricated fingers at the real culprits, who regularly spew atmospheric pollutants in the globe's eastern hemisphere. (Funny how it is always the United States which liberals always like to blame first). In reality, those who advocate extreme measures concerning carbon footprints and related and onerous corporate taxation, based upon these theories, really only seek the imposition of global socialism; they just don't want you to know it.

The fact is that the climate *is* changing, but it has absolutely nothing to do with the United States, nor human activity in any country, for that matter. The worldwide climate has gone through many eons of warming and cooling for millennia, long before primal man discovered how to warm himself and cook his food and harden and sharpen his spears with fire. Even since man's arrival, the world has experienced a multitude of ice ages and periods of global warming, just as the ocean tides ebb and flow. To suggest that man can cause any of this is egotistical at best and pure fantasy at worst, and yet there are those who say that "climate change deniers" should be silenced, censured, and even imprisoned, which shows the real and tangible hypocrisy that only liberals can truly evoke in their quest to indoctrinate the generation who follows us into adulthood. Unbelievable? Just try and suggest that these supposed "facts" of man- made climate change are merely theories that have not been empirically proved to a high school or college student today, and they will reply as though you have just told them that the earth is flat or that the sun revolves around the earth.

Certainly, mankind, being the most intelligent species on earth (some of these loons would even argue that point, by the way), has a custodial responsibility to practice good housekeeping with regards to our planet, but to take this to the extreme of destroying wholesale economies and food supplies in order to pacify the dictates of environmental extremists in government, academia, and the world politick is patently suicidal, immoral, and without justification, period.

Heresy, you say? So be it. Go ahead and burn me at the stake, if you will, but watch that carbon footprint, if you do.

9-11 Fourteen Years Later

11 September 2015

Once upon a time, when the world was young (and so were we), we naively believed that, by and large, we were safe from the ills that plague the Middle East. We told ourselves, "Yeah, it's pretty screwed up over there, but we are here, thank God, and all of that bad stuff is all over there, so why worry?"

Then a jet airliner flew right into one of the twin towers at New York's World Trade Center.

Our immediate reaction was, "That must be one screwed up pilot. How could he *possibly* have not seen that building on such a clear day?"

Then, a second jet airliner flew right into the other tower at New York's World Trade Center. And then we knew that these collisions were no accident.

Then, a third jet airliner flew into the Pentagon in Arlington, Virginia, and a fourth plane, bound for the United States Capitol dome, crashed into the fields of rural Pennsylvania. And then we knew that we were at war.

For an all-too-brief while, our country, the United States of America, which had a long-standing tradition of uniting during times of war, pulled together and resolved to do whatever it took in order to stop the sinister ideology that prompted such dastardly deeds. For a brief moment, we forgot our ideologies, we forgot our partisan affiliations, we forgot our creeds and our races and all of our identity groups and everything else that seeks to separate us, and we united behind the effort to get the sons of bitches who did this to us.

But then, partisan politics and advocacy journalism on the part of the mainstream media began creeping in and thus dividing us into partisan blocs, pitting liberals against conservatives, pitting Democrats against Republicans, pitting the poor and middle classes against the rich, pitting blacks against whites, nonbelievers against believers, gays against straights, etc., etc., *ad nauseam* until we were united no more.

Seven autumns later, these divisions, with complicit help from a mainstream media, bound and determined to do whatever it took to make history by ensuring the election of the nation's first black president, saw the election of a very different kind of president, a president who did not believe in American exceptionalism, a president who seemed to be above such childish notions of patriotism and "the American Way," a president who derided Americans who "cling to their guns and religion," a president who in reality had nothing but contempt for Americans and all that America has done over the many decades to preserve equality and freedom throughout the world. This new kind of president traveled the world, apologizing for all of his country's transgressions and telling all of the world that we are no better than they, and for this they awarded him a Nobel Prize for Peace, for having done nothing more than being elected and disrespecting his own country.

This new kind of president, one whose psychological makeup and ideology are vastly different from all of his forty-three predecessors, did everything he possibly could to tear down this country, to further divide this country, to set Americans against Americans, thus fulfilling his 2008 election night promise to "fundamentally transform the United States of America" by changing us from a country leading the world towards a better tomorrow to a country "leading from behind" in a concerted, determined effort to enable all of the world's many problems to visit our shores and infect our national psyche. Due to this one man and his nefarious agenda, race relations are worse today than they have been in sixty years. Due to this one man, we are far less safe today than we were, even on the sunny morning of September 11, 2001. Due to this one man and an imbecilic Secretary of State, he has struck a deal (a deal whose details have not been fully disclosed) with the most evil regime on earth, Iran- one that will assure their acquisition of nuclear weapons and intercontinental ballistic missiles with which to deliver these weapons on the shores of a nation they call "the Great Satan," the United States of America. This one man, who would have us believe that unsubstantiated claims of man-made climate change pose a greater threat to our national security than radical Islam, illegal immigration, and a nuclear Iran *combined*.

What have we, as a nation, learned since that sunny Tuesday morning, fourteen years ago?

Apparently, not a damned thing.

Back to School to What and Where

8 September 2015

Today, across the country (and depending on where they live), five- and six-year-old children are beginning their first day of kindergarten, thus embarking on a journey that will presumably see them graduate high school in the year 2028. Later that year, I will have reached the age of 70 (God willing), and I cannot begin to imagine what and where the world will be at that time.

When I journeyed off to kindergarten in the fall of 1964, kindergarten wasn't even offered in public schools within the Commonwealth of Virginia. One had to attend a private or parochial school for that level of preschool. I remember learning my numbers and letters, and we even remember learning to make change with play money, acting out the roles in a mock grocery store exercise, buying and selling empty boxes of oatmeal, cereal, and laundry soap which we had brought from home. As amazing as it may sound today, given the difficulty some store clerks have making change from a cash register, this was a skill I was required to master *in kindergarten*. By the time I entered first grade the following year, it was assumed that I knew the rudiments of addition and subtraction on day one. Calculators? Heck, I didn't even have access to an abacus!

By the time I entered the third grade, I started to notice changes being made in our school. Gone was school prayer and reading verses from the Bible, as I had routinely experienced in my first two years of public school. Kindergarten was being offered for the first time in my public school, and so was "new math," a form of learning arithmetic that bedeviled students, teachers, and parents alike. I remember my own parents shouting in frustration as I showed them how I was taught to do arithmetic, in a way very foreign from the way they had learned a generation before.

At the end of my fifth grade year, Circuit Judge Robert Mehridge, whose children attended a toady private school, handed down a court ruling that ordered the consolidation of county and city schools, a decision that would force suburban students to be bussed into inner city schools and urban kids to be bussed into suburban schools, in an ill-conceived attempt to equalize education. Ultimately, Mehridge's decision would be overturned in a landmark Supreme Court decision, but not before its unintended effect of swelling enrollments in parochial schools and in creating a plethora of new private schools within a year.

So I entered my sixth grade year attending a Catholic school, donning a uniform, and for the first time, white button down shirt, navy blue tie and slacks, dress shoes, and finding out the proper protocol for addressing a nun when I was summarily slapped for addressing her as "ma'am" instead of the more proper "Sister." What did I know? It wasn't all bad, though. The football team at the school for which I played had jerseys identical to the Baltimore Colts, and whenever I took the field for St. Bridget's, I found myself caught up in a juvenile fantasy that I was playing in Baltimore's Memorial Stadium, rather than a tree-lined field on Cary Street in Richmond's West End. Interestingly, St. Bridget's was still teaching "old math," far different from the "new math" which I had been taught in the latter years of public elementary school.

Three years later, I'd find myself at a Catholic military day school, which was now teaching "new math." It doesn't take much for one to infer the difficulty I had in mastering the idiosyncrasies of mathematics, given the back-and-forth means by which I was instructed over the relatively few years. After a year and one half of routinely marching "tours" to work off demerits, I left military school and returned to public school, where, as one might have guessed, they had returned to "old math," thus cementing forever the disdain I have for math, in general. But I digress.

Even with the variety of schools I attended and the variation of teaching methods that resulted from this variety, I did manage to learn the basics of that which was necessary to survive in an increasingly competitive and unforgiving real world, the one in which I find myself today, acting out an unforeseen role as a human ATM; the money comes in and goes right back out, as I struggle day to day in an effort to somehow keep myself afloat in a vastly changing world.

The retirement my parents enjoyed and the standard of living they realized will not be seen by their fourth child, but this is far from unique to this writer. Most all of my contemporaries are living a life that is one-half of an economic station below that of their parents, and his children are living a life that is a full economic station below the station of their grandparents. Then again, my parents were learning in high school much of what I learned in college, thus lending credence to the dumbing-down of educational curriculum that has been taking place during the last century. The fact that I have a Bachelor's degree from a large state university and that I am nevertheless challenged by standardized eighth grade testing from 1908 bears further witness to this unfortunate phenomena.

Granted, today's youth can run circles around me when it comes to operating computers and smart phones, but this does not mean they are better educated. Rather, they have been programmed to perform technological functions, thus preparing them to work in an increasingly technological world, where problem-solving has become more of a technological application and less of a cerebral function, requiring retrospection and intuition. While today's youth can cite me chapter and verse about the dogma of unsubstantiated man-made climate change, which they have been force-fed, they are challenged to identify the three branches of government and are virtually unable to correctly identify the century in which the American Civil War was fought. They know even less about the concept of representative democracy or the virtues of free-market capitalism, which can more than adequately explain why they tend to vote the way they do, but that is another topic for another day. While my parents were instilled with the value of self-sufficiency, many of my children's generation are indoctrinated with a mantra which says we are all responsible for caring for one another, a textbook (forgive the term) example of how good intentions can and do lead to bad policy and worse sociological modeling.

It's anybody's guess as to what today's kindergarteners will be taught during the next dozen years or so or where they will eventually land following graduation in 2028. Given the hyper-inflation of college tuitions, which is the direct result of government funding and the broad availability of student loans and the fact that what is being taught in colleges and universities is of increasingly questionable value, my guess is that either a) college and university education will become tuition-free; or b) far fewer students will be attending colleges and universities by the time today's kindergarteners will graduate from high school.

It can be certain if the trend continues away from broad-based, multifaceted education and towards homogeneous indoctrination and technological functionality, these children will grow up to become more functionary than intellectual, more codependent than independent, more orthodox and less imaginative, and it is for these reasons that I would not wish to change places with them, no, not by a long shot.

The Enemy Within– Targeting Domestic Terrorism

16 October 2015

In the midst of all of the news this week, it was quietly announced that the United States Department of Justice has created a Domestic Terrorism Unit to be headed by a yet-to- be-named Domestic Terrorism Counsel, whose job it will be to coordinate the creation of a database of those the administration designates as "lone wolf" and domestic terrorists and monitor their activity. If this were being initiated to monitor Islamic extremists or radical anarchists bent on mass destruction or violent overthrow of the federal government, such an effort would be in keeping with the administration's responsibility to secure the nation and protect its national security.

Sadly, however, this is not the case, no, not by a long shot.

This initiative is nothing less than an attempt by the Obama Administration to label those who it perceives to be their own political enemies and monitor all types of activities, from online blogging, to gun ownership to advocating political stances in the name of constitutionalism, conservativism, limited government, etc. No, folks, this is not a simple and laughable "enemies list" like the one Nixon maintained based upon those who criticized the thirty-seventh president; this involves actual monitoring in the style of George Orwell's "1984," with "Big Brother" watching every step of anyone who takes issue with Barack Obama's agenda to "fundamentally transform the United States of America," as he promised to do so on the evening he was elected in November of 2008.

Member of the NRA? Member of the Tea Party? Libertarian? Klansman? Pro-lifer? Someone advocating strict adherence to the U.S. Constitution, or limited government? Guess what, they'll all be lumped together in the same filing cabinet, the one labeled "Domestic Terrorist."

Strangely absent from this grouping are those associated with the New Black Panther Party, the anti-police Black Lives Matter movement, the Council on Islamic Relations (CAIR), Louis Farrakhan's Nation of Islam, the Communist Party USA (yes, it still exists), the Socialist Party, Greenpeace, or any movement advocating the annexation of large portions of the United States to Mexico.

Listed amongst the "domestic threats" are those who would firebomb synagogues and mosques, but NOT those who would firebomb churches, which brings the obvious question, "Why exclude churches?"

In other words, oppose Obama specifically and liberals in general, and one does so at his own peril. Here's the hitch; this is being done in coordination with Attorney General Loretta Lynch's "Strong Cities Network" in cooperation with, get this, the United Nations, as was announced at the end of September at the United Nations General Assembly in New York City. In coordination with the National Security Agency, the Obama administration seeks to silence *any* opposition by citizens of the United States under threat of force levied by the full weight of the federal government.

Essentially, in the name of "safety" and "national security," our rights to free speech, free assembly, gun ownership, the right to address grievances perpetrated by the government, and in some cases, religious expression and affiliation will become a thing of the past, if Obama and his henchmen get away with what appears to be the single most egregious and coordinated attack on constitutional freedoms in the history of the United States.

If you believe that the enemy within wears a hijab or shouts "Allah Akbar!," you *may* be correct with regards to specific individuals, but the *real* enemy within, the one who truly seeks to destroy this country, wears pinstriped suits, works on Pennsylvania Avenue and, while we are distracted with working our jobs and paying our bills and watching our televisions, is doing everything possible to control our citizenry and erase our liberties.

Be aware, be VERY aware, and keep in mind those presidential candidates and other politicians who advocate and seek to perpetuate these policies.

Christmas in the Winter of Our Discontent

21 December 2015

"Now is the winter of our discontent . . . "
—Act 1, Scene 1, *Richard III*, by William Shakespeare

Some two thousand eighteen years ago, give or take a year or two, a child was born to a young Jewish woman in Bethlehem, because her espoused husband had returned to that city to be registered in a census ordered by Caesar Augustus. The birth of that child, Jesus Christ of Nazareth, marked the beginning of Christianity and also served as the point of demarcation between the ancient world and the world which followed in human history.

Raised as a Jew in His stepfather's home of Nazareth, not much is known of His early life, other than His circumcision being recorded, where He was officially named by His stepfather, and preaching to astonished rabbis at the ceremony of His bar mitzvah thirteen years later. Yet this child would change forever the concept of the meaning of life itself and challenge all, believers, or non, to seek peace within ourselves and in the way we treat one another. His life, His teachings, His death, and resurrection would lead to the creation of the world's largest monotheistic religion, Christianity, which was based upon the Judaism of His own mother, Mary, but with the added promise of everlasting life for those who believe in Him.

In the two millennia that followed the life of Jesus Christ, the world saw war upon war upon war, much of which was based upon religious differences, within and outside Christianity itself. Supposedly, we live in a country where the freedom *of* (and *not* "from," as some would have us otherwise believe) religion is constitutionally assured by virtue of our First Amendment rights. Yet, in a country which supposedly assures all the freedom to worship as we deem fit, whereby there is no state-sanctioned denomination (also established in the First Amendment), it seems today that some religions or, for that matter non-religions, are more equal than others.

Say something against Islam, for example, and Attorney General Loretta Lynch has promised that doing so will invite criminal prosecution. Make a video which insults the prophet Muhammed, and one might find themselves jailed without the benefit of habeas corpus protections *for years*.

Host a holiday party at a public school, one that features a non-religious character in a red suit with a white beard, and just one single complaint by an agnostic or an atheist can bring on a lawsuit by the American Civil Liberties Union (ACLU), effectively shutting down such a holiday celebration. Add a crèche (manger scene) to a public square where a menorah is displayed, and both symbols of the season are brought down based upon the wiles of malcontented non-believers who wish to impose *their* views on the rest of us.

Work at a store or a business or in a government agency and utter the phrase "Merry Christmas," and find out just how quickly the denizens of political correctness are ready to issue a verbal warning that you are flirting with unemployment.

Such is *not* the separation of church and state, but rather an all-out assault against religion generally and Christianity specifically. Left unchecked, the generations of infants born in this new century will witness the outright censure of Christianity as a religion and the banishment of Christmas as a holiday itself. How sad that a true religion of peace is proscribed from celebrating the birth of its Savior by the politically correct classes that only seek to destroy our freedoms and our culture, and how sad for the youngest among us who must bear witness to the acrimony surrounding something as simple as a jolly old elf bringing toys down a chimney.

So while we are still not legally estopped from saying so, at this juncture in our history, please allow us to extend our heartfelt wishes for a Merry Christmas and Happy New Year to all who should read this post.

Chapter 3

Foreign Policy

An Angry Storm Approaches- a poem

22 March 2014

There's a storm a-brewin', upon a distant shore,
Slowly headin' our way, and knockin' at our door,
There's a wind a-blowin', the stench is in the air,
And don't think it can't happen, because we're almost there . . .
A seeping hatred overseas has festered for so long,
No matter what we've tried to do, all they see is wrong,
We've given the world our treasure; too often shed our blood,
And this is how they thank us, by dragging us through mud . . .

They gave Obama a Nobel Prize, for sayin' we've been wrong,
While all this time he weakened us and planned this all along;
"A house divided cannot stand," and so it soon shall fall
And if we fail to stop the tide, we soon will lose it all;
So listen brothers and sisters, too, it's time to raise your voices,
And scream a clarion call to all to make the toughest choices,
America is slipping from our grasp; we're losing it, somehow,
An angry storm is headed here unless we stop it now . . .

Wars and Rumors of Wars

13 June 2014

I believe it was Aeschylus (525 BC-456 BC), the Greek tragic dramatist, who once wrote that "In war, truth is the first casualty," and all of us must consider this purview with regard to what is taking place in the world today.

I am going to say something that is not popular, not politically correct, and would certainly not be uttered by President Obama, not by his predecessors, Bush (both), Clinton, not even Reagan, nor by any leader in Europe or elsewhere. Nevertheless, I am going to say it because it needs to be said, whether or not we want to own up to it, and that is that we are at war with radical Islam. There, I have said it, and I will say it again. We are at war with radical Islam.

Why?

Simple. Radical Islam is at war with us. They know it, they say it, and we don't, which places us at a tremendous disadvantage. No war can ever be won unless the enemy can be identified and called by its name. History has borne this out. For instance, in the World Wars, we were at war with Imperial and then Nazi Germany, which is not to say that we were at war with Germans, per se, but rather with their rulers, a slight and delicate distinction, perhaps, but altogether meaningful and substantial. We identified the enemy, and we defeated the enemy twice in a span of thirty years. So to be clear, we are not at war with Muslims; we are at war with radical Islam, and this distinction must be made clear lest the point of this missive be missed.

In southeast Asia, in the hills of Asia minor, in the Middle East, and in Northern Africa, radical Islam is waging war against the west, and by "the west," I mean the United States, western Europe, and, of course, Israel. Just as this war is being waged in Iraq, Iran, Syria, Afghanistan, Pakistan, Malaysia, and all over the Muslim world, it is also being waged in Europe, including Great Britain and here even in the United States. The problem is that the western concepts of sensitivity, inclusion, and political correctness will not allow us to own up to this very fact, but it is a fact.

When Nidal Hassan launched his murderous rampage at Ft Hood, Texas, does anyone with half a brain in his head want to say that this was merely a case of workplace violence, as the Obama administration would have us believe, rather than an attack by a radical Islamist in the name of jihad? Does anyone think that the bombing at the Boston marathon last year was anything other than an attack by radical Islamist brothers for the purpose of waging jihad? Just how many of these acts, not to mention the 9/11 attacks, will it take for we in the west to realize just who the enemy is, be willing to call the enemy by its real name, and wage war against it?

Please forgive me for saying so, but "terrorism," as it is so often used today, is nothing more than a generic euphemism orchestrated to hide the real truth, and that truth is that we are at war with radical Islam, not Muslims, nor even with the silent, so called "moderate Muslims" who refuse to condemn the radical counterparts within their same religion, but we are at war with radical Islam, and we will lose that war unless we as a society grow up, say what needs to be said without regard to sensitivity, inclusion, or political correctness, and wage this war with the righteous determination- bent on victory that is so necessary in what is most certainly not a rumor of war, but of a real war itself. If we fail to do so, we are finished, period.

Israel

23 July 2014

First, please consider the following three passages, in the context of today:

"And it shall come to pass in that day, that I will make Jerusalem a stone of burden for all the peoples; all that burden themselves with it shall be sore wounded; and all the nations of the earth shall be gathered together against it."

—Zechariah 12:3

"For behold, in those days and at that time, when I restore the fortunes of Judah and Jerusalem, I will gather all the nations and bring them down to the Valley of Jehoshaphat. And I will enter into judgment with them there, on behalf of my people and my heritage Israel, because they have scattered them among the nations and have divided up my land."

—Joel 3: 1-2

"See the fig tree, and all the trees. When they are already budding, you see it and know by your own selves that the summer is already near. Even so you also, when you see these things happening, know that the Kingdom of God is near. Most certainly I tell you, this generation will not pass away until all things are accomplished. Heaven and earth will pass away, but my words will by no means pass away."

—Luke 21:29-33

The nation of Israel, with an area smaller than that of New Jersey and a population less than that of Virginia, figures prominently in both the Old and New Testaments, particularly when it comes to Biblical eschatology. All of the Hebrew prophets, most all of the New Testament prophecies, and, according to three of the gospels, Jesus himself spoke of Israel in the last days. The first citation above refers to the nations of the earth coming against Israel, the second regards God's judgment against these nations, and the third refers to Israel's rebirth in 1948, indicating that the generation who was alive at that time to witness Israeli statehood would not pass away until all of these things had been consummated.

Sixty-six years later, what do we see? Israel, the sole democracy in the Middle East, surrounded on three sides by nations committed to its destruction, and who stands beside Israel? No one, not even the United States under its present regime, supports Israel's right to defend itself against aggression from without. Israel, far and away, the only middle eastern country that truly has freedom of religion and representative democracy and embraces the concept of tolerance, a concept unheard of in Saudi Arabia, Iran, Egypt, Iraq (under ISIS), Syria, and in the West Bank and Gaza strip, whose Palestinian authorities (Hamas) is unwilling to even acknowledge Israel's very right to exist and uses its own civilian women and children as human shields to protect the rockets that are used to bombard Israel.

Who gets the condemnation? Israel, from the United Nations, from the major media, and even our President and Secretary of State, who once again play the "Moral Equivalency" card, saying that peace must be attained by both sides, when knowing full well that one of those sides will not even acknowledge the other's right to exist and is wholly determined to annihilate the Jewish people.

While conservatives in the United States tend to back Israel and its efforts to survive aggression from all sides, liberals here predictably back the Palestinians and others who are dedicated to its destruction, liberals who pretend to be tolerant except when it comes to Christianity anywhere and Judaism everywhere. Both of these two religions are under assault all over the Islamic world, but to even mention this is to bring on charges of Islamophobia, when, in fact, Islam is the most intolerant of the world's monotheistic religions, which underscores liberal hypocrisy yet again.

How much land will Israel have to cede to its enemies once again in pursuit of peace? Answer: "All of it," say the Palestinians, who ironically are shunned even by their own Arab neighbors. Even then, if all of Israel were given to the Palestinians, the

Jewish people of Israel would not have peace, but would instead have no homeland in which to exist. So why should Israel cede a single acre to those bent on their destruction? Why shouldn't they invade the Gaza strip in order to destroy the tunnels with which Hamas smuggles its missiles and weaponry into Israel to wreak havoc and destruction on Israeli civilians?

More importantly, why should the nations of the world, including the United States under its current regime, condemn Israel for being committed to its own survival? With anti-Semitism exploding all over Europe once again and the world aligning itself with those who seek the destruction of Israel, it seems that we are living out the script in a play written thousands of years ago, a play whose final act may only serve to bring about our own demise.

Pearl Harbor Revisited

8 December 2014

" . . . what's past is prologue . . . "
—William Shakespeare, *The Tempest*, Act 2, Scene I

Seventy-three years ago, President Franklin Delano Roosevelt addressed a Joint Session of Congress. What follows is an excerpt of that address . . .

"Yesterday, December 7th, 1941—a date which will live in infamy—the United States of America was suddenly and deliberately attacked, by naval and air forces of the Empire of Japan. The United States was at peace with that nation and, at the solicitation of Japan, was still in conversation with its government and its emperor looking toward the maintenance of peace in the Pacific. Indeed, one hour after Japanese air squadrons had commenced bombing in the American island of Oahu, the Japanese ambassador to the United States and his colleague delivered to our Secretary of State a formal reply to a recent American message. And while this reply stated that it seemed useless to continue the existing diplomatic negotiations, it contained no threat or hint of war or of armed attack. It will be recorded that the distance of Hawaii from Japan makes it obvious that the attack was deliberately planned many days or even weeks ago. During the intervening time, the Japanese government has deliberately sought to deceive the United States by false statements and expressions of hope for continued peace . . . Hostilities exist. There is no blinking at the fact that our people, our territory, and our interests are in grave danger. With confidence in our armed forces, with the unbounding determination of our people, we will gain the inevitable triumph—so help us God. I ask that the Congress declare that since the unprovoked and dastardly attack by Japan on Sunday, December 7th, 1941, a state of war has existed between the United States and the Japanese empire."

–Franklin Delano Roosevelt, Address to Joint Session of
Congress, 8 December 1941

In the course of history there are occurrences which, despite
the seemingly isolated context of their respective contemporary
settings, nevertheless have ramifications which last for
decades. The Japanese attack on Pearl Harbor was just such an
occurrence. It set into motion a chain of events that united the
American people to support a war effort like no other before or
since, introduced nuclear warfare, led to the ultimate destruction
of totalitarianism in both Europe and the Pacific, ushered in a
decades-long Cold War, and established the United States as a
world superpower, just to name a few.

Sadly, however, the passage of time has eroded and faded
into oblivion the central lesson of Pearl Harbor, that isolationism
and living in denial of a real world can leave a nation and a people
open to attack and ultimately result in profound and lasting
changes to their way of life. Think September 11th, 2001, whose
own central lesson has begun to fade, especially with the young
people who have now grown to the age of electoral suffrage.

We did not seek war with Japan (nor Germany, nor Italy),
nor did we seek war with radical Islam. Yet both were thrust
upon us, in one form or another, because of our naiveté and
because we fell into a false sense of isolation, one that insidiously
told us "those problems are over there; we need to stay out," a
recipe for ultimate disaster and vastly increased carnage.

There are those who insist to this day that both of the attacks
on Pearl Harbor and on 9/11 might well have been avoided if we
had done a better job of appeasing those who were bent on our
ultimate destruction. There are also those who attempt to play a
moral equivalency card, one that expresses the egregious lie that
the attacks on Pearl Harbor and 9/11 were somehow justified
from the perspective of those who perpetrated these acts. Such
folly may sell in the cloistered world of academia and theological
seminary and may even persuade young and impressionable
minds of their supposed enlightenment to the point of advocacy
and active protest. Yet in the real world, the world where we
unfortunately find ourselves living, putting into place national
policy which espouses this fantasy can and only will lead to our

own demise and quite possibly our own destruction.

It would be nice if, in the words of Rodney King, we could "all just get along." Go try that one on a radical jihadist and see how long your head remains attached to your torso if you are a man, and how long your virtue remains intact if you are a woman. Like the Japanese who beheaded our prisoners of war and made wholesale rape a policy of occupation in China, radical Islam, in the form of ISIS, is employing the very same stratagem.

Just as the Japanese "suddenly and deliberately" launched a premeditated attack on the United States in 1941, radical Islam "suddenly and deliberately" launched an attack on the United States sixty years later. Americans were united in their resolve to annihilate the Japanese as a result and did so. It's too bad that we lack such resolve as a nation today to destroy the evil that is radical Islam. Without such resolve, we will most certainly *not "gain the inevitable victory, so help us God," and it is we the people who ultimately, ignobly, and finally bear the responsibility of our own demise.*

Netanyahu

3 March 2015

Not since January 17, 1952, when British Prime Minister Winston Churchill warned the United States of an Iron Curtain descending upon Europe, has there been a more important speech from a foreign dignitary to a joint session of the United States Congress. Yet today, Israeli Prime Minister Benjamin Netanyahu addressed a joint session of Congress in a speech as far reaching as Churchill's in 1952. In it, he implored the members of Congress to think long and hard about the consequences of lifting sanctions on the Islamic Republic of Iran, which would be part and parcel of an agreement that President Obama is desperately seeking with Iran in an inane attempt to thwart Iran's nuclear ambitions.

Specifically, Prime Minister Netanyahu took issue with two crucial elements of this nascent treaty presently being negotiated in Geneva, Switzerland by Secretary of State John Kerry. The first and by far the most important issue is the "sunset clause" whereby Iran would only be held to its terms for a period of ten years, after which they would be free and clear to develop a stockpile of nuclear weapons. Secondly, Iran would retain its entire nuclear enrichment program and thus geometrically increase the amount of centrifuges designed to enrich uranium, a key component to the creation of atomic weapons. Quite rightly, Netanyahu warned the Congress that this treaty would not do anything to thwart Iran's nuclear ambitions, but rather pave the way for Iran to become the latest member to the world's nuclear club and, given the nature of a regime that has been in place for thirty-six years, thus create an existential threat to the survival of Israel, since it is this same regime that has publicly and repeatedly called for Israel's annihilation.

Netanyahu documented the history of Iran's hatred of Israel, recalling from ancient history the attempt by Persia's Haman to destroy Israel, a plot that was thwarted by Esther and to this day is observed in the feast of Purim. He recounted the history of Iran's current regime since its inception in 1979 when the incumbent government, under Shah Reza Pahlavi, was overthrown by Islamic Radicals under the Ayatollah Khomeini, a regime that captured American diplomats and held them captive for 444 days in 1979-1980 and then a few years later was responsible for the death of 230 U.S. Marines in Beirut, Lebanon. He reminded the Congress that it is this Iranian regime that has extended its hegemony over four nations, Iraq, Syria, Yemen and Lebanon, and that it seeks to expand its domination of the Middle East, vying only with ISIS for such control. Conversely, it is the Obama administration which naively believes that this rivalry with ISIS represents a signal of Iran's willingness to take on ISIS as a pathway to friendlier relations with the Iranian regime, but it is indeed the exact opposite. As Netanyahu so succinctly put it, in this particular case, "the enemy of your enemy is your enemy."

Asininely, fifty-four Democratic representatives and eight Democratic senators boycotted the address by the Israeli Prime Minister in lockstep agreement with the Obama administration, who did not allow a single member of its team to attend the address by Netanyahu. All Americans must ask themselves the following question: "Why?"

Why is the Obama administration so resolutely opposed to Israel's Prime Minister addressing our Congress?

Why is it more important for the Obama administration to so lamely and desperately seek such a bad deal with the Iranians, one that would imperil the survival of the world's lone Jewish state?

Why would the President of the United States skip such an opportunity to sit down with Israel's Prime Minister and discuss with him what he sees to be the advantages of such an agreement, when he will not even disclose to the American people the reasons he is pursuing this ill-begotten treaty in the first place?

Is it because the narcissistic president is so consumed with his own legacy that he would wager the very survival of our closest ally in the Middle East just to be able to say at the end of his presidency, "I got Iran to agree?"

We have seen the folly of such agreements in the past, most notably when Churchill's predecessor Neville Chamberlain boasted that he had negotiated "peace for our time" with Adolf

Hitler by wagering away a sovereign Czechoslovakia on Hitler's promise not to invade eastern Europe, a promise broken when Germany invaded Poland less than a year later, touching off the Second World War. Twenty million lives later, the world learned the lesson of such folly and why a bad deal is far, far worse than no deal at all.

Or is it indeed the case that, in the long view of world history, we have forgotten this lesson?

Friday the 13th- The Attacks in Paris

16 November 2015

On Friday, the thirteenth of June, 2014, I wrote an essay entitled, "Wars, and Rumors of Wars." In that essay we indicated that we in the West are at war with radical Islam, for the simple reason that radical Islam is at war with us. Also in that essay, I took note of the fact that *they* know it, *they* say it, and *we* won't, which is why they are at a distinct advantage, essentially arguing that if one cannot name their enemy, one cannot possibly defeat their enemy.

On the evening of Friday the 13th of November, 2015, Paris was attacked by an ISIS-backed cabal in six separate, albeit coordinated, incidents, and the carnage was severe: one hundred twenty-nine dead, hundreds of others injured. Planned by one Abdelhamid Abaaoud, a 27-year-old Belgian national of Moroccan descent, these attacks answered, once and for all, questions concerning the wisdom of allowing Syrian refugees into Europe by the tens of thousands, something that Barack Obama has begun here in the United States.

Hand it to the French, who wasted no time in responding militarily with an aerial attack on an ISIS stronghold in Raqqa, Syria, and with law enforcement as well, launching one hundred sixty raids, making twenty arrests and confiscating hundreds of weapons in the context of these raids. Some of the assailants were indeed supposed refugees, whose real intent was not to escape ISIS, but rather act as enemy combatants cowardly murdering innocent victims who were doing nothing more than eating at a restaurant, attending a concert in one venue and, along with French President François Hollande, attending a soccer match at a stadium in Paris. In other words, innocent people were only doing what westerners like to do on weekends and thereby becoming sacrificial lambs at the hands of vicious radical Muslims. That's right, radical Muslims.

Amazingly, not twenty-four hours had passed when the Democrat's Presidential debate was taking place, and each of the Democrat candidates were falling over one another to avoid naming radical Islam as the culprit, thus following the same ridiculous reticence on the part of President Barack Obama, who would much rather hurl insults and admonitions at Christians, Republicans, Jews, Americans, and Israelis, then publicly admit that ISIS (which he calls ISIL) and the horrific attacks they perpetrate is at root an extension of radical Islamic theology. More disturbingly, each of the three candidates, Hillary Clinton, Martin O'Malley, and Bernie Sanders, agree with and want to expand upon a program that would import tens of thousands of Syrian refugees into this country, despite the fact that a plurality of these so-called refugees are in fact *men* between the ages of seventeen and forty years of age.

Setting aside the very real possibility that Obama (and Clinton and O'Malley and Sanders) and many of his Democrat allies in Congress are either naïve or stupid, there can be at long last only one realistic conclusion that can be drawn from the advocacy of such suicidal policies, as well as the extreme reluctance on their part, to name radical Islam as the enemy of the West. That is to say, as much as we otherwise are loathe to do so, Obama and his cohorts *want* ISIS to win, and they *want* to import into the United States that which took place in Paris Friday night.

As Pogo the possum once famously said in Walt Kelly's cartoon strip of the same name, when it comes to our feckless President who prefers to lead from behind, "We have met the enemy, and he is us." January 20, 2017 cannot arrive soon enough. God willing, may this country live to see that day.

A Most Disturbing Reincarnation

18 January 2016

It was a news story that might have been easily missed, but a news story all the same. For the first time since World War II, an all-new edition of *Mein Kampf*, the despicable and diabolical autobiography/manifesto of Adolf Hitler and printed in German, was placed on sale *in Germany* and was sold out (4,000 copies) in less than a week.

For more than seventy years, the publication and distribution of this book was banned by the German government, but on the expiration of the copyright which had heretofore placed this ban into effect, it became public property, which essentially allowed its republication. Worse, the German public has seized upon its availability, and it has become an instant bestseller in that country.

Nothing could prove to be more incendiary nor have a greater potential for misuse than the republication and distribution of Adolf Hitler's political and social commentary as contained in this book, which includes his twisted vision of anti-Semitism, lebensraum, and militant Aryanism. Written during his imprisonment in Landsberg following the failed "Beer Hall Putsch" in Munich, on 8-9 November, 1923 and dictated to Rudolf Hess, it sold more than ten million copies in Germany prior to the end of the Second World War. In effect, it became the pro-forma bible and textbook of National Socialism and poisoned the minds of Germans who came to regard their Fuhrer as something short of a deity, blindly following him and his henchmen into a holocaustic abyss, which resulted in the systematic slaughter of eleven million, including six million Jews.

Even more horrific than the Holocaust itself is the fact that this nightmare took place a little more than seventy years ago, barely a second ago on the proverbial clock that is the grand scheme of world history. Indeed, if it can happen as it did so relatively recently, it can easily happen again in the not-so-distant future, which is why the book's republication has so much potential danger.

In a present-day Germany, where tens of thousands of Syrian refugees have been permitted entry and where hordes of Muslim men have been engaging in mass rapes and other forms of sexual assault on German women in Cologne and other regions of that country, it is easy to see that such an environment can cause enough panic to lead otherwise thinking people to places that they should not venture, specifically into ideologies that are as sick and twisted as those espoused in Nazism. History has shown that time and time again, a void in the political power structure can lead to its replacement by dangerous policies and ideologies that can lead to cataclysm.

All it takes is for a U.S. President to ignore his own "line-in-the-sand" by effectively standing back and permitting a Bashar Assad regime to use chemical weapons to commit genocide on his own people, and a German Chancellor, Angela Merkel, to open the door to a quarter million of these refugees, many of whom are young men whose twisted ideology and radical interpretation of Islamic ideology permit and sanction the rape of "improperly dressed infidels" to create a potential powder keg in a European continent whose culture and Christianity is under constant assault from without and within as well.

Now, into that void has entered a book that should never have been published, a book which should have never been sold, a book whose most disturbing reincarnation and regrettable re-distribution is flying off the shelves of German booksellers, laying the groundwork for a reactionary response that will only serve to inflame and inspire an ideology that was once thought to be extinguished and rendered asunder.

Chapter 4

Racial Tensions

Ferguson

25 November 2014

It's an all-too-familiar story, and one we have heard many, many times since (at least) April of 1992. The legal process is followed in strict accordance with established standards of jurisprudence, a white officer(s) is exonerated of alleged crimes in the performance of duty, and the result is met with disproportionate rage, expressed in violent behavior by disenchanted blacks and others taking advantage of a specific situation, far removed from their own respective existence.

Four policemen, three of whom were white (along with one Hispanic) are acquitted in Los Angeles of assault and excessive force in the beating of an intoxicated black driver who led police on a dangerous, high-speed chase. Rodney King survived the attack, but fifty-three people were killed and 2,000 people were injured in the riots that followed. Approximately 1,100 buildings were destroyed. 3,600 fires were lit, and countless businesses were looted, many of which were owned by businessmen of Korean and other Asian minorities, who seemed to be particularly targeted.

Fast forward twenty-two years. In Ferguson, Missouri, part of the greater St. Louis metropolis, an 18-year-old black man is shot by a white police officer six times. Supposed eye-witness accounts initially allege he was shot in the back, despite undeniable forensic evidence to the contrary. All hell breaks loose in Ferguson and other places immediately following the shooting. Two people are shot, others injured, and a bacchanalia of looting and vandalism takes place, destroying businesses and livelihoods as a result. These riots, encouraged by well-practiced race-baiters like presidential advisor Al Sharpton and perpetrated by malcontents in the form of the New Black Panther Party and the Revolutionary Communist Party USA, are particularly and precisely engineered to wreak havoc by organized groups who have absolutely no connection to the officer, Darren Wilson, nor to Michael Brown, the man who was shot and killed.

In strict accordance with Missouri law, a grand jury comprising of nine whites and three blacks spends three months painstakingly reviewing all evidence and eyewitness testimony in order to determine whether criminal charges be filed against the officer. The county's District Attorney spends twenty-five minutes on live television, explaining in copious detail the process, the findings, and ultimately the determination by the grand jury, which was no charges of criminal conduct would be filed against Officer Wilson. And what happens?

Demonstrations take place across major cities in the United States, showing in some cases professionally preprinted signs and well-organized gatherings that required much planning and little regard for the rule of law. Worse, Ferguson again erupts in violence, vandalism, looting, and destructions of lives, livelihoods, and property. Shots are fired, automobiles are set afire, and stores are looted by individuals taking sheer and perverse advantage of the discordant disarray that ensues.

Meanwhile, in Washington DC, a president who was purportedly elected to be "a uniter and not a divider" pulls out the moral equivalency card once again, equating the street rage with law enforcement, as though both are on the same altruistic level of moral authority. This same president, whose Attorney General, Eric Holder, has been extremely and undeniably selective in the pursuit of cases where race is involved, ignoring cases where whites are victimized and exploiting cases where blacks are victimized, has done nothing but fan the flames of racial discord in this country, thus taking us back to a regrettable time where racial hatred was more the norm and less the exception. Once again, this country is being ripped apart because of certain highly placed individuals who make their living off of the misfortune of others. But don't tell this to the miscreants in Ferguson who broke into area liquor stores and availed themselves of free spirits. That would be racist, right? Think about it. For the sake of our country and our world, for God's sake, just think about it.

Ferguson (Part II)

13 March 2015

One of the missing elements in all of the hubris about what has taken place in Ferguson, Missouri is the cause, the root cause, of the death of Michael Brown, which prompted all of the protests, all of the violence, all of the looting, all of the unrest and, most recently, the shooting of two police officers there and the shooting of police officers elsewhere as well.

There is no doubt that the likes of Al Sharpton, emboldened by his friends at the Justice Department, outgoing Attorney General Eric Holder, and the White House, President Barack Obama, incinerated a small fire into a conflagration. For their part, Holder and Obama have not helped ameliorate the all-too-incendiary atmosphere when it comes to Ferguson. In fact, they have exacerbated the situation and, through their grandstanding and postulations, have nationalized an atmosphere of mistrust, resentment, and tension. It is not a stretch to suggest that President Barack Obama, ironically, the first African-American to be elected President of the United States, has set race relations back more than fifty years, as if the days of Selma and of Montgomery and of dozens of towns across the South and elsewhere have been time-warped to 1964, when racial upheaval found its boiling point in the midst of a decade which saw multiple boiling points.

Yet even beyond all of that, the one thing that has not been discussed, the one element that has not been mentioned is the young man whose death proved to be the spark of this unrest: Michael Brown. As much as liberals would like to blame the white man, blame the cops, blame a "racist society" that placed him into a situation where he lost his life, the fault lies not elsewhere but rather in the way he was evidently raised by a mother, one Leslie McSpadden, who had this to say concerning the shooting of two policemen this week:

"F*** them 2 comps (sic) . . . Don't got no sympathy for them or they families . . . Ain't no fun when the Rabbit got the gun . . . If my fam woulda (sic) got justice in August, maybe those two comps (sic) wouldn't have got shot last night . . . "

As much as human nature would drive us to otherwise sympathize with a mother who has lost her son, when this is the kind of thing she says in writing and on Facebook, the true cause of Michael Brown's death is really an environment which encourages an attitude of hip-hop, gang-bang, shoplifting, "get even with whitey" and "it's all 'the man's' fault" attitude that is all too pervasive in America today.

So all we can offer to those who want to take to the streets and cause unrest is to "clean up your own house and stop blaming others for your own shortcomings."

Until that happens, there will be more Michael Browns and more dead cops, and the problem will be repeated over and over and over again. What's worse, a society that was once envisioned by Martin Luther King, Jr, will go down in flames as a result.

Baltimore (coming to a city near you)

28 April 2015

"I've made it very clear that I work with the police and instructed them to do everything that they could to make sure that the protesters were able to exercise their right to free speech. It's a very delicate balancing act, because while we tried to make sure that they were protected from the cars and the other things that were going on, we also gave those who wished to destroy space to do that as well."

—Stephanie Rawlings-Blake, Mayor of the City of Baltimore, 25 April, 2015

Angry mobs and rioting are nothing new to Baltimore.

For instance, the first bloodshed of the American Civil War took place on Pratt Street in April of 1861, when local sympathizers to the Southern cause pelted the Sixth Massachusetts Regiment with cobblestones while marching from the President Street Station in East Baltimore to Camden Station in West Baltimore, prompting the death of sixteen men and injuring thirty-six others when the soldiers opened fire on what were locally known as the "Punk Uglies." As a result, newly elected President Abraham Lincoln ordered cannon be placed atop Federal Hill overlooking the city's downtown, with orders to "level" the city in the event of further disturbances. This bloodshed and Lincoln's reaction to it prompted the writing of what later became Maryland's State song, *Maryland, My Maryland*, by James Randall, as a rallying cry for Marylanders to join the Confederacy. Lincoln summarily jailed pro-Southern legislators, suspending habeas corpus, and thus prevented Maryland's secession.

Fast forward precisely one hundred seven years later when in April, 1968, rioting erupted in Baltimore following the assassination of Martin Luther King, Jr. For seven days, blacks rioted in the streets of Baltimore, setting 1,200 fires, looting thousands of local businesses, and terrorizing a city already struggling with race relations. Six people died, and seven hundred others were injured, resulting in 5,800 arrests and $12 million in property damages, the worst taking place in the U.S. during that troubled year.

Fast forward once more forty-seven years. It is April, 2015, and the injury and subsequent death of a twenty-five year old black man, Freddie Gray, in the custody of the Baltimore Police, prompted demonstrations which began peacefully, but quickly turned violent on Saturday, April 25th just outside Oriole Park at Camden Yards, when marching demonstrators attacked white fans outside a nearby pub and the police were nowhere to be found. Two days later, in northwest Baltimore, high school kids, prompted by social media, begin pelting police officers with bricks and stones, setting patrol cars on fire and sending fifteen officers to area hospitals, in what was a textbook example of that which happens when local law enforcement officers are ordered by their superiors to give leeway in the face of assault and stand down on orders of the Baltimore powers-that-be. Baltimore Police had advanced warning of a "verifiable threat" when three black gangs, known as the Black Guerilla Family, the Crips, and the Bloods announced that they would join together in concerted effort to kill white cops, and the mayor of this city did basically nothing to stop what was to follow until far too late. Later denying what she had said two days before about "giving space to those who want to destroy," she was also late in calling on Maryland Governor Larry Hogan to bring out the National Guard and, incredulously, announcing a citywide curfew beginning *tonight* when she should have made it effective *last night*. Mayor Blake, who is also secretary of the Democratic National Committee, reportedly consulted with President Barack Obama, who advised both herself and the Maryland Governor to "show restraint" in dealing with the protestors and to give them leeway in their increasingly violent expressions of anger.

Welcome to Obama's America, where rioters and looters are labeled "victims of oppression" and anarchy reigns. We are quite familiar with this section of Baltimore, where our mother grew up a half dozen blocks from the CVS pharmacy that was looted by the "oppressed" and summarily set afire. Firefighters, attempting to put out the fire, were thwarted by other "oppressed" citizens, who used switchblades to render their fire hoses inoperable. The assault on the police officers by black high school students being incited to "purge" and thus create havoc did so at an intersection where our father once worked at a gasoline station to support his family during the Great Depression. His family lacked what these "oppressed" people are given (welfare, food stamps, assistance) freely, showing the ugly reality of "dogs biting the very hands that feed them." The looting continued; liquor stores, wig shops, all types of locally owned businesses were looted by more of the "oppressed," who in reality couldn't have picked out Freddie Gray in a lineup of three people if they had to do so. A City Councilman who was watching a liquor store being looted ordered the police to retreat and allow the looting to continue and then told a reporter that the looting was the result of "decades-long oppression and insensitivity to the needs of the poor people who needed community investment, jobs, and leniency from the police." My father, back in the day, must have missed the memo that says, "It's okay to loot a nearby business if you are poor," but this is the reality of what has become of a once-great American city, the city of William Donald Schaeffer, urban homesteading, inner-city revitalization projects like Harborplace, and new baseball and football stadiums. That Baltimore died last night. No one in their right mind would bring much-needed businesses to a city whose police are ordered not to protect the very businesses on which a community depends for jobs and economic opportunity.

Weep not for Baltimore, for what has taken place there is coming to a city near you, thanks to the lack of leadership at the highest levels of government, including the Mayor, the City Council, and yes, even the President of the United States.

Baltimore (coming to a city near you) Part II

30 April 2015

Warning- What you're about to read may arouse anger. Please read carefully to the end prior to jumping to conclusions.

When all is said and done, and when all tempers cool (God willing), the fact of the matter is that we will never *know* whether Freddie Gray injured himself on purpose or accidentally, or whether his injuries were as a result of the way he was handled by the Baltimore Police Department. Those who believe that Freddie Gray was a victim of police brutality will continue to believe this, despite any or all evidence to the contrary. Those who believe that Freddie Gray injured himself accidentally or on purpose as a means to achieve whatever he may have wanted to achieve will continue to believe this, despite any or all evidence to the contrary. Nothing will sway either position in the minds of those who have made up their minds, any and all evidence be damned.

And, at the end of the day, it doesn't matter.

What *does* matter, the thing that really sticks out, is how we are going to proceed from here.

No amount of protests, no amount of marching, no amount of screaming, no amount of looting, nor assaults on police officers, nor fires, nor arrests, nor speaking in platitudes is going to bring Freddie Gray back to life, nor will it calm a troubled city, nor will it achieve law and order, nor social justice, nor anything of value to society as a whole. No amount of spending public funds will help people better their lot in life. No politically-motivated study group will arrive at an answer on how to cure that which ails us, and no amount of political rhetoric is going to change people of all races in the way that they need to be changed. None.

What is needed in Baltimore, what is needed in America or for that matter the world itself, cannot and will not be purchased, nor legislated, nor forced through political correctness, nor force of arms, nor bullying by others. What is needed, quite simply, will not come from without, but rather from within, which is why the solution to that which ails us is so evasive, so delicate, so nuanced, and yet, so damned simple that it is tragic in its simplicity.

Each of us, all of us, myself included, need to reach deep inside and ask ourselves "how?" How are we going to get along with one another? How are we going to make our communities safe? How are we ever going to arrive upon that which has eluded humanity since Cain slew Abel? How are we going to make the world around us a better place for all of God's children?

This much is certain. If we as individuals, if we as a community, if we as a nation and as a world fail to search within ourselves and seek the light within all of the darkness, seek truth within the clamor of garish noise, seek peace within ourselves, and with those with whom we encounter, then we are doomed as a people and as a nation and as a world, whose most intelligent form of life is otherwise going to extinguish itself.

Massacre in Charleston

19 June 2015

Every once in a while, we learn of a crime so horrific, so absolutely and undeniably detestable in its perpetration, that mere words cannot begin to balance the totality of its impact, not only upon its victims and their families, but on the greater society as a whole.

Such is the massacre which took place Wednesday night, the 17th of June, 2015.

A deranged racist, one Dylann Roof, who had a history of arrests and drug use, attended a Bible study group in the basement of Mother Emmanuel AME Church in Charleston, South Carolina, participated in the study group for about an hour, and then summarily arose, and thus killed nine innocent people, starting with its pastor and State Senator Clementa Pinckney. The perpetrator of this heinous crime was a known user of the drug Suboxone, a powerful narcotic analgesic, one that is known to bring about sudden violent outbursts if used in excess of prescribed dosages. He was also a nascent white supremacist, who was involving himself in the ideology of neo-Nazi, skinhead, and other racist ideologies who spew the same kind of hatred that other such groups are known to disseminate. The fact that this malcontented miscreant chose to thrust his hatred upon a group of people who gathered in the basement of a church to read and pray and worship, all the while pretending to be part of this group, makes his deadly assault especially repugnant. This was not merely a crime of passion, nor even a crime of unbridled racism. This was a crime of absolute and unadulterated evil, the satanic nature of which cannot and must not be overlooked.

It will be some time before we know all that was coursing through the twisted mind of this evil young man. Yet at the end of the day, it is hardly a stretch to say that his motivations went far beyond racism, far beyond the twisted philosophy of white supremacism, far beyond the glorification of apartheid, as evidenced by an earlier photograph of Roof wearing a jacket adorned with the flags of apartheid South Africa and Rhodesia.

When all of the dust has settled, it will become a self-evident truth that what really motivated this twenty-one-year-old to kill such innocent people in the way he killed them in the place and circumstance of their killing was the presence of evil so invested into the soul of such a man, which can only and possibly be rooted in something far more sinister than sociology and pathology. Its root is in the evil incarnate and all-consuming perdition of Satan himself.

It is indeed no surprise that certain politicians, namely the President and the former Secretary of State, took the occasion to exploit this tragedy for political purposes by renewing calls for gun control legislation, exposing the depravity of their political aspirations by revealing how they would use the sacrifice of nine lives to suit their own agendas. Other politicians chose to suspend their campaign activities out of decency and respect for those whose lives were lost Wednesday night, but this is a topic for another day and another time.

Today, all of us must reconsider and duly recognize the fact that there is indeed absolute evil which exists in the world today, an evil which cannot be politicized, cannot be socialized, cannot be legislated away. It is an evil as old as mankind, as old as Cain and Abel, and as old and ruthless as the unabashed hatred with which it is commingled, and one in which we can only pray and hope and aspire to rid within our society and within the world at large.

Symbolism over Substance

24 June 2015

In the frenzy to remove and/or deface all things Confederate, be they flags, statues, memorials, and yes, even headstones, much more is lost than won over these vacuous gestures. Listening to the talking heads as they bloviate through their all-too-predictable mantras, one might be led to believe the lie that were it not for the Confederate battle flag flying on the South Carolina capital grounds in Columbia, Dylann Roof would not have perpetrated the murder of nine innocent people on the evening of June 17th in Charleston. Yeah, right.

Turn back the clock to a fortnight ago, when no one, *no one*, was talking about the Confederate flag or what they *think* is the Confederate flag.

The familiar banner, known during the Civil War as the Confederate Battle Flag, is not nor ever was, the flag of the Confederacy. What is erroneously referred to as the stars and bars was not that either. The "stars and bars" was actually a flag that was based on the American flag. It had three very broad stripes, two red and one white (the bars) with a field of blue in its upper left hand corner with seven stars in a circular pattern representing the original seven states (the stars) of the Confederacy. This flag was the original and first flag of the Confederate States of America. Show a picture of this flag to the talking heads, who are most opposed to the display of the Confederate flag, and damned few of these imbeciles would raise any ruckus about it, which only goes to show that the loudest of mouths are frequently in close proximity to the smallest of brains.

Because from a distance, the original Confederate flag looked too much like the American flag (often causing friendly fire on both sides during the early years of the Civil War), the more familiar Battle Flag of the Confederacy with its pattern of thirteen stars arranged in a blue "x" on a red field was adopted for the purposes of battlefield identification. This pattern, set in the upper left hand corner of subsequent Confederate flags, became the second, third, and fourth official flags of the Confederacy, not unlike the state flag of Mississippi, which is still flown today in the Magnolia State.

It is altogether understandable why the Battle Flag of the Confederacy is offensive to some, particularly black Americans, some of whose distant ancestors were slaves. It might even be understandable (this is a stretch) why the same flag is offensive to some white Americans, whose ancestors fought for the Union during the Civil War. What is not particularly so understandable is why this flag is so offensive to those who can claim neither connection, slavery nor service.

Liberals in particular love to "Monday morning quarterback" and thereby "second guess" the motives of people who are now long since dead, trying to apply current sensitivities of political correctness and contemporary ideas of moral right and wrong to those who struggled with divisive issues one hundred fifty years ago. They will tell you the big lie that every Confederate soldier taking up arms against the Union did so because he inherently believed in and was willing to die for the institution of slavery. This lie—and it's a whopper—conveniently dismisses the fact that only one percent of those fighting for the Confederacy were slaveholders and also conveniently dismisses the fact that thousands of black southerners fought for the South. Perhaps it is conjecture to believe that a majority of these men, too poor to own slaves, would risk their lives for an institution that did not benefit them in the least, but we seriously doubt it. Never mind explaining that to a liberal; their minds are made up that the Confederate army was the nineteenth century equivalent of the twentieth century Nazis.

It is said that history of all wars is written by the victors and that the passage of time tends to divorce history from that which actually took place. Nevertheless, it is a matter of historical record that the Civil War did not become the "war to free slaves" until January, 1863, when Lincoln's Emancipation Proclamation (which, by the way, exempted the border states of Maryland, Kentucky, and Missouri) was set forth. Until then, the war was about national unity versus states' rights (the right to secede), and even the songs soldiers on both sides sang lay credence to this all but forgotten reality.

It is also amazing that so many politicos, who once celebrated Confederate flags and monuments (Mrs. Clinton, anyone?), now find it politically expedient and contemporarily convenient to jump on the "take down the flag" bandwagon. Yet in the final analysis, people seem to forget that flags, like guns, do not and cannot kill; only evil people of all races and political persuasions can and all too often do kill, with absolutely no thought to any flag.

Today, we see that Confederate flags and Confederate monuments are coming down and being defaced, respectively. So what is next?

Well, on many campuses across the country, academic elitists are now sounding a similar clarion call to haul down Old Glory, because they and the students they indoctrinate with prevarications and revisionist history find that the flag of the United States is offensive, that it symbolizes American imperialism and American atrocities and other such tommyrot as they would have us believe. They have actively encouraged desecration of the American flag and have petitioned to have it hauled down so as not to offend the all-so-precious sensitivities of those who do not respect the flag or what it stands for.

So, to all of you who wish to see a flag from the past taken down, would you be so willing to see your country's flag, Old Glory, also taken down, because some people find that it is also offensive?

My, the crickets are chirping aloud this month of June, aren't they?

When Lives Matter

31 August 2015

Ferguson. Baltimore. Brooklyn. Charleston; Roanoke. Houston. And, like the Energizer Bunny®, the list just keeps going and going and going. But where?

Of all of the social movements that have grown out of the events referred to above, perhaps the most moronic, the most divisive, and alas, the most racist is the "Black Lives Matter" movement which has taken a stranglehold of the political left, with the blessing of the most divisive president in the history of the United States, Barack Hussein Obama. Like no other president in the last two hundred thirty-six years, Obama has done more to divide people along racial lines than the sum total of all his forty-three predecessors combined.

It is not without reasonable notice that the President of the United States has much to say about the evils of racism when a black man is killed by a white man, but when a white man is killed by a black man, either nothing is said OR the blame falls on the gun rather than the assailant. Given the fact that 95% of all black men killed by guns are killed by black men, the president is woefully silent with regard to black-on-black crime, instead blaming this violence on the lack of gun control laws. Never mind the statistical reality that gun violence is greatest in cities which have the strictest gun control laws enacted. Better to blame the weapon than the moral depravity of the assailant, and this is where the president's moral authority is most lacking. A president is supposed to lead ALL of the people, not just the people who support him, nor the people whose race with which he identifies, nor even the members of his own political party, but rather ALL of the people. To do otherwise is to engage in the malpractice of the politics of division, emulating the modus operandi of Lenin, Stalin, Hitler, Mao, Castro, and other megalomaniacs who sought power in precisely the same manner: conquest via division.

Do black lives matter, really matter? Well, of course, black lives matter, just as white lives matter, as do yellow lives, brown lives, red lives, and yes, even blue lives matter. In fact, *all* lives matter, and anyone who does not agree that *all* lives matter is the *real* racist. While a Martin O'Malley can apologize after saying that all lives matter, and while a Bernie Sanders can surrender his microphone to a black-lives-matter protester, and while a Hillary Clinton can exploit the black-lives-matter movement as a means to harvest a particular block of voters, these politicians are only serving to make matters worse by giving legitimacy to what in reality is a racist movement, one that implies that black lives matter more than other lives. To suggest otherwise is ironically deemed racist by the politically correct when actually the opposite ideology is true, All lives *do* matter.

We don't hear chants that police lives matter, despite the fact that twenty-three law enforcement officers have been killed so far in 2015 alone. We don't hear that Christian lives matter, despite the wholesale genocide of Christians in areas controlled by ISIS. We don't hear that unborn lives matter, despite the millions of babies whose organs are being harvested for profit by Planned Parenthood and other such organizations. The hypocrisy is quite obvious and revealing.

Whoever is elected the next president of the United States will unfortunately be placed into the unenviable position of having to clean up this horrible legacy of the Obama administration–a legacy which has set back race relations sixty years through pitting one race against another during the term of his presidency. Any candidate who lacks the moral courage to insist that *all* lives matter has no business being elected President of the United States, regardless of who they are or the party from which they are nominated. Anyone who does not agree with this premise should own up to being exactly what they are—inherently racist—and would serve this country best by surrendering their right to vote.

(author's note- Energizer Bunny® is a registered trademark of Energizer Holding, Inc., manufacturer of batteries under the same trademarked name.)

Race in America—The Myth of White Privilege

12 November 2015

Realizing fully well that there are those who will quickly jump to label me "racist" for merely writing the headline that is written above, I am nevertheless going to take issue with the concept of "white privilege" because to do otherwise would betray my own search for the truth as it exists in America today. I was born as the civil rights movement of the 1950s was just in its infancy, and I well remember a time when black Americans were not granted the full benefits of American citizenship. I remember watching on television the fire hoses and police dogs that were turned on those who were peacefully marching to demand racial equality, particularly in the Deep South. I remember the animosity of whites who were opposed to integration and desegregation of schools, churches, and businesses of all types. To deny this reality of race relations, as it existed in the 1950s and 1960s, is to deny the reality of that which occurred during that time period.

Then, as the 1960s turned into the 1970s, I witnessed a fundamental change in the civil rights movement, one that transformed peaceful demonstrations into militant and terroristic expressions and acts of violence, inspired by all- too-calculating and race-baiting opportunists who sought not justice, but rather power, the power to incite, the power to exploit, the power to destroy. I saw what had been an altruistic movement to achieve equality transcend into a seditious and corrosive desire for revenge and retribution. To deny this reality of race relations, which began in the 1970s, is to deny the reality of that which occurred during that time period.

Considering today, what is happening in large cities and university campuses across the country with regards to race relations, I am witnessing the slow but steady descent into anarchy, which is sowing the seeds of racial discord which we had once thought long dead, a generation or two ago. I see misguided young people, people who were not yet born in the early 1990s, taking to the streets and screaming that "black lives matter," absurdly suggesting that black lives matter more than white lives, matter more than brown lives, matter more than yellow lives, matter more than blue lives. I see feckless liberals in politics and academia cowardly caving in to the delusional demands of mindless youths, youths who are acting on lies that are being fed to them in the mainstream media, in the collegiate classrooms, and in the very streets by those who seek to profit by fomenting hatred and misery and by those who are encouraging the absolute breakdown of peaceful coexistence, individual liberty, and the freedom of expression and divergent ideas in a country whose very existence has been dedicated to all of these values.

To suggest that in these years, the two thousand teens, that there exists in the United States today an all-pervasive "white privilege" is nothing more than a dubious means to sanction anti-white racism by militant blacks, as well as white radicals, most of whom did not yet exist in an era where black people truly were second-class citizens, in an era before the Civil Rights Act of 1964, in an era before equal opportunity legislation and before affirmative action in hiring and university admissions. These young people have never experienced racism like that which was witnessed by their grandparents and great-grandparents and yet find themselves to be the hapless prey of politicians who seek nothing more than the offices of power by exploiting their useful anger to pursue their own nefarious agendas.

Worse, the visions of a truly color blind society, once expressed by men and women of all races who based their advocacy upon good will and hopeful desire of healing, are thus being rendered asunder in all of the screaming and yelling based on a lie, the lie that police officers are out to kill blacks, the lie that white people want to return to the days of "Jim Crow," the lie that white people only succeed due to "institutionalized white privilege," the lie that America is an evil place where only the few are allowed to succeed.

If in writing this I am to be labeled "racist," then so be it, but that is the truth as I see it. And no number of demagogues screaming to the contrary and no amount of political correctness or attempts to silence and censure can change this truth: that the concept of "white privilege" in the autumn of 2015 is nothing more than an evil lie, designed to divide rather than unite us as a people and as a nation.

Part II
Political Monsters

Chapter 5

Barack Obama

The Wrong Side of History

4 March 2012

Where would we be, in response to the 1915 sinking of the RMS Lusitania, if Woodrow Wilson would have responded with, "Kaiser Wilhelm II is on the wrong side of history?"

Where would we be, in response to the 1939 invasion of Poland by Germany, if Winston Churchill would have responded with, "Adolf Hitler is on the wrong side of history?"

Where would we be, in response to the 1941 Japanese attack on Pearl Harbor, if Franklin Roosevelt would have responded with, "Hideki Tojo is on the wrong side of history?"

Where would we be, in response to the 1950 invasion of South Korea by Communist North Korea, if Harry Truman would have responded with, "Kim Il Sung is on the wrong side of history?"

Where would we be, in response to the 1961 erection of the Berlin Wall, if John F. Kennedy would have responded with, "Walter Ulbricht is on the wrong side of history?"

Where would we be, in response to the 1962 Cuban Missile Crisis, if John F. Kennedy would have responded with, "Nikita Khrushchev is on the wrong side of history?"

Where would we be, in response to the buildup of Soviet armaments in the 1980s, if Ronald Reagan would have responded with, "Leonid Brezhnev is on the wrong side of history?"

Where would we be, in response to the 1991 Iraqi invasion of Kuwait, if George H.W. Bush would have responded with, "Saddam Hussein is on the wrong side of history?"

Where would we be, in response to the 9/11 attacks on New York and Washington, if George W. Bush had responded with, "Osama bin Laden is on the wrong side of history?"

And . . .

Where *are* we now, in response to the 2014 Russian invasion of the Ukraine, when Barack Hussein Obama responds with, "Vladimir Putin is on the wrong side of history?"

I'll tell you where we are, thanks to our feckless and irresponsible president. We are on the wrong side of history.

Election 2012 Forethoughts

21 Sept 2012

Up until lately, I was errant in believing that this election was going to largely hinge on the dismal economy that we have been experiencing going back to the final year of the Bush administration, an economy that on balance has not improved and in some cases has actually worsened under the current administration. Yet, as so often happens in presidential campaigns, outside events begin to affect the course of political campaigns and the elections that result. The spate of violence erupting overseas has brought foreign policy into the debate of who is best suited to lead our nation in times of peril, times where our economic woes are now beset with the woes of world events taking shape as this is written. President Obama came into office promising a change in the way our nation conducts its foreign policy, with particular regards to how he would approach the means of communicating with the Islamic nations where there is so much turmoil taking place. What is often referred to as "the apology tour," he thought erroneously that if he could project a United States as somewhat humbled and contrite, that those who had been against us during the Bush administration would somehow reach out to us in appreciation for our new-found humility. For these efforts, he was awarded a Nobel Peace prize by an international community starving for a US president who would downplay US exceptionalism, a dubious award for a dubious reason at best.

As the Arab spring unfolded, Obama continued this approach in hopes that with the downfall of the Hosni Mubarak and Muhammar Khadafy regimes in Egypt and Libya, respectively, democracy would take hold and usher in a new era of peace in the region. Essentially, this naiveté in his approach has rendered a far more unstable situation across the region, where even our closest allies question the resolve and strategy that the United States brings to bear. While trying to pretend that this eruption of violence was merely a backlash against a poorly-produced YouTube video insulting Muhammad, anyone with half a brain knows that these events took place on the eleventh anniversary of the 9/11, that these attacks were carried out by a well-orchestrated campaign whose operatives were armed with assault weapons and RPGs, hardly the equipment usually in the hands of mere protesters. This pretense by the Obama administration was a cover-up to hide the real culprit, which is basically a direct result of the naive and feckless foreign policy that this administration has put into effect in a world which has become ever-more closer to the brink of destruction. A weaker foreign policy is no way to engage an enemy who hates us, something that history has told us over and over and over again at the costs of millions of lives.

If the president cannot protect Americans—American lives, American interests, American freedoms—then all of the other debates about education, the economy, the environment, etc., are rendered moot. This president has failed in all of these regards (the killing of Bin Laden doesn't change this), and for those of you who are thinking of casting your vote to continue this downward spiral by re-electing Barack Obama, I would ask that you think about your decision first before you cast this vote. Mitt Romney is not a perfect candidate to be certain. His campaign has been largely inept, to be sure. But the central questions of this election year are simply these:

"Does President Obama deserve for more years?"

"Does the United States want to continue down the path of its own self-destruction?"

Ask yourselves these questions for the sake of our future and futures of our children we so cherish.

This, friends, I beg of you.

When All of the Dust Settles,
What Will We Have Learned?

11 October 2012

We have been told for many weeks now that the president's re-election is something just short of a lock. Pollsters have been drumming the line that Republican challenger Mitt Romney doesn't stand a chance in the swing states that will ultimately decide this election, even saying recently that in the crucial state of Ohio, Barack Obama holds a ten-point lead, and in the Commonwealth of Virginia, a six-point lead. Yet it's almost a given that pollsters get it wrong, and we are reminded of Reagan's admonition that "the only poll that counts is the one on Election Day." I must admit myself that, prior to last week's debate between President Obama and Governor Romney, I gave the Republican nominee only four chances in ten that he might edge out the incumbent. But then, I saw the debate.

Casting aside the policy and philosophical divisions which separate the two candidates, I, along with most of the seventy million who watched the debate, gave the round to Romney, and it wasn't even close by a longshot. On one side, we saw a contestant who was commanding and forthright about what he intended to accomplish in the next four years. On the other, we saw his rival looking distracted, peevish, and in search of a message that would stick, and found to be woefully wanting. Of the two candidates, one looked like a president, the other like a "wannabe." Ironically, the one who appeared presidential does not currently hold the office. The postmortem began with the line that the sitting president was "off his game" then, that he hadn't adequately prepared for the debate, and then, when all else failed to resonate, that the apparent winner "must have lied." Hmmm. I am reminded of the fox which, having leapt at the reflection of grapes in the water, leapt to no avail and uttered, "They must have been sour anyway."

I offer another theory as to why Barack Obama did poorly in the first debate. Going back to 2007 (and perhaps before that), the media has largely given Obama a pass on just about everything having to do with his candidacy. To say that the media was "in the tank" for Obama in 2008 is a gross understatement. They were practically praying that he would set history by being the first African-American elected to the nation's highest office. Then, on what became known as the "World Apology Tour," Obama received a Nobel Peace Prize for having accomplished nothing, save his own election, even before he took office. Throughout his term in office, he was largely unchallenged by the "fourth estate," who gave him a pass on just about everything that ensued during the last four years, be it the increasing deficit and national debt (these are two different things, by the way), the bailouts that didn't work, Guantanamo (it's still open), Solyndra, gun-walking, "Obamacare" and the way it was outsourced to Harry Reid and Nancy Pelosi, and, most recently, the way the administration handled the recent events in the Middle East. Compare the way Obama has been covered by the media to the way his immediate predecessor was covered by the media, and it doesn't take a rocket scientist to see a double standard in the media's treatment of Obama as it compares to George W. Bush.

Now, having such an advantage with the media produced an unexpected but all-too-predictable result, reminding me of a prizefighter who, having laid on the couch for four years while his opponent has rigorously trained, gets his butt kicked when having to go toe-to-toe in the ring for the first time. Obama, not having been seriously challenged, has grown soft in the adulation that he has been receiving for the better part of a decade, going back to his "Red America/Blue America" keynote speech at the 2004 Democratic Convention (you remember, the one that sent chills up the leg of Chris Matthews). In 2008, Obama was the inevitable choice of an adoring media, despite the fact that he didn't even have the credentials to be president that his opponent's vice presidential nominee, Sarah Palin, brought to bear.

Yet now, in 2012, having held the office for four years, we hear from him the he is "unable to fix Washington from the inside" and that his opponent won a debate only because "he lied?" Seriously?

I know not at this point in time how the remainder of the debates will go. Nor do I pretend to know what will be the result of what takes place on the 6th of November next. But this much

I do know. Whatever is held in store, once the dust settles on the decision that lies before us, the laundry of a complicit media will be shown one way or another, and the laundry will bear the stains of a national media who, having failed to do its job, will either render the election of a man who might just prove to be a great president or the re-election of a President Wannabe who has never held a real job and who hasn't the ability nor the inclination to get the job done.

An election of consequence? You bet your ass it is.

Election 2012 — Afterthoughts

7 November 2012

As many of us watched, Barack Obama managed to eke out an electoral victory, principally by winning the narrowest of margins in a handful of states, most notably my own. I had predicted that if Mitt Romney had won either Ohio or Wisconsin (not factoring Virginia, of course), he would most likely have won the election, but if Romney had lost both of these states, Obama would win. I was correct, and Obama won.

Half of the country is happy, and half of the country is disappointed. Half of the legislative branch retained its Democratic majority (the Senate), and half of it retained its Republican majority (The House), thus assuring a divided government which succinctly reflects a divided country. One look at the electoral map also reflects this division with the Northeast, Midwest and West Coast being blue and the South and most of the Western States being red.

So now what?

Well, a great president would reach out to the other side of the aisle and find ways to work out solutions to the problems our country faces; such is the purview of real statesmen. Yet sadly, there is nothing in Obama's makeup that would suggest that he is either capable of or inclined to working together with Republicans and Democrats alike to achieve consensus, because he is a politician and most assuredly not a statesman.

Rather, by the indications of how he has conducted himself during his first term and the way he conducted his campaign for re-election, his narcissistic and self-aggrandizing tendencies not to mention his far-left political bent, will bring to bear a further polarization of our nation. He will attempt to govern by fiat, essentially putting into place policies outside the legislative process through the power of bureaucracy and regulatory oversight that will surely mean a continued erosion of representative democracy in the United States. His reckless spending priorities will expand the dependency of people on government—something our founding fathers had very much warned against—and this will ultimately result in the loss of individual liberty.

The fiscal catastrophe that will result will surely mean confiscatory tax policies that will weaken the private sector, eviscerate our military and naval forces, and ultimately weaken America at home and abroad as well. Whether or not this is what he set out to do in 2008 when he promised to "fundamentally transform the United States of America" is now beside the point, for his re-election has assured that the United States will be weakened as a result, and history tells us that once there is an absence of power in the world, this void will be filled by another, and that "other" is what we should all dread most of all.

Executive Orders

17 February 2014

So far, there have been over 900 executive orders put forth from President Obama, and he is not even through his first term yet. He is creating a martial law Disneyland of control, covering everything imaginable. Some of the executive orders he has signed recently have been exposed thanks to "Friends of Conservative Action Alerts." They have compiled a choice list of "Emergency Powers, Martial law Executive Orders." Get your headache medication out while you still can without a prescription.

Executive Order 10990 allows the government to take over all modes of transportation and control of highways and seaports.

Executive Order 10995 allows the government to seize and control the communication media.

Executive Order 10997 allows the government to take over all electrical power, gas, petroleum, fuels, and minerals.

Executive Order 11000 allows the government to mobilize civilians into work brigades under government supervision.

Executive Order 11001 allows the government to take over all health, education, and welfare functions.

Executive Order 11002 designates the Postmaster General to operate a national registration of all persons.

Executive Order 11003 allows the government to take over all airports and aircraft, including commercial aircraft.

Executive Order 11004 allows the Housing and Finance Authority to relocate and establish new locations for populations.

Executive Order 11005 allows the government to take over railroads, inland waterways, and public storage facilities.

Executive Order 11049 assigns emergency preparedness function to federal departments and agencies, consolidating 21 operative Executive Orders issued over a fifteen-year period.

Executive Order 11051 specifies the responsibility of the Office of Emergency Planning and gives authorization to put all Executive Orders into effect in times of increased international tensions and economic or financial crisis.

Executive Order 11310 grants authority to the Department of Justice to enforce the plans set out in Executive Orders, to institute industrial support, to establish judicial and legislative liaison, to control all aliens, to operate penal and correctional institutions, and to advise and assist the President.

Executive Order 11921 allows the Federal Emergency Preparedness Agency to develop plans to establish control over the mechanisms of production and distribution of energy sources, wages, salaries, credit, and the flow of money in U.S. financial institutions in any undefined national emergency. It also provides that when the president declares a state of emergency, Congress cannot review the action for six months.

It is more than clear that Obama is planning for the total control and takeover of America via Martial Law. Food, energy, transportation, work, banking, and health. He has it covered.

While Obama is busy pulling executive orders out of his infernal regions, to control everything inside our country, he has also been issuing executive orders to force us to submit to international regulations instead of our Constitution. Sher Zieve exposed this in one of her recent articles. It is as though Barack Obama and his behind-the-scenes handler, Valerie Jarrett, are saying, "Damn the U.S. Constitution, damn the American people, and damn U.S. sovereignty."

We must send faxes and emails and make calls to all congressmen and demand they stop Obama's perverted, extreme, and unconstitutional abuse of Executive Orders. It is time to demand our elected leaders start protecting America, our sovereignty, and our Constitution. So far, they seem to be protecting the Obama/ Marxist takeover plans, peppered with a little U.N. and Islam-centrism.

The Seeds of Impeachment

20 June 2014

Every mighty tree that ever grew began as a seed, which buried in the soil sprouted a tap root that began to spread into branches of that tap root. Then its sprout penetrated upward through the ground's surface and likewise began to grow into a trunk which sprouted branches, until the tree dwarfed the seed of its origin.

In a similar matter, every time in our history that the "tree" of impeachment or a potential of impeachment grew, it started as a "seed" covered up in dirt and began to sprout the roots of discontent, and the branches of dishonesty bore the fruit of impeachment.

Forty years ago, a 1972 burglary of the Democratic National Committee grew into a scandal of cover-up that caused Richard Nixon to resign his presidency. The articles of impeachment that had been drawn up had nothing to do with the actual break-in and everything to do with the lengths to which Nixon and members of his administration to cover up and obstruct the investigation appertaining thereto.

Sixteen years ago, Bill Clinton was impeached on two counts of perjury and one count each of abuse of power and obstruction of justice, which grew out of the seeds of the Whitewater real estate investment scandals, sexual harassment of Paula Jones, and ultimately, fellatio performed on the President in the Oval Office by Monica Lewinsky. The actual articles of impeachment had nothing to do with semen on Lewinsky's dress and everything to do with the fact that Clinton perjured himself in a deposition to a grand jury, and he attempted to obstruct justice in the investigation of Whitewater.

By comparison to Nixon's Watergate break-in and Clinton's Whitewater investment scandal/sexual peccadillos, comparatively small seeds in terms of their effects on the American public, the Obama administration has engaged in the process of planting numerous, much larger seeds that are just beginning to sprout tap roots in what might well grow into a veritable grove of impeachment trees.

The Veterans Health Administration, in their false recordkeeping and delays of services, those being systematically covered up that have caused and continue to cause actual deaths of veterans awaiting medical services, is but one of these trees.

The ATF gun-walking scandal, also known as "Fast and Furious," which resulted in the death of US Border Patrol Agent Brian Terry, has already resulted in formal charges of contempt for Obama's Attorney General, Eric Holder, by the House of Representatives for failing to provide Congress with subpoenaed documents.

Then there is the Benghazi Raid and the failure of Hillary Clinton's State Department to provide adequate security to the consulate in Libya that resulted in the deaths of our Ambassador, Christopher Stevens and three others, and the attempt to fabricate a false narrative of a video to hide both the President's and Secretary's culpability in their refusal to provide adequate security before the raid and rescue operations during the raid, all because Obama was in the midst of a re-election campaign whose narrative was that the "Arab spring was a success and Al-Quada is on the run," both of which were not true. These three scandals, unlike Nixon's and Clinton's scandals, have actually resulted in the deaths of Americans.

And then there is the IRS targeting of conservative organizations applying for 501(c)(4) tax exemptions, originally and falsely blamed on rogue operatives in the IRA Cincinnati office, which have now been traced to the IRS Headquarters in Washington. The former Commissioner of the IRS, Doug Shulman, went to the White House 138 times during his tenure when the targeting was going on, but in Congressional testimony said that he could only recall an Easter egg hunt as the reason for one of these visits and could not remember why he went there on the other 137 occasions. Then two years after Lois Lerner's e-mails were subpoenaed by Congress, these e-mails suddenly have vanished into thin air due to a hard drive crash, and the subsequent disposal of the computer's hard drive conveniently waylaying and preventing investigation into e-mails Lerner had sent to government entities outside the Treasury Department, e-mails which might otherwise have revealed IRS communication to other government entities like OSHA and the FBI, which also launched investigations into businesses run by taxpayers who supported these same conservative organizations. Also noteworthy was the fact that seven other IRS officials, being tied to the IRS abuse scandals, also somehow had the 'misfortune" of hard drive crashes and lost e-mails. All the while, Obama insists that there is not smidgen of corruption in this arena.

Despite the fact that the major media has refused to acknowledge these scandals as anything but phony scandals and Republican partisan witch hunts and despite the efforts of Democratic House members who toe the same line for the Obama administration, these scandals are very real, in some cases deadly and, in the case of the IRS, affect thousands of Americans both in and outside our government. Worse yet, there are other instances of either incompetence or outright dishonesty that are threatening the ability of President Obama to lead our nation in very troubled times, both here and around the world. Even some of Obama's supporters in the media, cognizant of his declining approval numbers, are beginning to see that his ability to lead the country has all but ended. Such a diminishment of his moral authority, left unchecked, will ultimately result in public outcry for further investigations and impeachment, which can be accelerated with a Republican takeover of the U.S. Senate in November.

As these scandals grow branches and begin to bear ill fruit, coupled with the stagnant economy and troubles abroad, Obama is unwittingly and steadily fertilizing the seeds of his own demise, and the danger is that all of us will be forced to dine upon the fruits of his own design.

DREW NICKELL 99

Redistribution

1 July 2014

First, a parable:

Once upon a time, there was a father who gave his son an allowance of $1.00 per week. The father told his son that he would have to "live within his means." Over time the son ran up debts that averaged $2.00 per week. So the son went to the father and said, 'Dad, if you increase my allowance to $2.00 per week, I promise I will live within my means." So the father increased his allowance to $2.00 per week. After a while, the son ran up debts to an average of $4.00 per week. So the son went to his father and said, "Dad, if you will only increase my allowance to $4.00 per week, I promise that I will live within my means." So the father increased the allowance to $4.00 per week. Sure enough, the son ran up debts that amounted to $8.00 per week. So the son said to his dad, "Dad, if you can just give me an increase to $8.00 per week, I promise that this time, I will cut my spending and live within my means." Predictably, this cycle continued: $8.00, $16.00, $32.00, $64.00, $128.00, etc., etc. etc. Then one day, the son came home and saw a "For Sale" sign in front of the family home. When he asked his dad why the house was for sale, the father told him that he could no longer afford to pay the mortgage on the house, because there wasn't enough money left after giving his son an allowance and the debts that the son had continued to run up would have to be paid. The son said to his dad, "All this time, I thought you had enough money, and now you have to sell the house? Well, gee, Dad, can I still get my allowance after you sell the house?"

This story, which I originally wrote in 2012, is an illustration of largesse on the part of our government and its propensity to throw billions of dollars to fix a problem that, in the end, is not going to be fixed by throwing more and more money at it. Since the inception of redistribution in the United States going back to LBJ's Great Society programs and even FDR's New Deal, there has been an effort to redistribute private wealth for the "public good," in other words taking from the "haves" and giving to the "have-nots." What was once a noble effort on the part of our society to provide for those who are truly in need has grown to the point of multigenerational dependency growing ever larger to the extent that we have arrived at a place where upwards of fifty millions of our citizens are receiving EBT benefits, while forty-five percent of our population is receiving some form of assistance from our government, all in the name of compassion, yet altogether unsustainable, in any way imaginable, as these numbers continue to grow.

To even mention these facts to anyone brings on the predictable accusations of insensitivity and selfishness, as though the national wealth is something that should be shared equally without any regard to the source of this wealth. There are those, largely Obama supporters and their liberal allies, who advocate such wholesale redistribution, and it is no wonder.

As far back as 2001, Barack Obama was advocating legislative action to make mandatory the wholesale redistribution of wealth in a radio discussion ("Odyssey" Chicago Public Radio, 18 Jan. 2001) he was having with two law professors while he was an Illinois state senator, citing specifically the failure of the civil rights movement to include legislative requirements that would mandate wholesale redistribution of private wealth to the less fortunate. Ladies and gentlemen, this is nothing less than radical socialism, and this point of view has now found discretionary power in our nation's highest office.

There is an inherent, tangible problem with this philosophy. If we took 100% of all of the assets of the wealthy in this country and distributed all of this wealth to the poor in this country, the net result would be a poverty level of 100%, which to some seems "fair," but to anyone who can look past the end of their nose is the recipe for national failure and the basis of our own destruction. It was Margaret Thatcher who epitomized this reality when she said, "The problem with socialism is that, eventually, you run out of other people's money."

Add this to the problem of illegal immigrants flooding an all-too-porous border who have been assured by this administration that they and their children will be cared for, and now we see an intent on the part of this administration to completely and intentionally wreck our economy and subsequently introduce the concept of the "collective" into the American system as a replacement for free enterprise. And this, ladies and gentlemen, is called Communism.

Going back to his formative years, most all of Obama's mentors were card-carrying communists, and they did a splendid job of indoctrinating their young protégé on the doctrine of communism, sealing the philosophy that he has endeared ever since. His promise to "fundamentally transform the United States of America" on Election Night, 2008 is now well under way, as evidenced by the dramatic rise in the numbers of people on public assistance that has taken place since he was inaugurated in January, 2009.

Those who have opposed him politically have faced substantial and punitive repercussions, most notably on the part of the IRS, but this fundamental transformation has not stopped there. We now live in a country where, thanks to his administration and their priorities, our government provides better health care to Guantanamo detainees than they do our own service veterans. The poor, the imprisoned, and indigent illegals who enter this country also are provided better health care than those who served our country, fought our wars, and sacrificed themselves so that we may enjoy freedom.

To even mention these things is to bring on charges of racism, insensitivity, callousness, and the predictable labels of "Right Wing Nut Job," all because, in their efforts to indoctrinate the minions who support them, the political left has committed wholesale larceny of the language itself, aided and abetted by a complicit media who failed in their duties to expose the hidden agenda of Barack Hussein Obama, and now we are all having to suffer the consequences of their failure to do so.

At the end of this week, we observe Independence Day, which is supposed to be an observance of the very thing that always made this country the greatest on earth, namely, Independence. Yet in increasing dependency on the part of millions, we are unwittingly undoing this spirit of independence and unknowingly playing into the designs of those who would tear us asunder. If we as a nation fail to awake and see what is taking place before our very eyes, America will cease to exist, and on that day all of us will come to suffer and rue the day that Obama and his acolytes came into power.

An Extremely "Foreign" Policy

21 July 2014

Last week's missile attack on Malaysia Flight 17 near the Russian-Ukrainian border, which caused the death of 298 innocent and unsuspecting people, was part and parcel of the proxy war that Russia has been conducting in efforts to reincarnate the Soviet Union. Vladimir Putin, well-schooled in the clandestine arts when he was an agent with the KGB, plays a deadly game of wit and parry, using separatists to lay siege to a sovereign Ukrainian nation, fully arming these separatists, providing enhanced training, and allegedly also providing Russian troops and equipment, conveniently devoid of any Russian military insignia on either.

Keep in mind that while not a full-fledged member of NATO, Ukraine has been a fully-fledged member of NATO's Partnership for Peace, having signed the NATO-Ukraine Action Plan in 2002, which essentially obligates NATO to treat Ukraine as a *de facto* partner in the event of outside aggression.

When Russia essentially annexed the Crimean peninsula in February, 2014, Ukraine's most southern and strategically-important region, NATO responded vis-à-vis the United States (nothing happens in NATO without the United States taking the lead), responded by providing MREs, Meals Ready to Eat, and nothing else. On face value this is at best a feckless initiative on the part of the Obama administration to tacitly show support for Ukrainian sovereignty. In fact, however, Vladimir Putin has nothing to fear from NATO with Obama as president of its strongest member, when this is the only support we are willing to provide.

Why is this relevant? Well, first of all, it brings to mind a comment made by Barack Obama to then-outgoing Russian President Dmitry Medvedev in March of 2012, not realizing that the microphone was still turned on, where he said, "This is my last election. After my election I have more flexibility."

To this, Medvedev replied, "I understand. I will transmit this information to Vladimir," presumably referring to then-incoming Russian president Vladimir Putin.

Now to any observer, this would suggest that Barack Obama was in effect telling his Russian counterpart that, following the 2012 Election, he would be in a better position to go along with what has turned out to be a nefarious design on the part of Putin to take a more aggressive stance in Eastern Europe, which is exactly what happened, beginning with Russia's annexation of Crimea in March of this year.

Now we have a situation where a civilian airliner en route from the Netherlands to Malaysia is shot down out of the sky by an extremely sophisticated Russian SAM (surface-to-air missile), and Obama's response screams in its tepidness and lack of moral outrage. Even his UN ambassador, Samantha Power, hardly anything but a pacifist herself, expressed an admirable level of outrage in demanding Russia to "end this war," while on the very same afternoon Obama played his oft-used moral equivalency card, saying it was up to Russia, the separatists, and the Ukrainians to come to the table and seek an agreement to end the hostilities, in other words intoning that all were equally to blame, which is a lie, plain and simple.

Compare for a moment Obama's response and his insistence to follow through on attending yet another fundraiser in New York to President Ronald Reagan's response to Russia's downing of Korea Air Lines Flight 007 in 1983, and it is easy to see the difference between political expediency and fecklessness on the part of Barack Obama, as opposed to Reagan's moral clarity and righteous determination to call out Russian aggression for what it is.

In short, if this is what Obama meant promising "more flexibility" to Medvedev and Putin, back in 2012, then it is certainly not a stretch to say that this is an "extremely foreign policy," foreign to the American tradition of righteousness and moral clarity. By its effects, the Obama administration is thereby complicit in its tolerance of the reincarnation of the evil empire whose demise President Reagan worked so hard to achieve, and it is to our peril that Obama so dithers.

Being Cool

28 July 2014

Those of us who have attained a certain age, remember well that the definitive example of being cool. For my contemporaries in the mid-1970s, it was a television character ironically offered as a "greaser" from the late 1950s named Arthur Fonzarelli, expertly portrayed by Henry Winkler. "The Fonz," as he was popularly known, was an Italian-American, leather-jacketed motorcyclist, quite ironic, considering that Henry Winkler in real life was a diminutive Jewish boy who, outside of his role as "the Fonz," was a soft-spoken, sensitive actor boasting a Master of Fine Arts from Yale. Conversely, the epitome of "cool" in the actual decade in which "Happy Days" was situated was another actor, James Dean, who made but three movies prior to his death in a 1955 automobile accident.

There were other examples of "cool" well outside of the acting profession. In sports, it was Johnny Unitas, the Baltimore Colts' quarterback with ice water running in his veins, facing the eye of the storm in the 1958 NFL Championship, leading his team down the field to put the Colts in "sudden death" overtime, which eventually the Colts won against the New York Giants on another classic Unitas drive downfield. The Beatles redefined cool in the 1960s, dethroning popular music's previous king of cool, Elvis Presley, who had taken that title from Frank Sinatra a decade before.

Politically, it was John F. Kennedy, not only cool in bearing and appearance, but in substance, as best substantiated in how his administration handled the 1962 Cuban missile crisis, thus averting what might have become an unthinkable nuclear war with the Soviet Union. Comically and pathetically, Richard Nixon tried to be cool, appearing on "Rowan and Martin's Laugh-In," delivering the show's tagline in question form: "Sock it to *me*?" It didn't work, and history would show that, in his handling of the Watergate scandal, he socked it to himself and ended up resigning the presidency. Jimmy Carter tried to portray being cool with a longer hairstyle evocative of the late 1970s and walking from the Capitol to the White House with his daughter by his side

following his own inauguration. His all-too-cool approach to the
Iranian Hostage crisis of 1979 led to his downfall, however, when
Americans realized that being cool without substance leads one
to assume reckless detachment and incompetence. Bill Clinton
revived the concept of a cool president, playing his saxophone
wearing Ray Ban sunglasses, answering hip questions about his
preference in underwear ("boxers or briefs"), which Monica
Lewinsky came to know all about first hand, and he was
impeached for perjury and obstruction of justice by playing it too
cool in testimony in federal court. So much for being cool.

It has oft been said that much of the young voters' attraction
to Barack Obama is based upon his being cool. There is no
doubt that Obama plays the cool front quite well, bounding up
staircases in a jaunty jog, offering fist- and chest-bumps with
much aplomb, and turning on the hip-hop rhetorical inflection
at will whenever addressing young voters and ethnic supporters.

Substantively, there is nothing wrong with his playing the
"cool card" up to a point, that is, and now it appears that the
president has reached and passed that point, a point of
diminishing returns. A recent poll of voters, undertaken across
the country by CNN, has shown that a 53% majority of voters,
given the chance to do it over again, say they would have voted for
Mitt Romney, instead, by a landslide margin of nine
percentage points, the equivalent of an electoral "buyers'
remorse," if there ever was such a thing.

What does this all mean? It means that it's okay to play it
cool if you have substance to back it up. However, given the
president's complete lack of leadership on a wide variety
of fronts, his coolness comes across as detached aloofness,
so symbolic of the man who worked so hard to attain the
trappings of office, only to let them slip away in the
apparent lack of interest in anything presidential except
raising funds for his Democratic Party allies. While
virtually and substantively ignoring domestic and
international flash points too numerous to count, Barack
Obama has overplayed the cool card to the extent that,
politically speaking, he has now left himself out in the cold,
and in so doing, created a vacuum of leadership here at home
and around the world.

Asleep at the Wheel

3 September 2014

Thirty years ago, when I was a district sales manager for a manufacturer of safety equipment based in Reading, Pennsylvania, the territory I managed comprised of seven states, which I had to cover by car. In order to do this effectively, I averaged driving about 1,700 miles per week, in addition to riding with my distributor representatives in their automobiles. Needless to say, I was either driving or riding in an automobile eleven hours a day. My biggest fear in those days was falling asleep at the wheel. To have done so would have surely brought about my own demise and might well have resulted in the death of others as well. Fortunately, between listening to talk radio and feebly practicing impersonations, I managed to stay awake during the years I had such a demanding schedule. Yet the fear of falling asleep at the wheel has remained with me, even though my road trips have diminished considerably in recent years.

Just as falling asleep behind the wheel of a motor vehicle presents potentially disastrous consequences, particularly for those who must make their living on the road, falling asleep behind the wheel of state has the potential of bringing down a presidency, as well as a nation, in this day and age. With crises brewing around a hostile world, it is indeed unfortunate, not to mention potentially perilous, that the President of the United States seems to be asleep at the helm of our nation.

Russia is flexing their muscles to a greater degree than at any time since the 1980s, as evidenced by the assault on the Ukraine which has already resulted in the annexation of Crimea and continued military operations against the Ukrainian Republic. At one point, Russian President Vladimir Putin recently reminded the west that Russia is a nuclear nation, something that a Russian leader has not done since Nikita Khrushchev in the early 1960s when he deployed intermediate-range ballistic missiles in Cuba. Putin did this knowing full well that Obama's response would be feckless, tepid, or nonexistent, *which is exactly what happened*. Putin would never had been so bold with Ronald Reagan or, for that matter, either George Bush (father and son) or Bill Clinton, which differentiates Barack Obama from his (count 'em) four immediate predecessors in a way no real American would ever want their commander-in-chief so differentiated. It is even arguable that Jimmy Carter, as feckless and incompetent as he most certainly was, would not have appeared as weak and as vapid in the international arena as Barack Obama appears to our friends and our foes alike.

And then there is ISIS, or ISIL, if you prefer. Regardless of what label you want to put on these murderous bastards, they pose a far greater threat than Al Quada ever did. In the wake of Obama's retreat from Iraq, a conflict that was surely won as the result of the surge during the closing years of the Bush administration, the void that Obama left behind was just as surely filled by Islamic radicals the likes of which we have never seen before. Equipped with military hardware that we left behind for the run-away Iraqi military and funding from Islamic organizations the world over that dwarfs any resources that Osama bin Laden had at his own disposal, ISIS has exponentially expanded its grip on the eastern half of Syria to the northern third of Iraq and has done so largely without response from Iraq's military, NATO, Turkey, nor the United States itself. Its members routinely rape children, abduct and rape women, murder religious minorities to a degree not seen since the Nazi holocaust, sever the heads of western journalists, and are the fearsome front line of radical Islam's war on the West, a war that we refuse to call by name or even acknowledge that it so exists, while our president attends fundraiser after fundraiser, improves his game on the links, and spends his political capital assaulting Republicans as if the GOP was the real enemy of the United States instead. He has yet to formulate a cohesive strategy to deal with such threats as ISIS and Russia present and in the vacuum of such nonexistent leadership allows bad actors to dominate the world's stage instead.

In essence, Barack Obama remains asleep at the wheel of our nation and in doing so, imperils us to a far greater degree than even the months leading up to the attacks on September 11, 2001. Regardless of whether one agrees or disagrees with Obama's domestic agenda, failing to defend our nation in the face of such threats renders such a domestic agenda pointless when our worst fears may well soon be realized. So I ask, "Is this really what we want in a president?"

Political Poison

13 November 2014

How badly has Barack Obama, along with help from Harry Reid, Nancy Pelosi and Debbie Wasserman-Schultz poisoned their Democrat Party? This badly:

> Since the election of 2008, the Democrats have lost (and the Republicans have won) a net 13 seats in the United States Senate; that's a 23% drop for the Democrats.
> Since the same election in 2008, the Democrats have lost (and the Republicans have won) a net 72 seats in the House of Representatives; that's a 28% drop for the Democrats.
> Since the same election in 2008, the Democrats have lost (and the Republicans have won) a net 7 Gubernatorial Elections; that's a 24% drop for the Democrats

Much has been made about the toxicity of Barack Obama's intention to bypass the legislature and evoke yet another Executive Order, thereby granting millions of illegal aliens amnesty for having entered the United States illegally. Well, considering that the President of the United States is sworn to uphold the laws of the United States and to preserve, protect, and defend the Constitution of the United States, such a move on his part would indeed be toxic, to say the least, and quite possibly in violation of the Constitution of the United States in practical terms.

Not that he cares. Singlehandedly, he has destroyed our credibility overseas, completely erased any semblance of a mandate he received in 2008, weakened the United States' position all over the world, alienated our allies, and emboldened our enemies to an extent not seen in the history of the United States. Not bad for a community organizer whose birth certificate is somewhat questionable, whose collegiate records remain sealed, and whose citizenship is not entirely established, not completely, that is. With the help of resident dingbats like

Nancy Pelosi, Debbie Wasserman Schultz, and Harry Reid, he has also destroyed his own political party, and that is saying something, considering that the Republicans are not exactly well loved in this country.

In short, Barack Hussein Obama is poison, toxic to his country, toxic to our allies, toxic to the world's stability (if there ever was such a thing), and toxic even unto his own political party. So the question is, "Does he give a rat's hindquarters?"

Not in the very least. And that is the very real problem we face today.

American Dystopia—
Obama's Demolition of America

21 November 2014

Nation- (nay-shuhn) – n. 1) a large body of people, associated with a particular territory, that is sufficiently conscious of its unity, to seek or to possess a government, peculiarly its own; 2) the territory or country itself, separated by borders.

Last night at 8:00 p.m. EST, the President of the United States, Barack Hussein Obama, announced that he is going to sign an executive order which begins the unravelling of our nation. Despite his dubious and pejorative claims as to presidential precedence, it is the first time in our nation's history that a chief executive has taken it upon himself to declare that a law no longer exists without supporting legislation to do so. In effect, he has unilaterally decided that he will cease and desist with the deportation of over one-third of the aliens who have entered this country illegally, and he has done so without regards to Congress, the electorate, and the wishes of the American people.

He has done this in spite of all of the aliens who have entered this country legally and all of the immigrants who have played by the rules in the hope of attaining full citizenship in the United States.

In a word, he has done this with complete contempt and total disregard for the American people.

In effect, he has opened the floodgates of even more illegal entry than ever before along with its resulting humanitarian crises, and in so doing, he has effectively eliminated the national sovereignty of the United States of America.

We should not be surprised by any of this.

After all, he was elected and re-elected largely by margins made up of illegal and multiple voting (remember ACORN?). He has done this in the hopes of geometrically expanding a voting bloc which he has deigned to broaden legislative control by his own Democratic Party. He has done this as a cynical stunt to goad the GOP into a possible governmental shutdown and/or impeachment proceedings, knowing full well that such moves would largely serve to encourage further resentment of the Republican legislators, in spite of the recent and nationwide Republican landslides in the last two midterm elections. In effect, he has raised his middle finger to the Republicans in general and a majority of those who voted in 2014 specifically.

Why?

Barack Obama is part of an effete and elitist cadre of academics who, having been indoctrinated in radical ideology, disdain the concept of national identity. These radicals who have infected college and university campuses across the country inherently believe:

1. that the United States is the source of most, if not all, of the world's ills;
2. that anyone should be allowed to cast a ballot, without regards to citizenship;
3. that the borders of the United States should be open, and that anyone and everyone should be allowed to enter this country and avail themselves of all of our government's largesse, be it welfare, healthcare and education (all of which they believe should be free for all);
4. and by effect, that the United States should be marginalized to the level of a third-world nation as punishment for its perceived sins of the past.

Everything this president has done in office is completely and irrefutively commensurate with this twisted, albeit prevalent mindset which has taken over academia and is now meandering its way down to the elementary and secondary schools as well. One look at the Common Core curriculum of today, juxtaposed against the curriculum that prior generations were taught, bears out this fact in due course.

Left unchecked, the end result of these endeavors by the President of the United States and his academic allies will surely bring about the utter demolition of the United States as we know it and usher in an era of American Dystopia, a society in which no sane person would ever wish to inhabit, and thus subject the watching world into an abyss from which there will be no one capable of extricating mankind as a result.

Noshowbama

12 January 2015

Noshowbama is not a city in Japan, but rather an approach to foreign policy by the current administration when it comes to world leadership or, rather, the lack thereof. While leaders of the free and not-so-free world united in clasped arms to march in support of peaceful expression and against extremist terrorism, word has it that our dear leader, Barack Obama, was taking in NFL playoff games in the privacy and comfort of his digs at 1600 Pennsylvania Avenue. The "company line," as it were, is that the security requirements entailed for "His Arrogance" to participate, along with millions marching in Paris, were so great as to negatively impact the march itself, which is a load of horse-hockey, and that's saying something, given the fertilizer factory that is this administration.

Marching, not even ten feet apart from one another, were Israeli Prime Minister Benjamin Netanyahu and Palestinian Leader Mahmoud Abbas, both of whom had the sense of noblesse oblige to join with other world leaders in a joint demonstration of the sentiment that "enough is enough" when it comes to Islamic extremism, something that the Obama administration cannot even vocalize at the end of the day. Attorney General Eric Holder was even in the same city earlier that morning, but this Administration couldn't even arrange for his representation in the parade, which says a lot about the priorities of Obama and his world view, which is basically this: "Disrespect your allies and kiss the hind-quarters of your enemy."

Even the Russians, hardly the bastions of civil liberties, had the wherewithal to send their foreign minister, but the United States couldn't manage to ante in a vice president (Biden), secretary of state (Kerry), or attorney general (Holder) when, in fact, our president (Obama) could and should have been there. For all the world to see, by this absence, Obama has certified his own credentials to his oft-stated view that the United States is not exceptional, nor even classy.

This ranks right up (or, I should say, down) there with his presentation to the Queen of England, in honor of her sixtieth jubilee as reigning monarch, an iPod containing a collection of his own speeches, along with a "take-this-bust-and-shove-it" 2010 return of Winston Churchill's bust, which had been presented to former President Lyndon B. Johnson forty-five years before.

If this is what passes for leadership in the free world, then the free world is as screwed as is ever can or could be. Here we have a sitting U. S. president who cares more about seeing who will make the NFL's final four than leading millions of men and women and leaders across the globe, united to stand and march against totalitarianism and extremism.

It's enough to make any *real* American barf up his/her bouillabaisse.

If there is anyone in the United States that still is under the complete and fantastic misconception that Barack Obama is a great leader in the free world and a great president, then let such a person give him- or herself an overdue swirlee in their own toilet and wake the hell up.

Obama is a coward, a miscreant, and utterly unworthy of the office to which he was twice elected, and his exit cannot come quickly enough to a watching world, which at long last has come to see the light of day, that we are at war with Islamic barbarism and that the fate of civilization depends on its very outcome.

The State of the (dis-)Union

20 January 2015

The Constitution of the United States, in Article II, Sec. 3, requires that the President of the United States from time to time provide to Congress a report on the state of our union. This requirement has over the decades become an annual address outlining the president's recommendation on his own legislative agenda, more so than a report on the actual state of our union, as it were. On rare occasions, the president has elected not to provide such a report, and the vaguely referenced requirement in our Constitution provides for this leeway.

In the past, most notably when presidents have faced defeat (typically following the midterm congressional elections), they have reached out to the opposing party and proposed consensus-building initiatives for the greater good of the country. For example, when President Clinton suffered such a defeat in the midterm election of 1994, he used the State of the Union address to reach across the aisle to engage the Newt Gingrich-led Republicans, and the result was fruitful in providing for needed welfare reform and, thanks to a change in the accounting procedures which moved some of the country's financial obligations "off the books," a so-called balanced budget as well. These two initiatives proved better for the country at large, and business responded favorably.

In essence, Bill Clinton decided that it was better for the country for him to work with the opposition than it was for him to stick with his partisan base and continue to try to ram through ideologically-driven initiatives, such as "Hillary-care" which would have divided the country and promoted even more legislative inaction.

This past autumn Barack Obama suffered, far and away, the worst electoral midterm defeat of any president since the 1930s. Nine senate seats changed hands, and the House Republicans picked up an additional forty-seven seats, giving the GOP the largest share of House seats since the Great Depression. Not that "His Arrogance" was bothered in the least, as he inferred that the election results were nothing more than a reflection of poor voter turnout, which reminded us of someone who throws the blanket over their head when they flatulate in bed. Tonight he will deliver his state of the union speech and, rather than putting the country ahead of his own lofty ego, he is going ahead with plans to further drive a divisive and toxic wedge into our country's electorate by once again driving home the dubious point that the rich need to do their "fair share" and pay even more in taxes than they already pay. That is not exactly a legislative initiative that seeks to spur economic growth, according to any economist with half a brain, aside from Paul Krugman who, it would seem, only has half a brain. Some people, like Obama and Krugman, will never get it, the "it" being that communism doesn't work, socialism doesn't work, and taxing the rich doesn't work either. Again, Obama couldn't care less. Should the country go down the tubes, he'd still be more than satisfied in the scent of his own flatulence, so why in the sand hill would he want to reach across to Republicans at this point in his presidency and accomplish something good for the country?

He'll swagger his pen and insist upon continuing to act as though he were some kind of monarch and run down a list of executive orders that he intends to issue, Congress be damned. The useful idiots in the major media will continue to jump over each other in voicing ejaculatory praise for his lofty vision, a vision designed to further marginalize what was once a truly an exceptional nation, because his presidency has proved to be nothing more than an expression of his determination to make the United States of America no better than any other nation in the world. In other words, his stratagem is this: "if you cannot lift up the rest of the world through the example of your own leadership, than the best thing to do is lower the United States to the level of the rest of the world, ensuring international equality." In a world view where equality trumps excellence, nothing improves and, by definition, everything deteriorates instead. That will prove to be the legacy of Barack Obama.

When all of us are dead and gone, historians will surely say of him, "He brought us down to make us equal." That's some legacy indeed. God help us.

At What Price Obama?

20 February 2015

In the past few weeks, we have heard President Barack Obama tell us the following:

> that we as Americans should avoid getting on our high horse about ISIL, due to similar occurrences under Jim Crow and the crusades;
> that we should refrain from connecting their religious beliefs with ISIL because doing so constitutes a lie, despite the fact that everything they do is in the name of Allah;
> that the shooting of five Jews in Paris at a kosher delicatessen was just a random act of violence that had nothing to do with the victim's nationality or creed;
> that it is the duty of all Americans to defend Islam whenever it is slandered (conveniently omitting Judaism or Christianity);
> that we, as a nation, are not a Judeo-Christian nation, but rather one whose greatness originates with Islam, going back to our nation's founding;
> that we need to be more understanding of the legitimate grievances of Muslims, here at home and around the world (again conveniently omitting such grievances on the part of Christians and Jews);
> that we need to put more treasure into countries where ISIL is gaining power, so that an enhanced standard of living and increased job opportunities will dissuade young Muslims from joining ISIL and becoming radicalized;
> that the beheadings of Coptic Christians in Libya by ISIS terrorists were an act perpetrated by bad people, having nothing to do or say about the religion of either the perpetrators or the victims;
> that a three-day White House symposium on extremism, which omitted both military assets and

representatives of the Christian and Jewish religions, but replete with Muslims both "moderate" and radical, including one man who blamed 9/11 on the Israelis, was in order.

This is just *part* of what President Obama has done JUST on the subject of the very subject he won't name, that being Radical Islam.

Then we hear that, despite all of the evidence pointing to the contrary, his departing Attorney General Eric Holder, in his last act as AG, is now suing the Ferguson, Missouri Police Department for racism in the shooting death of Michael Brown, By the way, there was no mention of race baiting on his part, on the part of his boss, or their buddy, Al Sharpton, which encouraged the rioting and looting that followed.

The former mayor of New York, Rudy Giuliani, was roundly excoriated for suggesting that this president lacks love for his country in a way that no other president has done, based largely on the president's constant criticism of America, reaching back to the days before he became president and the comments Obama has made since, as referenced above. If anything, Giuliani is far from being a dyed-in-the-wool conservative Republican, and even liberal Democrats are now calling to question Obama's reticence in labeling Radical Islam for what it really is and are expressing vocal skepticism on his approach to dealing with Iran as well as ISIL. The president has even lost MSNBC's Chris Matthews, the same guy who suffered chills up his leg during Obama's keynote address to the 2004 Democratic National Convention.

So at what price must we continue to be led by such a man as Barack Obama? Is he worth the increasing polarization of our country's citizens to a degree not seen since the 1850s? Is he worth the growing threat of Islamist terrorism both here at home and around the world? Is he worth the continued alienation of our allies in Europe, Asia, and the Middle East? Is he worth the continued strengthening of America's enemies, including countries who have expressed their goal to destroy the United States and Israel?

In short, is Barack Hussein Obama worth it?

Presidential Self-Esteem

3 June 2015

"There is no limit to what a man can do, or where he can go, if he doesn't mind who gets the credit."
> – Ronald Wilson Reagan, Fortieth President of the United States

One of the intangible qualities that separate the great presidents from the rest of our presidents is an abiding sense of humility, the idea that whatever a president (or, for that matter, any leader) achieves is the result of long hours and hard work, done by others, in pursuit of the greater good. Ronald Reagan had it. George Washington had it. Abraham Lincoln had it. Even George W. Bush and his father, George H. W. Bush, though certainly not great presidents, per se, still had an abiding sense of humility in the way they approached their respective tenures as president.

Barack Obama, quite simply, does not, which is the principal reason why he will never achieve greatness, period.

Certainly, there have been other presidents (actually, most presidents) who have missed the mark of greatness, largely as the result of either: grave misfortune (i.e., John F. Kennedy), perjury (i.e., Bill Clinton), impeachment (i.e., Bill Clinton and Andrew Johnson), incompetence (i.e., Jimmy Carter), dishonesty (i.e., Richard Nixon), bad timing (i.e., Herbert Hoover), or, even in some cases, outright corruption (i.e., Warren Harding). Yet when it comes to the absolute avoidance of greatness, nothing ensures lack of greatness like an overabundance of self-esteem, in which history is replete with examples going back millennia.

Barack Obama is nothing, if not arrogantly egotistical to the point of pathos. Yet, it's not entirely his fault. No, not entirely. After all, when a young man is awarded academic honors befitting far more deserving students who actually display academic promise, it's no wonder that such a man begins to believe that he is the smartest thing on two legs. Anyone who has experience working with Obama will tell you that he acts like he is the smartest one in the room; when a man is elected to the nation's highest office without having achieved anything tangible to merit such a political victory, it's not a stretch to understand that such a man begins to believe that his sense of greatness is self-evident. Obama is awash in his own sense of greatness; when a man is awarded, for instance, a Nobel Prize for Peace for having done nothing (other than to besmirch his own country on a post election "apology" international speaking tour) to earn such distinction, it's not surprising that then the man's head might swell up a bit or, in Obama's case, a lot; when a man is re-elected to that highest office with the assistance of a fawning mass media who works, along with his campaign, to marginalize and discredit his opposition and to gloss over any shortcomings (and there were many) during the incumbent's first term, it's no surprise that such a man begins to take on the trappings of a celebrity teen idol, and let's be honest about this. Barack Obama is so saturated with adoration all around him, it's no wonder he acts like an older version of Justin Bieber.

So, even if Barack Obama achieved something, *anything* of substance, while in office, his own self-adoration would take away from such achievement. Even if the policies which he advocates were retrospectively deemed to be truly beneficial to the United States or even tangibly contributed to the peace and security of the free world, his ego would belittle such advocacy.

So it is with these thoughts in mind that we should consider his statement that he alone has "improved the Unites States' standing in the world" and that American prestige and respect in the world "is at an all-time high," when quite the opposite is true. Such statements are the sad utterings of an uber-narcissist, completely divorced from any sense of reality.

In short, our friends do not trust us, our enemies do not fear us, and Barack Obama, in six short years, has in fact, "fundamentally transformed the United States of America" from Reagan's "Shining City on a Hill" to the international equivalent of "Comedy Central," whose adoring audience includes Russia, China, Iran, Syria, ISIS, and host of other bad actors who are rolling in the aisles of Obama's pathetic theater, the "Theater of the Absurd." Send in the clowns, folks, be it Hillary Clinton, Elizabeth Warren, Joe Biden, Bernie Sanders, or Martin O'Malley. After all, what *else* is left for us to lose?

2016- The Election That Wasn't?

8 July 2015

On March 28, 2013, President Barack Obama signed the following Executive Order, which established his authority, among other things, to control and even indefinitely postpone, as outlined in section 3a, part x, a Presidential Election. Essentially, by declaring a "National Emergency," President Barack Obama can use such an emergency to remain in office on January 21, 2017, and thereafter. This Executive Order reads as follows:

"Executive Order—Establishment of the Presidential Commission of Election Administration

By the authority vested in me as President by the Constitution and the laws of the United States of America, and in order to promote the efficient administration of Federal elections and to improve the experience of all voters, it is hereby ordered as follows:

Section 1. Establishment.

> There is established the Presidential Commission on Election Administration (hereto after referred to as "the Commission").

Section 2. Membership.

> (a) The Commission shall be composed of not more than nine members appointed by the President. The members shall be drawn from among distinguished individuals with knowledge about or experience in the administration of State or local elections, as well as representatives of successful customer service-oriented businesses, and any other individuals with knowledge or experience determined by the President to be of value to the Commission.
> (b) The President shall designate two members of the Commission to serve as Co-Chairs.

Sec. 3. Mission.

(a) The Commission shall identify best practices and otherwise make recommendations to promote the efficient administration of elections in order to ensure that all eligible voters have the opportunity to cast their ballots without undue delay and to improve the experience of voters facing other obstacles in casting their ballots, such as members of the military, overseas voters, voters with disabilities, and voters with limited English proficiency. In doing so, the Commission shall consider as appropriate:

(i) the number, location, management, operation, and design of polling places;

(ii) the training, recruitment, and number of poll workers;

(iii) voting accessibility for uniformed and overseas voters;

(iv) the efficient management of voter rolls and poll books;

(v) voting machine capacity and technology;

(vi) ballot simplicity and voter education;

(vii) voting accessibility for individuals with disabilities, limited English proficiency, and other special needs;

(viii) management of issuing and processing provisional ballots in the polling place on Election Day;

(ix) the issues presented by the administration of absentee ballot programs;

(x) the adequacy of contingency plans for natural disasters and other emergencies that may disrupt elections; and

(xi) other issues related to the efficient administration of elections that the Co-Chairs agree are necessary and appropriate to the Commission's work.

(b) The Commission shall be advisory in nature and shall submit a final report to the President within 6 months of the date of the Commission's first public meeting.

Sec. 4. Administration.

a) The Commission shall hold public meetings and engage with Federal, State, and local officials, technical advisers, and nongovernmental organizations, as necessary to carry out its mission.

(b) In carrying out its mission, the Commission shall be informed by, and shall strive to avoid duplicating, the efforts of other governmental entities.

(c) The Commission shall have a staff, which shall provide support for the functions of the Commission.

Sec. 5. Termination.

The Commission shall terminate 30 days after it presents its final report to the President.

Sec. 6. General Provisions.

(a) To the extent permitted by law, and subject to the availability of appropriations, the General Services Administration shall provide the Commission with such administrative services, funds, facilities, staff, equipment, and other support services as may be necessary to carry out its mission on a reimbursable basis.

(b) Insofar as the Federal Advisory Committee Act, as amended (5 U.S.C. App.) (the "Act"), may apply to the Commission, any functions of the President under that Act, except for those in section 6 of the Act, shall be performed by the

Administrator of General Services.

(c) Members of the Commission shall serve without any additional compensation for their work on the Commission, but shall be allowed travel expenses, including per diem in lieu of subsistence, to the extent permitted by law for persons serving intermittently in the Government service (5 U.S.C. 5701-5707).

(d) Nothing in this order shall be construed to impair or otherwise affect:

(i) the authority granted by law to a department, agency, or the head thereof; or

(ii) the functions of the Director of the Office of Management and Budget relating to budgetary, administrative, or legislative proposals.

(e) This order is not intended to, and does not, create any right or benefit, substantive or procedural, enforceable at law or in equity by any party against the United States, its departments, agencies, or entities, its officers, employees, or agents, or any other person.

(signed) "BARACK OBAMA"

(source wh.gov)

Do not even begin to think that it cannot happen, for it will not take much for President Obama, a president who is quite adept at ignoring the Constitution, to indefinitely postpone the 2016 election under the guise of a "national emergency." Do not make a fool's mistake of believing that such a move is not beyond this president, no, not for a second.

Dealing with the Devil

14 July 2015

This morning we awoke to news that, after months and months of negotiations, President Obama announced that we have struck a deal with Iran concerning their nuclear enrichment activities and their pursuit of nuclear weapons. The same regime in Tehran which held hostage our diplomats for 444 days in 1979-1980 and which has funded, promoted, and facilitated terrorist activities throughout the Middle East and around the world ever since and which has as its mantra "Death to Israel and Death to the Great Satan (meaning the United States)", this same regime is now to be trusted with its promise to export 80% of its enriched uranium and refrain from developing nuclear weapons for ten, fifteen, twenty-five years (take your pick), or forever (according to Secretary of States John Kerry) because "we have a deal." (Pfft!)

Well, let's consider this little troublesome fact. The whole premise of "the deal" depends upon the ability of the International Atomic Energy Agency to inspect *some* (but *not* all) of Iran's enrichment facilities with (get this) two weeks' advanced notice. In exchange of this ability, the economic sanctions which purportedly brought the Iranians to the negotiations in the first place would be lifted in stages, and if they are found to have violated the deal, such sanctions (which are difficult, if not impossible to be imposed) would suddenly (get this) be "snapped back."

Unbelievable!

Imagine for a moment a teenager's mom telling her teenage son that she will be periodically inspecting the top drawer of his dresser for marijuana *and* will give him a fortnight's notice of such an inspection, each time she feels the need to inspect it, and then if she *does* find marijuana after said notice, he will lose his set of keys to the family car. What pot-smoking teenager would not accept *that* deal?

There is absolutely no difference between this scenario and "the deal" that the Obama administration has struck with Iran. None.

Except for one thing. We are not talking about the dangers of a teenager smoking some joints here. We are talking about an existential threat to one of our closest allies (Israel) and, given the fact that Iran is also developing intercontinental ballistic missiles (ICBMs), a national security threat to the United States of America.

This is the net result of electing a inexperienced, idealistic, naive community organizer to the most powerful position in the world, one whose Secretary of State, John Kerry, an anti- war protester who lied to Congress in the 1970s, slandering his fellow war veterans with unsubstantiated tales of US servicemen beheading enemy combatants in order to advance a narrative, is negotiating Israel's survival and our own national security with the most evil regime in the last thirty-six years. Can we all say a collective "WTF?"

It is this same president who has asked Israel to give up its defensive nuclear arsenal and is also insisting that Israel share its protective dome with the Palestinian State, a state which advocates Israel's destruction.

Meanwhile, Kerry's predecessor, one Hillary Rodham Clinton, has approved the deal's "key elements," which should only serve to give us and Israel much pause as to the possibility of her being elected the next president of the United States.

Stepping back to the scenario of the mom and her teenage son, we know what he is smoking. The question should be, "What are Obama, Kerry, and Mrs. Clinton smoking?"

Obama's Russian Delegation in the Middle East

30 September 2015

For more than forty years, the one constant in U.S. foreign policy had been the absolute resolve to prevent Soviet/Russian hegemony in the Middle East, a resolve that transcended both party and ideology. From the mid-1970s on, U. S. presidents were united in the construct that Soviet/Russian influence in that troubled region be minimized, if not proscribed, by an activist U.S. sphere of influence in that troubled region.

And then Obama happened.

Whether or not one agrees with the wisdom of U.S. intervention in Iraq during the administration of George W. Bush, it is a matter of fact that a) weapons of mass destruction (WMDs), some 5,000 of them, according to a New York times article in April of 2013, *were* indeed present in Iraq under the regime of Saddam Hussein at the time the United States sent ground forces into Iraq; and b) following the 2007 surge of forces under General David Petraeus on orders from President Bush, the war in Iraq was most definitely won and Iraq was at long last stabilized.

And then Obama happened.

Running for president in 2008, Barack Obama's opposition to the war in Iraq was patently clear during his campaign for the presidency and, immediately following his election that November, he a) promised to "fundamentally transform the United States of America," and b) went on a world tour to apologize for America's transgressions, including our Iraqi intervention, and tell the world that the United States was no better than any other nation, for which he was dubiously awarded the Nobel Peace Prize. When he was inaugurated in January 2009, he reiterated his "apology tour" speeches, announced his intentions to withdraw from Iraq as quickly as possible and close the U.S. detention facility located at Guantanamo Bay, Cuba, where the "worst of the worst" terrorists were being held as *de facto* prisoners of war, a war on terror that began on September 12, 2001, following the attacks which took place the day before.

And then Obama happened.

Against strong advice to the contrary from a wide array of expertise in both political parties, Obama began the systematic dismantling of U.S. presence in the Middle East with a premature withdrawal of troops from Iraq, troops that would have provided the much-needed stability in Iraq following the war at a precious moment in time where such a presence, much like the post-war presence in Germany and Japan following World War II and South Korea following the Korean War, would have provided the security and conduit necessary to establish a stabilized government and U.S. ally in the Middle East, just as we had done in Europe and Asia.

In doing so, it was Barack Obama who created a vacuum of power in Iraq, which summarily led to the rise of ISIS/ISIL, enabled the Syrian dictator Bashar Assad to wage genocide on his own people by Obama's drawing a facetious "line-in-the-sand" about the use of chemical weapons against them and summarily allowed the continued atrocities being levied against Christians and noncompliant Muslims by not even being willing to identify the culprit as "radical Islam". His thorough disengagement from all presence in the region, not even providing requested weaponry and assistance to the one ally fighting against ISIS/ISIL, Jordan and, along with the unequivocal farce of his "deal with Iran," reveals his absolute intent to allow radical Islam, which words he dares not say, to take over an entire region.

Perhaps even worse, Barack Obama has allowed and abided the entry of Russian military forces into Syria by creating a void which Russian President Vladimir Putin was oh so happy and willing to fill. Today, it has been announced that Putin has ordered, *ordered* the United States to cease and desist from the very limited and targeted air strikes which have occasionally been taking place, in lieu of meaningful military action which could, if utilized without hand-wringing by the Obama administration, otherwise destroy both ISIS and the Assad regime.

In other words, while Barack Obama has absolutely no intention to oppose Russian aggression in the Ukraine, he is willing to allow Russian hegemony and thereby delegated to Vladimir Putin the authority to lord over an entire region in the Middle East, where all of his predecessors had committed themselves to preventing such a thing from happening in the first place.

When the day arrives in which an emboldened and resurgent Russia has the wherewithal to order the United States to "cease and desist" from doing anything at all, that day marks the beginning of the end for the United States as a world superpower, and the void which is then filled by a not-so-benevolent and oh-so-calculating Russian federation will no doubt usher in a scenario ending in the next world war.

Yes, Obama happened.

" . . . and he gets your gun . . . "—
Obama's Selective Outrage on Shooting Deaths

7 October 2015

Sometimes the predictable becomes oh-so-predictable, especially with a president who all too selectively shows passion and outrage when the political winds just happen to blow in the right direction.

Never mind the fact that, on any given week, twenty-five or more people are killed by gunfire in Chicago, while hundreds of others are wounded. To date, President Obama has yet to mention these staggering statistics in a city with some of the most restrictive gun-control laws in the land. Same goes for Baltimore, New York, and other cities that have done everything to restrict gun ownership, short of nullifying the Second Amendment of the United States Constitution.

A shooting in Charleston here, a shooting in Roanoke there and, most recently, a shooting at Umpqua Community College in Oregon, and the selective politicizer-in-chief, Barack Obama, gets on his soapbox demanding more and more gun control legislation, that is to say, legislation-as-a-concept, rather than legislation-as-a-specific, while the carnage continues unabated in the heavily gun-controlled urban meccas ruled by his Democrat allies for decades. Even in New York City, where former Mayor Rudolph Giuliani's "stop-and-frisk" policies had drastically reduced gun violence, this policy has been deemed "racist" by his race-baiting and opportunistic successor, Bill de Blasio, and by ending this "stop-and-frisk" policy, New Yorkers have now witnessed a spike in gun-related deaths. Such is the result of liberalism run amok.

In the most recent instance, it is tragically ironic that Umpqua Community College had been designated a "gun-free zone," which is what happens when liberal academia honestly believes that such platitudes and policies make their campus sanctuaries safe, when indeed the opposite is true. The result? Nine Christians, faithful to the point of becoming martyrs, dead for owning up to their faith in Christianity at the point of a gun, a factor oddly (but then again, come to think of it, not so oddly) omitted by a president who still believes that Islam is a wholly peaceful religion which remains to this day a victim of the 12th century Christian crusades. Remember Virginia Tech, anyone? Thirty-two deaths of defenseless victims occurred on a college campus which proscribes the possession of firearms.

That is the problem with gun control laws. Law-abiding people have a tendency to abide by gun control laws, leaving themselves defenseless victims to criminals who don't give a rat's ass about gun control laws in the first place. Listening to these liberal politicians, one would think that guns are so dangerous that they kill without willing human accomplices pulling triggers, as if to say homicide stops in the absence of firearms.

Those out there who would be so ready to ban guns because of shooting deaths should be asked as to whether or not they would be as ready to ban alcohol and ban automobiles because of all of the deaths related to driving under the influence (DUI). There is no difference between the two, except for liberal hypocrites who think otherwise. Death is death, and, in both instances, these deaths are not the fault of the gun, not the fault of the bottle, not the fault of the automobile, but rather the fault of the operator.

While there is no constitutional right, per se, to own or operate an automobile and, despite the end to prohibition by the twenty- first amendment which ended prohibition by the eighteenth amendment, while there is no constitutional right to imbibe, per se, there *is* a constitutional right for an individual to keep and bear arms without infringement, like the infringement of gun control laws in some of the most dangerous cities in America. Interestingly, it is the only stated constitutional right that is almost universally regulated by licensure, and in some cases, outright proscription. The second amendment was very distinctly added to the Bill of Rights to enable individual citizens the right to protect themselves and their property against aggression perpetrated by other individuals and even by the government itself. Remember that Adolf Hitler confiscated privately owned firearms in Germany, so as to leave the populace defenseless against a coming Nazi onslaught and holocaust against the Jews in Germany and Eastern Europe.

Given the president's opportunistic grandstanding, leave

it to all his would-be Democrat successors to jump on the bandwagon of gun control, with Hillary Clinton even stating quite clearly that she will do away with the second amendment entirely by executive order, which represents an entirely new frontier in executive overreach, where even Barack Obama has yet to venture.

So much for a nation of laws.

The World Turned Upside Down

8 December 2015

"Listen to me and you shall hear, news hath not been, this thousandth year:

Since Herod, Caesar, and many more, you never heard the like before.

Holy days are despised, new fashions are devised.

Old Christmas is kicked out of town

Yet let's be content, and the times lament, you see the world turned upside down . . . "

—"The World Turned Upside Down"
(old English ballad c.1642)

The first stanza of this old English ballad, which was first published in an English political broadside in the mid-1640s, was written in protest to a recently enacted law by Oliver Cromwell's Parliament, banning festive celebrations of Christmas. This same tune was played by Lord Cornwallis's military band during the surrender of his armies to George Washington on October 19, 1781, marking the effective end of the American Revolution. To those who opposed the banning of festive Christmas celebrations during the British Commonwealth period and to the once-thought invincible British Army one hundred forty years later, both events seemed to evoke the feeling that the world indeed had turned upside down.

In the few weeks remaining before Christmas, 2015, how prescient it seems to recall this ballad at this particular time and place in the course of world history.

Just seventy years ago, the United States and its allies defeated both Nazi Germany and Imperialist Japan concurrently in the greatest war ever fought since the dawn of mankind.

Both Germany and Japan boasted quite powerful military and naval assets, as well as very proficient commands which had engineered stunning victories across two theatres of war, and yet were defeated in a few short years by a determined alliance which had not previously been prepared to wage war.

The reason? Dogged determination and the will to win at any and all costs.

Seventy years hence, that same alliance, now united with its former foes, seems incapable of defeating a comparatively, logistically, and militarily inferior adversary.

The reason? The total lack of determination and will to win at any and all costs.

Seventy years ago, a wheelchair-bound and ailing progressive Democrat was spending the final weeks of his life finishing the work of wielding and waging war in a crusade to save the world from totalitarianism. Franklin Roosevelt put into motion America's industrial and military might to join with its allies to defeat Nazism and Imperialistic Japan *at the same time*. While he did not live to see the actual surrenders of Nazi Germany and Imperial Japan, he brought this country and her allies to the very threshold of victory, because he and his country were determined to do so at all and any costs.

Seventy years later, a healthy and physically robust progressive Democrat is spending the final fourteen months of his presidency shrinking from his duties to lead the world in its fight against radical Islamic totalitarianism. Barack Obama has been and is in a complete and utter state of denial about the evils of radical Islamic ideology and has decided to "sit this one out" and leave it to his successors to pick up where he has so ignobly left off, assuming that such successors arrive in time to save the world from its own intransigence.

The contrast in seventy short years could not be more ironic or more obvious.

Seventy years ago, the president led this country into waging war without reservation, without fear of offense, without misgivings or political correctness, because he saw with clarity what the world would become without doing so.

Seventy years later, the president chides this country for its love of freedom and independence, cautioning us against offending Islam by expressing misgivings about waging war against radical Islam (which he still won't name), and drowns us in his own vision of political correctness to the very precipice of surrender without a fight.

One need look no further than Obama's speech on the very

eve of the anniversary of the attack on Pearl Harbor which precipitated our entry into the Second World War to see that fecklessness and cowardice have now replaced what was once determination and resolve in the Oval Office in a "world turned upside down."

Constitutional Carousel—
Obama's Merry-Go-Round with Executive Orders

4 January 2016

Among his many other "firsts," President Barack Obama is the first U.S. President to have taught constitutional law at the university level, which he did at the University of Chicago from 1992-2004, first as a lecturer from 1992-1996 and then as a senior lecturer from 1996 until 2004. Ironically speaking, he is also quite possibly the most extra-constitutional president in U.S. history, which just goes to show that a university professor can and often does teach that in which he does not necessarily believe.

In short, Barack Obama's presidency is nothing if not an exercise in wholesale contempt for the Constitution of the United States, as evidenced by the wide-ranging scope of his executive orders designed to circumvent the Constitution and, in so doing, by his habitual bypass of the Congress. If anyone should know that it is the exclusive venue of the legislative branch to enact laws, it is certainly a man who once made his living teaching constitutional law.

Yet this is a man who boasts of "having a pen and a phone" and who carries through on his threats to impose his will when Congress doesn't act on his priorities accordingly. He gets away with this lawlessness, largely because Congress lacks the testicular fortitude to impeach "His Royal Arrogance" for doing so. Instead, they do what lawyers like to do, file lawsuits with the Supreme Court of the United States and leave it to the nine "robed wonders" to do the right thing and curtail Obama's furtive finaglings. Sometimes they do, and sometimes they don't, but at least by doing this, they manage to take the heat off of a Republican congressional leadership who would rather show that they can get along with the opposition than act like a party of opposition like they are supposed to do. It's as if the GOP leadership was nothing more than a branch of the Democratic National Committee, based upon their overall lack of loyal opposition and the way they repeatedly cave in to Obama and the Democrats.

These same GOP "leaders," a term which is used loosely, scratch their heads in amazement that three of the top five candidates in their own party's presidential sweepstakes are outright congressional outsiders (Trump, Carson and Christie), and a fourth (Cruz) is treated like a pariah within his own Senate caucus. Here's a news bulletin: the voters, namely the conservative voters who put them in power, are fed up with the go-along-with, get-along-with House and Senate GOP leadership and desperately want a true conservative to lead the country instead. If that means nominating a braggart like Trump, an ideologue like Cruz, a political novice like Carson, a bullhead like Christie, then so be it, but the days of "Republicratic" candidates like Jeb Bush or John Kasich or Lindsey Graham or George Pataki are numbered, primarily because the rank and file of their own electorate no longer believe in their resolve to turn things around in a way that they desperately need to be turned around.

So while the President consults with his dubious Attorney General this week on exactly how they can parlay yet another end run around Congress, this time by an all-out assault on the Second Amendment, look for the GOP leadership, the "Wonder Boy of Budgeting," House Speaker Paul Ryan, who gave Obama a veritable blank check through next September, and the "Blue-Lipped Wunderkind of Kentucky," Senate Majority Leader Mitch McConnell, to file yet another lawsuit with the Supreme Court, one that will not be adjudicated until Barack Obama has completed his final term of office. Meanwhile, the "Constitutional Carousel" continues to go merrily round and round and round, with Obama laughing all the way.

Something to Cry About—
Obama's War on the Second Amendment

6 January 2016

Anyone who has ever been the parent of a small child knows that there is nothing more effective at plucking the heartstrings of a parent than a child's tears. Whether genuine or crocodilian, the "waterworks" are pretty effective at motivating a parent's change of heart, that is, up to a point, that point being when a parent realizes that he or she is being "played." That's when a responsible parent, like the dad in the movie *A Christmas Story*, scolds Ralphie's younger brother, Randy, saying, "I'll give you something to cry about," or words to that effect.

Yesterday, we saw a stellar performance by the President of the United States, one worthy of an Academy Award nomination, as a matter of fact.

This president who has never publicly shed a tear for the hundreds of Christians being beheaded by ISIS, who has never publicly shed a tear for Americans being killed by the score in America and around the world by Islamic militants, who has never publicly shed a tear for the likes of Kate Steinly, killed by a repeatedly deported illegal alien in San Francisco, or the many victims of Nidal Hassan at Fort Hood, Texas, would have us believe that he is so passionate about curtailing gun violence that he is suddenly moved to tears.

"Sorry, Mr. President, but *thinking* people from both parties aren't buying what you're selling. Your tears are no more genuine than a spoiled child who is not getting his way and, truth be told, it is you who should be given something to cry about, like impeachment."

Having failed on multiple occasions to get the votes necessary to pass the gun control legislation he seeks, our petulant president decides to bypass the legislative branch, stomp his feet, and create an entirely new set of crimes by changing the laws regarding gun distribution and does so via fiat. Well, such a move would be fine in a dictatorship or in an absolute monarchy, but the unfortunate and inconvenient truth for Barack Obama is that we live in a representative democracy, governed by a

Constitution, the Second Amendment of which forbids ANY infringement on gun ownership by the government, period.

Obama's commitment to end gun violence might be more believable if he had previously directed the many branches of government, the FBI, the Department of Justice, the Bureau of Alcohol, Tobacco and Firearms (ATF), to more stringently enforce the laws on the books which address crimes committed with the use of firearms. His passion for gun control might be less suspect, had his own Justice Department, while under former Attorney General Eric Holder, hadn't allowed the ATF to distribute thousands of firearms in the drug cartel regions of Northern Mexico under Operation Fast and Furious, which led to the death of many Mexicans, as well as Border Patrol Agent Brian Terry.

Sure, there are those, the mass of uninformed voters, who truly believe that Obama's passion for ending gun violence is genuine and sincere and benevolent and that he truly cares about the victims of gun violence and that we should support him in this effort. Yet, having had the experience of raising children who tried many times to use their tears to get their way, I "ain't a-buyin' what he's a-sellin' ." Not me, and hopefully not the vast majority of Americans who believe that the Constitution of the United States is something more, much more than a quaint relic of distant history.

Chapter 6

Congress

Eric Cantor

11 June 2014

The defeat of House Majority Leader Eric Cantor in Virginia's Republican Primary at the hands of a relatively unknown Dave Brat should serve as a wakeup call to all of the incumbent Republicans in both Houses of Congress. Rep. Cantor came into office with the promise of conservative aspirations and had the strong backing of conservatives within his district. Yet with each year, his conservative credentials started to fade in the wake of, presumably, his own ambitions to become a party leader, and this proved to be his eventual downfall.

What the so-called "GOP establishment" has long failed to realize is the proper role of an opposition party. When Republicans try to moderate their message, they seem more and more like Democrats wearing Republican clothes, which is *not* why they were elected in the first place. The largely liberal media has shoved a false narrative down the throats of the Republican electorate: that they can only win by appearing moderate. This premise has repeatedly failed in the relatively recent nominations of moderate Republicans to national office: Gerald Ford in 1976,

George H. W. Bush in 1992, Bob Dole in 1996, John McCain in 2008, and Mitt Romney in 2012, all of whom lost in the general election. The only time that Republicans have won this election since the 1970s is when they have nominated true, unapologetic conservatives: Ronald Reagan in 1980 and 1984 and George W. Bush in 2000 and 2004.

If the Republican Party even hopes to gain the White House in 2016, they had better learn the lessons repeatedly taught to them and instead nominate true conservatives, simply because their base of support is NOT looking to elect those individuals who want to work with Democrats who in turn smugly laugh behind their backs and retain their power in the wake of such folly. The conservative electorate wants to elect those who will bring about substantive and lasting change, not by the moderation of a John Boehner or an Eric Cantor or a John McCain, but rather by the steadfast determination of conservative candidates who will not allow the stench of Washington to dilute their mission; and that mission is to undo more than sixty years of governmental largesse and return this country to the roots of its success, those being self-sufficiency, independence, and the pursuit of excellence in all things with determined and righteous indignation.

Immigration Reform and Congress

12 June 2014

Much has been made about the effect that his stance on Immigration Reform had on Eric Cantor's failed primary bid and the media's drumbeat on how this issue is splitting the Republican Party in half. Wishful thinking on their (the media's) part, but that alone is not splitting the Republican Party, nor does it mean that Democrats will somehow prevail in November. Immigration reform is, at best, a tactical diversion on the part of politicos to dodge the central issue of this fall's campaign, namely a referendum on the Obama Administration and how Congress will address the growing scandals within that administration going forward.

Presently, the investigations into scandals ranging from IRS to Benghazi to VA to Fast and Furious to the Bergdahl Exchange (and the list grows) can be summed up into four parts:

a.   House Committees investigate these scandals with Republican members of the committees asking questions, as their Democratic counterparts attempt to de-legitimize these investigations by inserting partisan counterstrikes on the questioners and providing diversionary cover for the Administration.

b.   Administration officials appear before these committees and answer with the following strategies, in consecutive order:

   1.   I don't recall;
   2.   We are investigating and will get back to you;
   3.   It will take a long time to turn over the documents (which, when turned over, prove to be largely redacted or substantially incomplete);
   4.   Indicate that they have already answered the questions;
   5.   Label the investigation as phony scandal or partisan witch hunt;

c.   The Attorney General, Eric Holder, refuses to appoint a Special Prosecutor;

d. The Senate, under the auspices of its Majority Leader, refuses to investigate, period.

Taken alone, it could be argued that ANY one of these scandals involve more serious crimes, loss of life, and Constitutional breach than Watergate or Iran Contra or the Impeachment of President Clinton. Taken together, it can be equally argued that we are faced with corruption and lawlessness not seen in any administration in U.S. history.

While his media allies hope beyond hope that Democrats retain control of the Senate, President Obama continues to slowly unravel the fabric of our country here at home, across our borders, and around the world. His latest attempt to import juvenile illegals across our borders and thus creating a humanitarian crisis unknown in the United States since the days of Native American relocation in the 18th and 19th centuries in an attempt to force upon the American people provisions of the Dream Act which have not been legislated or adjudicated, once again flaunting the Constitution and diverting attention away from the mounting scandals that grow with every week.

To be clear, there is not a single solitary sitting Republican in the House or the Senate that is or ever was "anti-Immigration." Having said this, there must be a distinction made between *legal* and *illegal* immigration, the latter of which has many opponents within and outside Capitol Hill. This is where the real debate lies on immigration reform, but thanks to the Democratic Party, the Obama Administration, the enabling lapdogs within the mainstream media, and what we'll call the "Go-along-with, Get-along-with establishment GOP," most Americans will never know this distinction, which suits Obama and his allies just fine.

The Coming Constitutional Crisis

27 June 2014

Created September 17, 1787 and ratified June 21, 1788, the Constitution of the United States, on which representative democracy is based, has long stood the test of time. It replaced the 1777 Articles of Confederation, which proved unworkable as the result of Shay's Rebellion in Massachusetts the preceding year. Born of this crisis in the early years of our republic, it has been the foundation of what it means to be an American and is the oldest constitution in the entire world still in use, an attestation to its brilliance in forming a government of, by, and for the people. Following the first ten amendments, known as the Bill of Rights, created September 25, 1789 and ratified December 15, 1791, it has been amended an additional seventeen times, amendments which have also proved, with the exception of the 18th Amendment, to be lasting.

Since its inception, there have been a few occasions in which there occurred a constitutional crisis. Most notable was the constitutional crisis of 1861, when eleven states seceded from the Union to form the Confederate States of America. This secession brought about the deadliest war in the history of the United States, as well as the Western Hemisphere, as civil wars throughout the world very often do prove to be so deadly. Another constitutional crisis erupted in 1937 when President Franklin Roosevelt attempted to pack the Supreme Court, which unanimously struck down FDR's National Recovery Act two years prior. Yet another constitutional crisis in 1974 brought about the resignation of President Nixon, following the Watergate scandal. Since then, the Constitution has been occasionally tested, most notably in 1998 when President Clinton obstructed justice and perjured himself in *Clinton vs Jones* that previous year, which resulted in the second impeachment of a president in US history. This week on the 25th of June, Speaker of the House John Boehner announced that he is introducing legislation to allow the House of Representatives to sue President Obama for his refusal to execute our laws, for exceeding his constitutional authority in the use of his executive actions, and for his continuous attempts to bypass Congress. This confrontation has been slowly percolating since prior to Obama's re-election and has, in the wake of the border crisis and many other brewing scandals, begun to boil over into a crisis within our federal government. Already, the Supreme Court has unanimously ruled against the president twice, in his attempt to make recess appointments to the National Labor Relations Board without consent of the Senate and in his attempt to have the National Security Agency monitor the cellular telephones of American citizens without due process.

Now it will ultimately be left to the courts to rule as to whether Speaker Boehner, at the behest of Congress, has legal standing to proceed with this lawsuit, perhaps and potentially the most important litigation in the history of our republic. If Boehner is successful, then the constitutional balance of powers, outlined in the Constitution's first three articles, will remain intact. If Boehner fails in his attempt to curtail Obama's overreach, then this delicate balance of power on which our nation has survived will forever be lost, and this president will have destroyed representative government as we know it. Under such a contingency, future presidents would become *de facto* dictators, and the legislative branch of government will be emasculated to the extent of outright impotence, rendering the United States Constitution irrelevant, thus completing the hidden agenda of Barack Obama and his nefarious allies.

How the GOP must not be succored into the Trap of Negotiation

10 November 2014

With all of this talk concerning Republicans who have recently won control of the Senate and broadened their control of the House and how they should negotiate with President Obama, I am beginning to see a pattern here, a pattern of self-destruction being promoted by the usual suspects in the media, based upon the supposed need for moderation on the part of the GOP, as though they should somehow be cowed by President Obama and the illegal actions he has taken as president. They seemed to be almost psyched by his finaglings, as if Obama was the strongest president since FDR.

History has shown quite the opposite. For instance, LBJ was far more effective at corralling bipartisan support for his agenda, and so were his successors, Ronald Reagan and Bill Clinton. All three of these presidents worked within and not outside the Constitution of the United States and for the greater good.

Another problem is the inherent corruption of the Obama administration. Obama's actions as president and those on the part of his cabinet and administration are, by metes and bounds, far beyond anything, *anything*, that occurred during the Nixon administration, the only, *only* difference being that Obama has had a complacent media covering for him, as opposed to Nixon having the media bound and determined to bring down his presidency.

This spirit of moderation and advocacy of cooperation that are presently being advocated, if so acted upon, are defeatist in the worst way, in effect having the GOP say, "We know the 2014 election was an anomaly, and we know our positions on the issues are wrong, so we will just be placeholders and allow the Democrats to re-attain their rightful majority in 2016." This is the unintended effect of that for which these "pundits of moderation" are advocating, a go-along-with, get-along-with restrained GOP which brought them to defeat with the nominations of Gerald Ford in 1976, Bob Dole in 1996, John McCain in 2008, and Mitt Romney in 2012, all of whom were GOP moderates who went down to defeat with their own respective, all-too-tempered tone. Unlike Obama, who knows that politics is war, what they and the voices of moderation within and outside the GOP advocate was and is a soft-spoken, well thought out, and oh so temperate strategy that will only serve to make people question what the difference is between liberal Democrats and moderate Republicans, of which there is absolutely none, and one which will assure a Democratic trifecta in the next election.

In order for negotiation to work, both, not one, but both sides must be pragmatic and thereby willing to negotiate on a bilateral basis. Such bilateral negotiations can and do work, to wit:

> LBJ effectively negotiated the Civil Rights Act of 1964 with Republicans, led by Everett Dirksen of Illinois;
> Ronald Reagan effectively negotiated the tax cuts of 1982 with Democrats, led by Dennis DeConcini of Arizona;
> Bill Clinton, once he lost both houses of Congress, effectively negotiated a balanced budget (in exchange of welfare reform) with Speaker Newt Gingrich in 1997.

All three of these presidents were, at day's end, pragmatists of the first order; hence, they were able to negotiate effective governance with members of their respective opposite parties.

Obama, on the other hand, is incapable of negotiation as he is neither a pragmatist, nor is he interested in the "pursuit of the greater good," as the predecessors I have listed. He is a dogmatic ideologue who can't even manage to negotiate with the hapless members of his own party, much less the members of the GOP. Our allies abroad don't trust him to keep his word, our enemies abroad don't fear his resolve (for there is none to be feared), and he cannot be trusted to keep his word with anyone, save for Valerie Jarrett and Michelle Obama. In essence, caving to Obama and his political operatives will never work, because there is no spirit of "give and take" in Obama- only take, take, take, *ad nauseam*. No one will ever negotiate anything with Obama, so it is pointless to try.

What Republicans *can* do, on the other hand, is to restrain the president through controlling the all-important purse strings.

For instance, if Obama signs an executive order on immigration, they can withhold funding for its implementation. They can do the same with Obamacare, which may end up being skewered in the Supreme Court anyway, due to pending litigation now in the works. Social issues such as gay marriage are facing similar scrutiny in pending litigation and may end up being decided on a state-by-state basis, which is where it should be decided anyway. In the end, negotiation and compromise only work if there is bilateral cooperation, and Obama has not yet shown any penchant for either, hence such a naïve and well-meaning approach will not work, not with this president, not ever.

In re 2015 — The Look Ahead

6 January 2015

The holidays have now passed, and we have returned to the realm of five-day workweeks, dietary comeuppances, weather that bites, and epidemic influenza, all attesting to the cruelty that is and always has been the month of January. God help us. Congress has returned to the nation's capital. Speaker John Boehner has survived a nominal challenge to his leadership, while Former Senate Majority Leader Harry Reid has suffered an electoral blow that must have felt very much like the actual blows he received as a result of his exercise equipment, whose resistance band knocked him for quite a blow as well. He'll still be in the Senate, but without the power to obstruct legislation that is sent from the House. This means that President Obama will be tasked with the onus of either:

a. signing Republican bills, many of which will have some Democrat support, such as Keystone Pipeline and ACA Medical Device Tax Elimination;

(or)

b. vetoing such legislation that will expose him to charges of obstructionism that he hasn't ever had to face before.

Well, Mr. President, it's time for you to "man-up" and stop hiding behind the skirts of Harry Reid, who won't be in a position to cover for you going forward.

The Republicans are in a position to actually govern, *but* they will have to "man up" as well. Doing so means that they will have to defund the President's recent executive order which effectively legalized illegal immigration, and there is no doubt this will require the kind of political courage not seen in recent decades. The same goes for (Supreme Court rulings notwithstanding) replacing or amending the Affordable Care Act (Obamacare), to alleviate the most economically onerous parts of the bill that legislators, many even on the Democrat sides of the aisles, wish they hadn't passed after all. Republicans might even have to resort to pulling on the president's purse strings (again, something that hasn't been done in memory) in order to keep the excesses of this all-too-excessive president in check. The major media will continue its Quixote-like quest to make Obama out to be a great president, in spite of the fact that he isn't or ever will be a great or even a good president. Nevertheless, they'll stay in the tank for their "dear leader," if for no other reason, to facilitate their entry into "Tank Hillary," soon to open in a campaign near you. Allegations that her husband is still philandering around (this time with minors) won't have any more ill-effect on her campaign than her refusal to comply with Rep. Trey Gowdy's subpoena for her Benghazi documents, because the major media has already decided they're in for Hillary, both to be nominated and elected; so much for what passes for journalism in these United States.

We will hear much about so-called "moderate Democrats" having to stave off the efforts of "extremist Republicans" because that is what the media keeps shoveling at us, and we for the most part aren't so up on things as to determine that which is being shoveled, the very same, in substance to that which is shoveled out of the stables at Pimlico. That's what happens when an electorate stops voting their heads and votes their hearts instead, as they have done in every election since 2008, save for the most recent which took place last November. The media let the 2014 election get by them, but they won't risk it next time around, to be sure. Whoever the Republicans nominate in 2016, he or she will be labeled an "extremist" by a mainstream media who amazingly proffers New York Mayor Bill de Blasio and Senator Elizabeth Warren as moderates. Such is the state of our fourth estate.

Sadly, the situations a-brewing overseas will continue to grow worse, much worse, partially due to an effete, nuanced, and altogether feckless foreign policy that Professor Obama espouses—he'll go to his grave thinking that America is not exceptional, after all, and he has spent all of his presidency attempting to ensure just that. As the result of his selective approach to law enforcement and his commentary regarding same, there will unfortunately be a continuation of racial unrest here at home not seen since the late 1960s, ironic that the nation's first African-American president and his Attorney General have only served to inflame racial hatreds that most of us had thought were put to bed two generations ago.

Congressional Impotency and the need for Viagra®

20 August 2015

One day recently at a church whose denomination will not be revealed, a children's service was taking place. The children, all of whom were under ten years of age, sat in the front row pews while their parents were sitting in the pews behind. The pastor, as is done frequently, asked the children if any of them knew the meaning of the word "resurrection." After a few moments, one of the children raised his hand and said, "I know if it lasts for more than four hours, you need to see a doctor." Predictably, the parents roared in laughter, and the pastor was beet red with embarrassment until he too doubled over in laughter.

Today we are bombarded with advertisements for medications which treat erectile dysfunction, but that is not the subject of this essay.

The impotence to which we reluctantly refer is the impotence of the GOP House and Senate leadership, whose all-too-tepid and milquetoast moderate stratagems are marginalizing what should be a party of opposition to the president. Ever since the House leadership went from Democrat Speaker Nancy Pelosi to Republican Speaker John Boehner and ever since the Senate Leadership went from Democrat Majority Leader Harry Reid to Republican Majority Leader Mitch McConnell, both amidst promises to curtail the president's overreach on a variety of issues, the Republican leadership has acted more like Democrat wannabes than Republican leaders. Their reluctance to lead has caused Republican voters to collectively ask, "Just who are these guys trying to impress, the mainstream media or their Democrat counterparts?" It would be nice if *someone, anyone* would take a hold of these two by the collar, shake them, and scream, "Grow a pair, for Pete's sake!"

Obamacare? It's still alive and kicking, despite promises to end this unpopular program. Executive Orders on amnesty? Nope, no action on this either. Planned Parenthood defunding? Yeah, hurry up and wait until September. It's absolutely nauseating to see the lengths these two clowns will go to just to avoid offending anyone, except their own party's base, that is to say.

Now, even with a few but growing list of Democrats who are rightfully opposed to Obama's farce of a "deal" with Iran and an all-but-unanimous Republican opposition to this deal, the Senate leadership seems to be dithering on the issue while the House Speaker mumbles something about appearing to have the votes to object to, but not block the worst foreign policy initiative ever put forth by a sitting US president and one which will just as surely escalate a nuclear arms race in the Middle East and practically ensure the destruction of Israel if allowed to be implemented. This deal, as has been recently learned, provides for **Iranian** inspections of Iranian centrifuges and enrichment sites.

Has someone lost their friggin' mind (besides President Obama, Secretary of State Kerry and the rest of what can laughingly be called a negotiation team)?!?

If the Speaker of the House and the Senate Majority Leader can't seem to (excuse the expression) "get it up" on this Iran deal, then the two of them need to step aside and allow others, ones who are capable of "getting it up," to replace them at once. No "little blue pill" will help these two, but maybe, just maybe, if their constituents start flooding the telephone lines at the U.S. Capitol, demanding immediate and swift action on this deal (not to mention Planned Parenthood defunding), someone up there will get the message and start acting like they "have a pair" after all. Otherwise, the president will continue to laugh at their "floppy jalopies" as he continues to march this country down the road to irrelevance.

(author's note- Viagra® is the registered trademark of Pfizer, Inc.)

Done In by a Done Deal

2 September 2015

Well, it's official. Thirty-four horses' asses in the United States Senate have put the proverbial screws to Israel and the American people. They have indicated that they will support Obama's Death Deal to Israel, otherwise known as the Iran Nuclear Treaty, and thereby prevent the Senate from overriding the very worst treaty ever signed by a sitting U.S. President.

Looking at the deal, Iran gets everything they want and more: $150 billion in assets to be released by the United States, twenty-four days advanced notice of inspections at some, but not all of their *civilian* nuclear enrichment sites, and all inspections to be performed *by themselves*; think about that for a moment . . . *by themselves*!

In return, we get *nothing*, not even the release of four American hostages.

In a prior essay entitled "Dealing with the Devil," written on the 14th July 2015, we likened this deal to the following scenario:

> "Imagine, for a moment, a teenager's mom telling her teenage son that she will be periodically inspecting the top drawer of his dresser for marijuana, AND will give him a fortnight's notice of such an inspection, each time she feels the need to inspect it, and then, if she *does* find marijuana after said notice, he will lose his set of keys to the family car. What pot-smoking teenager would not accept *that* deal?"

This was written *before* we knew about the *twenty-four* days' advanced notice and *before* we knew about the side deal whereby Iran would be conducting *their own* inspections. So let's amend the scenario:

> "Imagine, for a moment, a teenager's mom telling her teenage son that periodical inspections of the top drawer of his dresser drawer will take place, searching for marijuana, *and* he will be given twenty-four days of advanced notice of such an inspection each time she feels

the need for inspection, and that *he* is to conduct the inspection of his own dresser drawer, and then if *he, the teenager, does* find marijuana after said notice, he will lose his set of keys to the family car. What pot-smoking teenager would not accept *that* deal?"

There is absolutely no difference between this scenario and "the deal" that the Obama administration has struck with Iran, none.

Except for one thing. We are not talking about the dangers of a teenager smoking some joints here. We are talking about an existential threat to one of our closest allies (Israel) and, given the fact that Iran is also developing intercontinental ballistic missiles (ICBMs), a national security threat to the United States of America.

We might expect such outlandishly naïve deal-making from a president who is stupid enough to think that man-made climate change, a theory not even close to being empirically proved, is the greatest national security threat to the United States. We might even expect that many of his party's outgoing Senators might even prostitute their own better judgement by accepting favors from a president who puts his ignorant ideology before country on a regular basis. But to suggest that both they and the president would all but guarantee a nuclear arms race in the Middle East, all but guarantee an attack on Israel ushering in World War III, and all but guarantee that Iran, who is developing ICBM technology, will use this technology to attack what they still to this very day identify as the "Great Satan," that being us, the United States, to suggest that shows how low they can stoop and how little they can even consider the ramifications of what they have done.

Albert Einstein once said that while the next World War may be fought with nuclear weapons, "World War IV will be fought with sticks and stones," and thanks to Barack Obama and thirty-four U.S. Senators, the path to this scenario has now been advanced irrevocably.

Speaker Boehner Resigns—
The Tragedy of Strategy

28 September 2015

Amidst all of the many news items flashing across headlines at the end of last week, including the "Pope's Visit," "Obama Meets with Chinese Leader," "Obama to Meet with Putin," "Official e-mails Recovered on Hillary's 'Wiped' Server," one sent a shockwave throughout Washington like none other: "Boehner Steps Down from Speakership, to Leave Congress October 30th."

Setting aside the irony that the 30th of October happens to coincide with my fifty-seventh birthday, it was indeed a surprise that House Speaker John Boehner (R-OH) proffered his resignation the day after the Ohio congressman was seen repeatedly dabbing his tear-filled eyes during and following Pope Francis's address to Congress the day before. Whether or not one of these had to do with the other is something that will never be known, so we'll set aside any hypothesis that the two are related, as doing so would be nothing more than gross speculation.

More relevant to the Speaker's resignation was the Henrico County, Virginia electorate's ouster of his former Majority Leader Eric Cantor (R-VA) in June of 2014, when a relatively unknown conservative Republican and Tea Party favorite named Dave Brat mounted an old-fashioned, door-to-door campaign and wrested his party's nomination from a man who at the time was the second most powerful Republican in Congress. Eric Cantor, the epitome of the go-along-with, get-along-with oh- so-moderate Republicans in the Congress and Senate, was *so* confident in his incumbency that he forgot to campaign for and thereby defend his seat.

By pursuing a strategy of "let's not risk our power in Congress by confronting the Democrats and Obama," the loss of his seat was the warning shot across the bow of mainstream, establishment Republicans that they should start listening to their broad base of support, conservative Republicans who elected them into office. Yet, by and large they didn't listen.

Fast-forward to the midterm elections later that year. Then-Senate Minority Leader Mitch McConnell (R-KY), along with

House Speaker John Boehner (who had himself become Speaker in the midterm Election of 2010 when the GOP won a House majority overthrowing Speaker Nancy Pelosi (D-CA) and the Democrats), went out and told the country, "Give us a majority in the Senate, increase our power in the House, and we'll defund Obamacare and put the brakes on his executive overreach." The electorate responded in kind, drastically increasing the GOP caucus in the House, overturning nine seats in the Senate, ousting its erstwhile Majority Leader Harry Reid (D-NV), and delivered to the GOP leadership exactly what they asked for: a mid-term election of historic proportions, with the largest shift of power on Capitol Hill since the mid-1920s.

For all of their efforts, the Republican voters were awarded with (drum-roll please) absolutely nothing. The Republican leadership did an about-face and returned to their "go-along-with, get-along-with mainstream, establishment oh-so-moderate strategy" of "let's not risk our majority's standing by doing nothing instead," as if to say, "Screw our Republican base, they'll vote for us anyway, let's not make any waves, and by doing so, we'll consolidate our power."

So afraid was the GOP leadership in the House and the Senate that they wouldn't even risk the political fallout of a threatened government shutdown, on defunding/replacing the wildly unpopular Affordable Care Act (Obamacare) when they had an absolutely magnificent opportunity to do so, and now are doing the same with regards to the disaster that is the Iran Deal, and continued funding of Planned Parenthood in the wake of the baby-part-for-sale videos, both of which find vast opposition across the electorate by wide margins.

Often saying, "We don't have enough votes to override the president's veto," they instead surrender power to the president and the minority Democrats in both houses without waging any discernible opposition in the first place, essentially giving up the fight before the bout.

Wonder why the leading Republican candidates seeking the nomination are nonpoliticians, and why the leading politicians under them in the race for the GOP nod are the most conservative? Recent polls have shown that almost two-thirds of Republican voters (62%) "feel betrayed" by the GOP leadership in Washington.

Simply stated, the "go-along-with, get-along-with mainstream, establishment Republican Party" has gone the way of the dinosaur, which is why the Jeb Bushes, the Lindsay Grahams, and the John Kasichs of the world will not get the nomination of Republicans who have grown weary of being taken for granted by these Democrat "wannabes" and demand instead a truly conservative Republican Party as a true alternative to the increasingly socialist Democrat Party. Having been burned five times by moderate Republicans who went down to defeat in prior elections (Ford '76, Bush-the-elder '92, Dole '96, McCain '08, Romney '12) and barely squeaking by with a moderate/semiconservative George W. Bush twice ('00 & '04), they have since awakened and are thus demanding that a true conservative, along the lines of a Ronald Reagan, be nominated instead. If that doesn't work, they will settle on *any* Republican who is willing to call out Obama for what he is, Hillary for what she is, and the Democrats for what they are, because they are absolutely fed up with the oh-so-deferring and gentlemanly chivalrous Republicans, who have about as much fight in them as a wet dishrag.

One would think that the departure of Boehner and the demands for replacing the Senate Majority Leader Mitch McConnell would serve as a much-needed wakeup call to the rest of the GOP caucus to either "put up or shut up" by actually opposing through action legislation that would finally put Obama and the Democrats on the defensive for once. Yet leave it to a "blue-lipped wonder" like Mitch McConnell to stand by his principles and ignore the increasingly obvious handwriting on the wall that states quite plainly, "The analysis of paralysis is nothing more than a strategy of tragedy, and by sticking to it, you will give ALL of the power back to the party you pretend to oppose, while the country will suffer as a result of you own impotence."

It's the obvious that is most often difficult to grasp, when one cannot envision a forest for the sake of all of the trees instead.

Chapter 7

Hillary Clinton

How the White House conversation might have gone . . .

30 May 2014

The Conversation *might* have gone something like this:

CLINTON- "Mr. President, thank you for sitting down with me this morning."

OBAMA- "Hillary, what can I do for you?"

CLINTON- "As you know, our Democratic allies in the House are meeting to strategize on how to handle the Republican-led witch hunt into Benghazi, and we need to make sure our asses remain covered ...."

OBAMA- "*Our* asses? Come on, Hillary, you were in charge of State when this happened. And my team scoured the internet to find some cover for you. Thank God for YouTube."

CLINTON- "Yes, Mr. President, our asses. While you were upstairs with you-know-who, all of this shit was going down."

OBAMA- "You weren't in the situation room either,

and the way I hear it, you were busy yourself doing
. . . "

CLINTON- "Look, Mr. President, we all have our own
little secrets. Oh, shit. This meeting was supposed to
be secret, and I just let a picture be taken with one of
our allies at *People* magazine. I sure hope this doesn't
get tweeted out."

OBAMA- "That's your problem, Hillary. As you know,
I am up to my ass in VA, IRS, and all of the other
investigations going on down the street. And Holder
is nearly beside himself trying to run cover for me.
The last thing I need is this Benghazi bullsh- . . . "

CLINTON- "I am cutting you off right there, because
if I can't run for president because of this "Benghazi
bullshit" as you have called it, then I am gonna spill
on you and Eric and everybody else."

OBAMA- "Now hold on, Hillary, just a second. As
long as we have our allies in the House blocking and
thwarting Gowdy and the Republicans, nothing is
gonna come out that doesn't need to. Besides, we
have our secret weapon from Nevada in the Senate,
so you need to chill and let my operatives cover both
our asses, okay?"

CLINTON- "Works for me, okay, well, I gotta be off
now, tell Michelle I said 'hello.'"

OBAMA- "Who?"

CLINTON- "Michelle, you know, your wife?"

OBAMA- "Oh, yeah, okay, I will . . . "

Hillary

18 June 2014

Last night, having watched Hillary Clinton's interview with Bret Baier and Greta Van Susteren on Fox News, I thought a lot about what it could be that is driving support for her candidacy. To be charitable, I found Mrs. Clinton's demeanor to be glib, that to the extent of her ability, she did her level best to be charming. There is no doubt that she is articulate as well.

Yet I was also shocked to see that, after all of these many months, she is STILL trying to force feed us into accepting an entirely false narrative that the September 2012 attacks on the U.S. consulate in Benghazi were (now she says "in part") due to a YouTube video about Mohammed that Muslims found offensive. The very next morning following the attack, the president of Libya insisted that the attack had nothing, NOTHING to do with a video that was not even available to Libyans at that time. Yet the White House kept pushing that same false narrative for weeks, when they knew all along that it was nothing more than an attempt to deceive Americans, designed to lay credence to the fiction that Al Qaida "was on the run" and that Obama's foreign policy was a success. when in fact the opposite was true.

Since that time it has been discovered that on the very night of the attack, political operatives in the White House frantically started to search the internet, trying to find anything, ANYTHING on which they could lay blame for the attack in an attempt to provide cover for the president and his campaign narrative. Never mind the fact that the Ambassador to Libya, Chris Stevens, repeatedly pleaded with the State Department to provide more security and was repeatedly turned down by a State Department being run by Hillary Clinton. Amazingly, Hillary Clinton said, in one sentence, that she is responsible, but only to the extent that she feels the pain of their loss, and nothing more. Then she had the audacity last night to once again plug the false narrative of a video as being partially responsible for the attack. Talk about delusional narcissism!

There can only be three explanations for her performance:

1. She is suffering from complete dementia (the least likely)
2. She is completely devoid of even a shred of honesty (more likely)
3. She will say anything, ANYTHING, to fend off any criticism whatsoever, and ethics be damned in the process (most likely)

Is this what we want in our next president? Haven't we, as a nation, had our nauseous fill of narcissistic and self-serving demagogy that is so very present in the current administration? More importantly, can't even the most partisan and sycophantic supporters of the Clintons see through her deceptions and own up to the fact that Hillary Clinton is most definitely not what the country needs in a successor to Obama?

I leave the answers to these questions to those who would support her candidacy, with a respectful request to explain just why they would continue to support her, aside from the fact that she is a woman, and aside from the fact that she is a Democrat. I suspect that many of these same supporters also supported Barack Obama, principally because he is African-American and also a Democrat.

A *real* president needs to be much more than a member of a sex or a race or even a member of a political party. He/ she needs to be a leader who believes in the things that sets our country apart (American exceptionalism), is willing to defend the values of freedom and individual liberty wherever they may be threatened, and defend and uphold the Constitution in its entirety. When we elect officials based solely on their own demographics and not on these values, we endanger our country and the world in which we live.

Barack Obama is not such a president, and Hillary Rodham Clinton most certainly would not be either.

The Magna Carta Revisited

11 March 2015

This coming June 15th will mark the eight hundredth anniversary of what was to become the first attempt by the English to evoke the concept of equal justice under law. On the fields and plains of Runnymede, near Windsor, England, the Magna Carta came into being when the Archbishop of Canterbury attempted to make peace with the vastly unpopular King John and a small group of rebel barons who opposed the monarch for what they saw as an infringement of their rights. It also marked the first attempt to subject the English crown to English law. Though later nullified by Pope Innocent III, it was reinstated by King John's heir, Henry III, the following year, and its eventual progeny was the Constitution of the United States, which assured the young nation that no man nor woman was above the law, no one.

It is indeed ironic that, eight hundred years later, we are still struggling with the concept of who is and who isn't subject to the laws of the United States. It seems that certain politicians of a certain political party manage to skate above the law time and time again.

In the summer of our youth, twice-elected President Richard Nixon was forced to resign his office because he lied about having knowledge after the fact of the Watergate break-in. It is a matter of historical record that a young lawyer investigating the Nixon Administration for the Watergate Select Committee was summarily discharged from her duties due to ethics violations on her own part. Her name? Hillary Rodham Clinton. The same Hillary Rodham Clinton who later became the First Lady of Arkansas, the First Lady of the United States, a Senator from New York, and, under President Barack Obama, Secretary of State.

Hillary Rodham Clinton and her husband, the former President William Jefferson Clinton, have amassed such a dubious record of achievement and such a lengthy list of crimes and ethical violations as to make William Marcy Tweed of Tammany Hall, President Warren Harding of the Teapot Dome Scandal, and Richard Milhous Nixon look like comparative angels, and yet they have managed to effectively lie and dance their way out of legal jeopardy through means that have, at times even become violent, but nevertheless very much aided and abetted by a complicit mainstream media. President Barack Obama, no *real* friend of the Clintons by the way, has taken a page from their own playbook and has managed to remain in office despite having presided over far and away the most corrupt and criminal presidential administration in U.S. History. Obama has managed to do this through threats, intimidation, use of governmental agencies like the IRS and the Justice Department, again with the unabridged assistance from an all-admiring mainstream media. His administration's list of scandals, some of which also touch the Clintons, is indeed mind boggling, and yet, there he sits.

The list of crimes perpetrated by both the Clintons and the Obamas have and would fill volumes, but somehow they manage to escape intact, due largely to the political party of which they are a part. Had they been Republicans, they would have summarily been impeached and imprisoned for high crimes and misdemeanors, but instead, they manage to benefit from a double standard that sows the seeds of our own undoing and one that places the concepts of representative government, individual liberty, constitutional freedom, and equal justice under law in grave peril. So it comes down to one thing. Do we as a nation give a damn?

Hillary Clinton Faces the Benghazi Committee — The Theatre of the Absurd

23 October 2015

Absurd, in a word, is possibly the best way, given the confines of the English language, to describe Hillary Clinton's long-awaited appearance before the House Benghazi Committee yesterday. The former first lady, senator and Secretary of State rightfully deserves an Academy Award for Best Actress, given her portrayal of the oh-so-caring, oh-so-thoughtful, oh-so beleaguered victim of those horrible Republican meanies bent on destroying her candidacy.

Not that she didn't have the supporting cast of sycophantic "ass-clowns" supporting her performance, as the Democrat members of the Committee were practically drooling in her presence, stepping all over one another and stepping *on* their fellow Republican committee members in an all-out effort to run interference for their "lady-in-waiting," who just happens to be their best and only shot at retaining the White House within the confines of their own party.

It was quite absurd, really, especially when the oh-so-sanctimonious Democrat members scolded the Republicans for wasting, yes, WASTING some four-and-a-half million dollars investigating the attacks on the diplomatic mission in Benghazi on September 11, 2012. Heaven help us all when Democrats, of all people, lecture Republicans about wasting taxpayers' money, or have they not heard of their own president's program that spent five hundred million dollars to train five, count 'em, *five* Syrian "freedom fighters?"

It was quite absurd, really, that these same Democrat representatives spent their time kvetching about the committee's inability to uncover new information about what happened before, during, and after the raid on Benghazi, especially since they spent most of their allotted time making speeches and postulating about the unfairness of it all and defaming their Republican colleagues on the Committee instead of questioning the witness herself. It's rather hard to uncover new information while making speeches, isn't it? The only Democrat who asked any substantive questions was Rep. Tammy Duckworth (D-IL), and even there it was obvious that Hillary knew exactly what she was going to ask, as Hillary answered her questions with prepared statements, reading from a script on the table in front of her.

The Republicans on the committee, by comparison, acted professionally, asking probing questions about the processes State Department officials used (or didn't use, for that matter) to address the security requests—there were over 600 of them—by Hillary's "friend," slain Ambassador Christopher Stevens, and the comparative access to Hillary Clinton of the slain ambassador juxtaposed against her "long-time friend" Sidney Blumenthal. The former had practically no access, while the latter had unlimited access, according to her own testimony. When pressed as to why no administrative action was taken against her underlings, who were directly responsible for refusing the ambassador's request for additional security, Hillary responded with a lame excuse of being constrained by federal law, an actual "first" for her, considering the hundreds of occasions over the years when Hillary has not felt so constrained. Having repeatedly maintained that all of the e-mails she received from Blumenthal were unsolicited, she changed this stance to "well, unsolicited, at first" when the evidence presented showed that she constantly solicited more and more e-mails from Blumenthal, a man who she was told not to engage with on any official basis by the Obama Administration, while pleading complete ignorance of the hundreds of requests by Ambassador Stevens to enhance security at the Benghazi mission.

Sitting behind Mrs. Clinton were half a dozen of her own attorneys, most notably Cheryl Mills, who was at one time concurrently Mrs. Clinton's personal attorney and Chief of Staff during Clinton's tenure as Secretary of State, and none other than David E. Kendall, who was her husband's own attorney during the Monica Lewinsky scandal and also represented former President Clinton during the trial *Paula Jones vs William Jefferson Clinton*, where the former president perjured himself, resulting in his impeachment. This begs the question that if this committee hearing was only a "political witch hunt," as asserted by Hillary and Ranking Member Elijah Cummings (D-

MD), then why the need for all of these lawyers? Answer: the ongoing FBI investigation into Hillary's e-mail server. Potentially, Mrs. Clinton has already opened herself up to charges of perjury and obstruction of justice by repeating that she had turned over all of the relevant e-mails, when clearly she hasn't. Whether or not the Obama Administration will eventually allow the FBI to pursue an eventual indictment is beside the point. It is obvious to anyone with an impartial mind that Mrs. Clinton is a pathological and serial liar.

This was never more perfectly illustrated when it was revealed during yesterday's hearing that, at the very moment and instant she was telling Americans and, specifically, the families of the slain personnel that the attack was the result of a protest mob spurred on by an internet video insulting the Islamic prophet Muhammed, she notified the Egyptian Prime Minister and her own daughter, Chelsea, the attack was an organized, preplanned raid by an Al Quaida-affiliated terrorist network, having absolutely nothing to do with the video. It was also revealed that she started the bogus video narrative while the attack was still under way on the night of September 11, 2012.

Nothing new, huh? Well, unlike the seven preceding hearings which probed bits and pieces of the Benghazi attack, this one had the benefit of her own e-mails as evidence, e-mails she and the State Department spent three years trying not to reveal and attempting to defy Congressional subpoenas.

Democrats should ask themselves honestly (assuming that they are capable of doing so) that if indeed the roles were reversed and this was a Republican Secretary of State being questioned by a House Committee led by a Democrat majority, would they have been as appalled as they professed to being yesterday?

Perhaps this is the *one* question that needn't be asked.

Chapter 8

Donald Trump

The Call of the Trump(-et)

22 July 2015

Love him, like him, admire him, or hate him as you will, but there be no doubt that when Donald Trump does something, he does it in a in a big way. Whether he is opening a golf course, a hotel/casino, or even a presidential campaign, he is a whiz at garnering attention. While that in and of itself can be a double-edged sword in the world of politics, there are more than a dozen of his rivals for the Republican presidential nomination who absolutely and undeniably covet the attention that he is commanding in this summer before the convention summer of 2016. And he is not backing down, not anytime soon.

His advantages are obvious. He has the requisite wealth to pursue his quest without having to kowtow to donors, hat in hand, begging them for the cash necessary to mount a serious national campaign. When he speaks, he commands attention, and he does so without consulting pollsters and advisors who all-too-often bind a candidate from saying anything that carries any meaning whatsoever. He is honest when he voices his opinion, albeit perhaps to a fault, but honest nevertheless. Above all else, he lacks the fear to do so that is so sickeningly obvious in so many other politicos, right and left. He carries the bombastic delivery of a Theodore Roosevelt, the self-confidence of a Ronald Reagan, and the fighting spirit of an Andrew Jackson. When he is lambasted or insulted, he has the cajones to reply in kind and with the artful modus operandi of a prizefighter, as most recently displayed when he "served" South Carolina Senator Lindsay Graham after Graham called him a jackass by forcing the Senator to go through the inconvenience of having to change his wireless phone number. That is absolutely priceless in a world saturated with enough sensitivity and political correctness to make even "Miss Manners" gag on the saccharine soliloquy of acceptable social intercourse that is politics. Senator Graham will no doubt think twice the next time he wants to start a scrape with "the Donald."

His disadvantages are equally obvious. He has no political experience, per se, aside from donating to multiple candidates over the years from both parties. His brazenness, part schmaltz, part shtick, with a heavy dose of New York City guile, turns off a lot of people in the hinterlands, particularly in the South and the Midwest, where abrasiveness is not so tolerable due to regional social norms which exists, by and large, in those areas. His generally ritzy bearing in all manners of dress and style makes him seem incapable of relating to the "average joe," much the same as Hillary Clinton's icy seclusion makes her seem out of touch in the same manner. Seemingly devoid of any sense of humility, he has a tendency to sing the song of a braggadocio, which only serves to fuel the disdain that such behavior elicits. Most importantly, he often lacks restraint in what he says, which, when he says something corrosive, makes political observers take pause in what otherwise would be the efficacy of a populist campaign.

As things stand now, in this all-too-early presidential campaign, it remains to be seen whether "the Donald" can master his foibles while continuing to capitalize on his considerable gifts of showmanship. Republicans will rightfully fear the possibility of his pulling a "Perot" and running as a third party candidate, should he be locked out or denied the nomination. Democrats will just as rightfully fear what he would do facing Hillary in a debate. For the time being, and it's damned early, the nomination appears to be his to lose, but there is absolutely no doubt that he has drawn a tremendous amount of interest during a time that usually draws little interest and, left unchallenged, makes him a formidable and viable candidate by any measure. It just depends on whether this Trump(-et) plays "Charge" or "Taps" at the end of the day.

Populism Reincarnated—
The Rise of the Anti-Politician

24 August 2015

All of us *should have* seen this coming from some time back: cycle upon cycle of professional politicians promising one thing and, if not delivering the complete opposite, delivering nothing at all. While the balance of power has shifted to and fro in both the White House and in the halls of Congress between two major political parties, very little has changed, and what *has* changed has been for the worse.

When taken to excess, moderation breeds mediocrity, and the excessive constraints on free speech, illegitimately bred from the demands of political correctness, have strangled and suffocated political speech to the point of utter silence. The professional political class has been emasculated to the point of irrelevance, and what do they have to show for it? An electorate whose trust in public service has reached an all-time low and the vacuum that has thus been created has resulted in the rise of the anti-politician.

The anti-politician is the candidate who is deemed outside the political mainstream. On the left, a Bernie Sanders fits the mold of the anti-politician, a self-styled and self-identified socialist who wants to end free-market capitalism in toto. Sanders is Barack Obama on steroids and has capitalized (forgive the term) on the leftward lurch of the Democratic Party that came into fruition with the nomination of Obama in 2008. Elizabeth Warren also fits the mold, wanting to take this country to a place it would otherwise dare not go. The only difference between these two is that the former, Sanders, admits he *is* a socialist and is officially running for the Democratic nomination, while the latter, Warren, admits nothing and is not running, not yet, anyway. Warren is just one Hillary Clinton indictment away from tossing her hat into the ring, for she is smart enough to know that neither Sanders, nor Joe Biden, nor Lincoln Chafee, nor Martin O'Malley, nor Jim Webb, nor an *indicted* Hillary have the goods to ultimately be elected president. Were she *actually* a Native American instead of pretending to be one, her Native-

American name might be "Waiting in the Wings" Warren.

On the other side, there are several anti-politicians vying for the presidency. Most talked about is Donald Trump, the real estate mogul who has a history of patronizing career politicians from both parties in order to do his bidding, and, bravely, he not only admits it, he *brags* about it to boot. Ben Carson, a noted pediatric neurosurgeon, and Carly Fiorina, a former business executive, have virtually no political experience at all, but these two candidates have elevated their respective standings in the Republican Party at the expense of established politicians like Rick Perry, Chris Christie, Rick Santorum, George Pataki, and Lindsay Graham. Despite what all agree was a very poor debate performance, "the Donald" has managed to keep his dominance of the GOP field intact and has miraculously enhanced his numbers over establishment rivals like Jeb Bush, Scott Walker, Marco Rubio, and Ted Cruz, the latter being the "outsider inside Washington" whose unforgiving conservative credentials account for his solid standing in a soon-to-be-shrinking field of seventeen wannabes.

While the reporting class (a.k.a. the mainstream media) and the political class (i.e., Jeb Bush, Rand Paul, et al) collectively wring their hands and gnash their teeth about the prospect of a Donald Trump grabbing the nomination, the growing legion of Trump supporters couldn't care any less. They continue to fill stadiums, which ensures that their candidate will get the attention he seeks. The same holds true for the leftist loons who believe in their hearts that Bernie Sanders or Elizabeth Warren can lead them to the promised land of a European-styled socialist utopia despite the reality that Europeans who live in such socialist utopias do not view their countries as utopian, no, not by a long shot. Sanders and Warren are merely trying to grab the baton from Barrack Obama and run us further down the road into mediocrity, a road that Obama has paved quite thoroughly here at home and around the world.

The moral to the story, and the message to the political class, is simply this: just keep screwing around with the demands of the people while you continue to marginalize their message, and eventually the people will marginalize the politician and cleave to the anti-politician instead.

Crossed Wires — Trump and the Problem
America has with Islam and Obama

11 December 2015

Hand it to "the Donald." No one in a generation or two, perhaps even going back to FDR in the 1930s, has mastered the art of media manipulation the way that Donald Trump has done, and with such little effort.

Be it "the wall" he wants to have built or the "temporary ban" on Muslims entering the United States from the war-torn Middle East or the multiple slams against members of the media or his political opponents in both parties, every time the man says something that no one else has the "cajones" to say, the media goes into a hissy-fit, and his poll numbers rise and rise and rise again.

Such a phenomenon is making even the most arrogant media pundits scratch their collective heads and wonder in bewilderment how this can possibly happen in an America whose thought processes were once believed to be under their strict and presumptive control.

The short answer is that they just don't get it, "they" meaning the Obama Administration, the Democratic National Committee, the Democrat candidates for president, the Republican National Committee, most of the Republican candidates for president, both the Republican and Democrat leadership in the U.S. House and Senate, and most of the media including Fox News who are ALL screaming about Donald Trump's latest proposal to delay Muslim immigration *temporarily* until we can improve our procedures for screening Muslim immigrants and visitors alike.

This can only mean one thing. They are all deathly afraid that the man can win the Republican nomination and win the election. And here is what they don't seem to get. Often in the course of history, Americans have elected a president as a direct result of and in absolutely polar opposition to his immediate predecessor. In 1920, Americans were fed up with Woodrow Wilson's internationalism and, realizing the futility of our entry into Europe's "Great War," elected a Republican isolationist, one Warren G. Harding, who ran on a simple platform of returning to "normalcy." While the term was coined at the time and never really cogently defined, Americans knew what he meant, and he was swept into the White House by a substantial margin.

In 1932, Americans were fed up with Republican Herbert Hoover's laissez-faire approach to the Great Depression and elected a progressive Democrat who promised a "New Deal," one Franklin D. Roosevelt, despite warnings that much of what FDR advocated was socialism bordering on bolshevism.

In 1952, Americans were fed up with Democrat Harry Truman and his "police action" taking place in Korea, which was costing tens of thousands of American lives with little to show for it, and elected a Republican "nonpolitician," one Dwight D. Eisenhower, who promised to go to Korea and end the stalemate. In 1960, Americans were fed up with the bland and blasé Republican Eisenhower administration and elected a Democrat with movie star good looks who promised to "get America moving again," one John F. Kennedy, who spoke of a "new frontier," which sounded exciting as America entered the 1960s. In 1968, Americans were fed up with the Democrats' JFK- LBJ war in Viet Nam and its domestic backlash here at home and elected Republican Richard Nixon, who supposedly spoke for the "great silent majority" of Americans who wanted this country to return to a time and place where such upheaval did not exist.

In 1976, Americans were fed up with Nixonian corruption and Republican Gerald Ford's pardon of his predecessor and summarily elected an unknown Democrat, one Jimmy Carter, who ran on nothing more than a promise to tell the truth.

In 1980, Americans were fed up with the fecklessness and incompetence of Jimmy Carter's lack of effective response to Iranian Revolutionaries who had kidnapped American hostages and elected Republican Ronald Reagan, who ran on a platform touting a "New Beginning for America."

In 1992, Republican George Bush was turned out of office by a combination of baby boomers who sought the election of one of their own, aided and abetted by a third-party run by Bush's nemesis, H. Ross Perot, and that is how Democrat Bill Clinton got elected.

In 2000, Americans were fed up with corruption in the Clinton White House and weary of Clinton's womanizing ways and elected Republican George W. Bush, a born-again, religious man whose marriage and family life more equated the values of Middle America.

In 2008, Americans were fed up with Republican Bush's wars in Iraq and Afghanistan and, with the help of an adoring media who failed to properly vet the unknown "outsider," elected Democrat Barack Obama president.

Approaching 2016, America finds itself fed up with Barack Obama and his insistence that radical Islam is not the problem associated with terrorism here in the United States and across much of the world. Americans are fed up with a politically-correct mantra of not offending anyone, be they illegal immigrants from Mexico or radical Muslims coming here from the Middle East, when most Americans know, even in their own silence for fear of being labeled a "bigot," that open borders and lack of proper screening of Muslim refugees from Syria and other parts of the Middle East pose the potential of great peril for our own national security.

And into that void enters a man who is not afraid to say what many Americans, admittedly or not, are thinking. "We need to seal our borders, and we need to arrive upon the means by which we can better screen immigrants from countries and cultures who wish us harm." One Donald Trump. Donald Trump is nothing if not a man of the times in which he exists and the all-American antidote to a feckless and cowardly apologist for Islamic extremism, one Barack Hussein Obama. He is (or seems to be) to Obama, what Harding was to Wilson, what FDR was to Hoover, what Eisenhower was to Truman, what Kennedy was to Eisenhower, what Nixon was to JFK-LBJ, what Carter was to Nixon and Ford, what Reagan was to Carter, what Bill Clinton was to the elder Bush, what the younger Bush was to Clinton, and what Obama himself was once to the younger Bush. And yet . . .

They *still* just don't get it!

Part III
Electioneering

Chapter 9

Political Correctness

Flag Day

12 June 2015

Sunday, June 14th, is Flag Day, a day set aside to honor the flag of the United States. Without any sense of clairvoyance, we can easily close our eyes and see, almost word for word, the news stories in print and on television for the following day, Monday, June 15th. Some group of university students will exercise their Supreme Court-sanctioned right to tromp on, stomp on, burn, and otherwise desecrate the American Flag, while another group of students- students not sanctioned by their respective faculties and administrations, will attempt to counter-protest by waving the American Flag (which on some campuses now constitutes "hate speech," believe it or not) and tussling with the faculty-and-administration-approved flag burners. Believe it, for it is as predictable as the daily sunrise.

Why?

It can be universally assumed, by both the right and the left, that the Stars and Stripes, constructed of red, white and blue fibers, is something more than a mere piece of cloth or nylon. It is a symbol, albeit loved or loathed, of Americanism, the idea of freedom, independence, and self-determination, as well as the cost of that freedom, paid several times over, in both national treasure and the blood of our soldiers, sailors, marines, and airmen. Generally speaking, it is these values that are as loved by the right as they are scorned by the left in the constant war of words exchanged between the two.

Elitists in academia, having been well schooled in the religion (and, yes, it has become a religion) of anti-Americanism from the 1960s radicals who flocked to academia in the 1970s, now wantonly encourage their students to view America as something to be scorned, hated, and vilified and give tacit as well as enthusiastic approval to desecration of the flag as an expression of this anti-Americanism. In reality, these young minds who do this will robotically recite a litany of all of the supposed sins of America's past and present, while being willfully ignorant of all of the great things America has given and continues to give to the world. While these students bemoan America's supposed "imperialism," they blithely ignore American generosity, individual, governmental, and, yes, corporate generosity which tangibly aids other countries in times of disaster, and ironically funds their dubious academic studies, to a degree that no other nation in the world can approach.

Talk about dogs biting the very hands that feed them!

Just once, would we like these imbeciles and their mentors to face the reality of what would occur, if the largesse of government and the wealthy patrons who they so despise suddenly dried up. Just once, would we like to see these indoctrinated idiots, now in the third generation of anti-Americanism in the ivied lecture halls of universities across the land, see how free they would be to march in protest and burn the national flag in many of the countries they admire, countries which guarantee none of the rights to do so. In reality, they would face long terms of imprisonment, forced labor, or, worse, the gallows, a firing squad, or beheading by the very same governments they so admire, because of an imaginary social justice they foolishly believe exists in those places.

Just once would we like to see these effete elitists tour a veterans' hospital and explain to those hospitalized there just why it is that their missing arms and legs were supposedly sacrificed for naught, or worse.

No one who would so easily stomp on, tromp on, or otherwise desecrate or destroy the flag they despise would dare face any of the above scenarios, for they lack the intestinal fortitude of their own corrosive convictions to do so.

Essentially, these malcontents are nothing more than narcissistic ne'er-do-wells who only express themselves, not so much to trash a piece of cloth or nylon, but rather to shove their hatred of America down the throats of those who think otherwise. Regard them as the pathetic cowards they are and pity them for their delusions, for by and large, they know not whence they come, nor where they would take us, if given the power to do so.

On Sunday, June 14th, we'll celebrate Flag Day by flying the Star-Spangled Banner outside our doorstep. As an advisory to anyone who would exercise their freedom of expression to take it down and desecrate it, we want them to know that we will, in turn, be expressing our freedom to protect our home and our flag by summarily opening a can of good ole' American whoop-ass should they try to do so. This is not a threat, by the way; this is privileged information, so we hope they consider themselves duly privileged.

Political Correctness

8 July 2014

Last year, I posted a tongue-in-cheek letter to the president, written to mock the all-too-pervasive speech codes that are the illegitimate, albeit predictable progeny of political correctness. Before we delve into the issue of political correctness and how it is destroying the freedom of expression in this country, here is that letter.

An open letter to the President of the United States

Dear Mr. President,

I am writing to you today (nothing against yesterday or tomorrow) to express my concern (I am not unpatriotic) about the direction (not a geographical reference) our country (nothing against cities) is headed. To be clear (not meant to plagiarize your favorite phrase), and in the interests of full disclosure (not exposing myself indecently), I did not vote for you (I'm sorry) in either of the last two presidential elections (please do not audit me). I am a 54-year old (nothing against young people) straight (nothing against gays) white (not a racist) male (not a sexist) who usually votes Republican (not a right-wing extremist nor a fascist) and one who believes in monogamy (nothing against polygamists or "players").

My father (nothing against fatherless children) served his country (he was not a warmonger) as a Corpsman (not a Corpse-man, but a Corpsman –pronounced "korman") in the Navy (nothing against the other branches of service or those who chose not to serve) in World War II. He has passed away (nothing against the living) a few years ago, but at the time of his passing, was worried about the future (nothing against the past or present) of our country (he was not an extremist either). He worked (nothing against those who don't) all of his life, just as my mother did (nothing against stay-at-home moms) and wanted only to pursue the American (nothing against other countries) dream.

Like my parents (nothing against orphans), I too

have worked (nothing against those who haven't) all of my life and am afforded (nothing against those who aren't) health insurance (nothing against Obamacare, oops, I meant to say the Affordable Healthcare Act, sorry!) by my employer (please don't audit them either) and every once in a while, (nothing against those who do so more or less frequently) like to fly (please don't put me on a no-fly list) to see other places (nothing against persons or things) but find that it's getting harder to do so (nothing against those that don't) because of rising taxes (not anti-government) and, therefore, less (nothing against more) take home pay. I drive a car (please forgive my carbon footprint), have air conditioning (ditto carbon footprint), and just want to continue to live freely (nothing against those who don't) and independently (not a militia member) in the greatest (nothing against those who don't think so) country (nothing against other countries) on earth (nothing against other planets). I read the newspapers (please don't hack my phone, internet, or communications), I watch Fox News (not a co-conspirator) as well as other news outlets (just to be fair), and hope that my children (nothing against my elders) and grandchildren (nothing against grandparents) will continue enjoy the blessings (nothing against non-believers) of liberty (nothing against the imprisoned) and be able to worship (nothing against those who don't) God (nothing against other names, beliefs, or lack thereof) as they deem fit.

So please (nothing against you if you're not pleased) take my (nothing against others) letter (nothing against tweets) into consideration when performing (nothing against not performing) the duties of the office (nothing against those without an office) to which you were elected (nothing against your operatives who weren't), and I promise to continue to be a good (nothing against bad) citizen (nothing against aliens, legal or otherwise, undocumented workers, and visiting diplomats).

Very truly (nothing against the untruly) yours (nothing against mine, his, hers, theirs, ours),

-Drew Nickell

Seriously speaking, the inherent problem with political correctness is the all-too-intended effect of creating speech codes, which are nothing more than the attempt of the political left to silence, ostracize, and alienate the political right. Criticize the president's policies, and one is labeled a racist. Focus attention on the problems at our southern border, and one is called anti-Hispanic. Question public funding of abortion, and one is accused of sexism; same holds true for those who might object to "free" birth control. Any attempt to identify or quantify the source of terrorism around the world carries with it the moniker of Islamophobia. Advocacy of traditional marriage brings on charges of homophobia. Question measures to reign in carbon emissions here in the United States or dubious "scientific" claims of man-made global warning, and one is identified with a "flat earth" mentality. Being a Christian and admitting to it brings on multiple labels of intolerance, ignorance, and living in a fantasy world. *Anything* in support of Israel, and one is automatically a Zionist occupier of the "peaceful" Palestinian territory. Question any use of EBT cards and the expansion of Medicaid, and one is callous, insensitive to the needy or greedy for not wanting to share the wealth. Comparatively trivial, perhaps, even though I am a Baltimore Ravens fan and not a Washington Redskins fan, I feel their pain because now dedicated Redskins fans are ignobly identified as anti-Native American. And the list goes on and on *ad nauseam*.

Ironically, this destruction of dissent originated in the halls of academia, the one-time center of intellectual pursuit and erstwhile venue of the exchange of ideas. Coincidentally and concurrently, the "blame America first" ideology began in these institutions of higher learning during the early days of the 20th century and took root in the 1970s following the Viet Nam war. Its ignominious influence spread to the newsrooms and editorial boards of publishing concerns ranging from book publishers to newspapers in the decades that followed. Now it has crept in to all manners and means of public discourse. Just ask any student with conservative leanings on just about any college campus in the United States, and they will tell you that even their grades are adversely affected if they so much as even question the liberal dogma being spewed by their professors. In essence, if they want to pass the course, they keep their opinions to themselves and end up being forced to feed into the egotistical monster behind the lectern, whose purpose is not to educate, but rather to indoctrinate. Ask yourself this question, "Why is it that former domestic terrorists such as a Bill Ayers or a Bernadine Dohrn are given tenured faculty positions at the very same universities which would never allow Former Secretary of State Condoleezza Rice to give a commencement speech?" The answer, sadly, is self-evident.

These efforts to silence the opposition to liberal orthodoxy are nothing new. We saw it in Soviet Russia until the Gorbachev era. We saw it in Nazi Germany (remember that National Socialism grew from the German Labor Party and is actually a leftist ideology, not what the liberal left would have us otherwise believe). We saw it during the Cultural Revolution in Communist China, and the result? *Hundreds of millions* killed during the 20th century.

Even the very term "liberal" has been so corrupted. What was once considered to be advocacy for inclusion and the exchange of ideas has now been denigrated to mean the proselytizing of radical ideology and the forced quarantine of political conservatism.

In their attempt to silence opposition, such measures unwittingly fuel the fires of discontent here at home and wherever free men and women who cherish the concept of liberty and freedom may live. Squash a person's freedom of expression today, and such expression will surely take on a less-than-civil means of communication tomorrow, and then things can get ugly very quickly, given the right impetus. Ladies and gentlemen, therein lies the true danger of political correctness and why we must demand that all be heard, on campus, in the newsrooms, and in the halls of Washington and beyond. Failure to do so will just as surely lead to the extinction of individual liberty as we know it and send the entire world into an abysmal return to the Dark Ages, whence we come.

The Inadmissibility of the Left

15 October 2014

Disclaimer: Some of my very best friends are liberals. I don't know why this is the case, given the fact that I am pretty conservative in my own political beliefs. Perhaps, in the end, I just feel sorry for these otherwise deplorable Democrat dolts (talk about alliteration) because, at the end of the day, they are usually proved to be wrong but never, *ever* admit to having been proven wrong. You just gotta love such stupendous stubborn stupidity (okay, enough of the alliteration) when, in the face of facts which eventually bear out, they just can't admit they had it all wrong. Cases in point:

> "Ronald Reagan is just an 'amiable dunce,' a 'reckless cowboy' who will get us into nuclear war with the Soviets." As it turns out, Reagan was an erudite reader, who actually studied up on the issues, made the right decisions despite advice to the contrary from his own cabinet, and his policies brought about the end of the Soviet Union without having fired a single shot.
>
> "By 2013, the polar icecaps will have completely melted, causing a catastrophic rise in the sea levels which will obliterate coastal cities in the United States." Al Gore's blathering, once taken so seriously, have been completely debunked, and that "Man-made Global Warming" is nothing more than a farce, not supported by scientific data, but a farce that made him quite wealthy, nevertheless.
>
> "George Bush is an idiot who thinks that if Obama pulls the troops out of Iraq too soon, that a force more dangerous than Al Quada will take over large parts of Iraq and cause death and destruction on a scale not yet seen," Ummm, ISIS anyone?
>
> "There are no weapons of mass destruction in Iraq; it's just a lie made up by that dunce, George Bush, and his evil counterpart, Dick Cheney, as a lame attempt

to justify an illegal War in Iraq." Well, as a *New York Times* article published just this morning by one C.J. Chivers has pointed out, there were WMDs in Iraq, lots of them, and they even caused injury to our soldiers there. Here is an excerpt from that article:

> 'From 2004 to 2011, American and American-trained Iraqi troopsrepeatedly encountered, and on at least six occasions were wounded by, chemical weapons remaining from years earlier in Saddam Hussein's rule. In all, American troops secretly reported finding roughly 5,000 chemical warheads, shells, or aviation bombs, according to interviews with dozens of participants, Iraqi and American officials, and heavily redacted intelligence documents obtained under the Freedom of Information Act.'"

And then, there's this:

> "Our experts here at the CDC and across our government agree that the chances of an Ebola outbreak here in the United States are extremely low. We've been taking the necessary precautions, including working with countries in West Africa to increase screening at airports so that someone with the virus doesn't get on a plane for the United States,"—President Barack Obama, 13 Sept. 2014.

As it turns out, someone with the virus got on a plane to the United States, and so far, two of the health workers tending to him in Dallas have become infected with the virus. In short, it's here.

So, do you think all of these liberals will ever admit that they had it wrong about Reagan? Wrong about Bush and Cheney? Wrong about WMDs? Wrong about pulling out of Iraq too early? Wrong about the wisdom of Obama easing travel restrictions on flights from Western African nations where Ebola has become pandemic? Don't hold your breath. At this very moment, these same liberals are now *blaming Bush* for the Ebola virus coming to the United States.

In essence, the Inadmissibility of the Left is a nothing more than a play on self-righteous indignation, one whose asinine arrogance is only exceeded by the president they elected twice, whose very own asinine arrogance has now brought a disease into the United States for the first time since its first outbreak in 1976.

In a word, dangerous men, given power, beget dangerous results to those who empower them, and those of us who saw through the lies of liberalism must now suffer along with the fools who refused to see otherwise.

True or False

25 February 2015

Just *one* of the following ten statements is true, so to test whether or not you can discern fact from fiction, identify the one *true* statement out of the list of the following:

1. President Barack Obama is upholding the oath of his office by preserving, protecting, and defending the Constitution of the United States of America and is making this world a far better place by promoting hope and change for all people everywhere.
2. Hillary Rodham Clinton, in her heart, truly cares about women, the plight of the poor, and other disadvantaged people here, at home, and around the world.
3. Global warming has already accounted for 90 percent of the icebergs being melted and will cause the oceans to rise twenty-five feet in the next century.
4. The biggest terrorist threat facing the United States of America are right-wing, extremist Tea Party types who support the NRA, the Republican Party, and border security.
5. Islam is the world's most tolerant religion, and Christians and Jews alike should open up their hearts and try to be more understanding of the plight of Muslims here in this country and around the world.
6. There has been absolutely no change in the opportunities that African Americans enjoy today, when compared to the opportunities that they enjoyed during the 1940s.
7. There is equally a war on women being perpetrated by the Republican Party, who wishes to outlaw all kinds of birth control, including oral contraceptives, and that Republicans want to force women out of the workplace and back into the kitchen, pregnant and without shoes.
8. Israel faces an existential threat from Iran, specifically relating to Iran's efforts to produce a nuclear weapon

through the enrichment of uranium.

9. Ninety percent of police officers in the United States are racists who want to kill young black men.

10. Allegations that Bill Clinton has been unfaithful during his marriage to Hillary Rodham Clinton and that Hillary Clinton attempted to silence such "bimbo eruptions" (her words) are based solely on a vast, right-wing conspiracy perpetrated by a Republican-controlled mainstream media

Now that you have determined which one of the preceding statements is true, think about which groups of political activists are perpetrating the lies contained in the other nine statements and then ask yourself, "What is the agenda at play in perpetrating such lies?"

The Sesquicentennial

8 April 2015

The ninth of April, 1865 was a seasonably cool, yet mostly sunny Palm Sunday, and for the first time in four years, guns were silent and cannons stilled. The armies' movements were halted, and all was quiet in the tiny hamlet of Appomattox, Virginia. Accompanied by his personal secretary, his orderly, and another cavalry soldier bearing a white flag of truce, General Robert Edward Lee, commanding officer of the Army of Northern Virginia, rode his white horse "Traveler" slowly toward a recently-relocated house owned by Wilbur McLean. The house which, ironically, once stood near Manassas, Virginia, when the War Between the States had begun four years earlier, was offered by its owner as a meeting place for Union General Ulysses Grant to receive General Lee in order to discuss the terms of surrender of the armies under Lee's command.

Lee really had no choice but to approach Grant that Sunday morning. His armies—starved, ill-equipped, decimated, and vastly outnumbered—were virtually surrounded by the armies under Grant's command—better equipped, fed, uniformed, and vastly superior in numbers. The day before saw the last skirmishes between the two sides, and facing certain annihilation, Robert E. Lee was quoted as saying, "There's nothing now left for me to do, but go and speak with General Grant."

Dressed in his finest uniform, General Lee climbed the steps of McLean's house and entered the parlor, along with his personal secretary, and the two generals began reminiscing about their shared service during the Mexican War twenty years before. Lee, the one-time stellar lieutenant under General Winfield Scott, was well known during the Mexican War, while Grant was virtually unknown at that time. Grant remembered Lee quite well from that conflict, but Lee regrettably did not remember Grant at all.

After some awkward moments, the two generals stumbled into the conversations that would effectively end the American Civil War. Magnanimous in victory, Grant offered his vanquished foe generous terms in the proposed surrender. Confederate officers would be allowed to retain their sidearms, provided they sign an oath to never again take up arms against the North. Any man who claimed to own a horse would be allowed to retain the horse so that they could "plow their little farms" for spring planting, to which Lee responded, "that will have great effect" upon the morale of his decimated soldiers. All of the Confederate army would be "paroled until exchanged," which effectively meant that they could return to the states that they called home, present themselves at their respective courthouses, sign a loyalty oath to the United States, and return to their families in due course.

Amongst these tattered remnants was my great, great-grandfather, Private Edward James Nickell, a man in his late thirties who had black hair and stood all of five feet, seven inches. His father, Andrew Nickell, had been a captain serving his country in the War of 1812, and his grandfather, Thomas, had fought in the French and Indian Wars under British General Braddock, then at the Battle of Point Pleasant under Colonel Andrew Lewis in Dunmore's War, and finally under General Washington in the American Revolutionary War. His grandson and our great, great-grandfather, Edward, spent much of the Civil War stationed at a railroad depot in nearby Lynchburg, Virginia, and performed courier duties on horseback, far away from his remote homestead, located in Monroe County, in what was to become West Virginia. He would journey to Charleston, sign his loyalty oath, return whence he came, and live for the next thirty-six years on the small farm near Pickaway, where he died in 1901.

Something else happened in Appomattox on that particular morning, though nobody present would realize it until many years later. Prior to this war, far and away America's costliest (civil wars tend to be the bloodiest), the United States were referred to in the plural (i.e., "they"), placing emphasis on the states which comprised the union. Following the war, the United States would be referred to in the singular (i.e., "it"), placing emphasis on the union, itself. This lays credence to the fact that the Civil War was primarily fought to settle a constitutional crisis and ultimately determine whether any state or group of states could secede from the union. It wasn't until January of 1863, when Abraham Lincoln signed the "Emancipation Proclamation," that the war took on the secondary cause of freeing the slaves in the Confederate states (the "border states" of Maryland, Kentucky, and Missouri, which had not seceded, were exempted from this emancipation order). My great, great-grandfather, whose family was hardscrabble poor and owned no slaves, threw his lot in with the Confederacy because he felt more loyalty to his home state (then, Virginia) than he did toward the nation of which it was a part, just as most of his fellow soldiers had done. Following Lee's surrender, he went home to live his life as an American, beaten in war yet not defeated in spirit, which should be the important lesson of that which took place 150 years ago when two generals sat down and settled a conflict, one which politicians, left to their own devices, could not settle and one which took the lives of some 600,000 men.

Historical revisionism, left to the wiles of contemporary political correctness, has done a remarkable job in redefining both the cause and the meaning of America's Civil War and in demonizing the confederacy and those who fought for the South (someone once said that history is written by the victors, after all). Yet, in the stillness of Appomattox, the truth remains that it was there where a divided nation became one nation, an inclusive, forgiving, and united nation, where all could claim to be American at long last. Lee knew it when, returning to his army, he told his men to "go home and be good citizens." Grant knew it and dissuaded his army from exacting revenge and engaging in raucous celebrations of victory. It's just too bad that, 150 years later, people today tend not to realize what all of this means, really means, in the grand scheme of things.

Chapter 10

Politics as Usual

Selective Disservice

17 July 2014

Let us begin with the concept of law. We have oft heard it said that we are a "Nation of Laws" and not a "Nation of Men." According to our Constitution, the legislative branch enacts our laws through a designedly complicated process, the executive branch upholds and enforces our laws, and the judiciary interprets our laws—the perfect balance in an imperfect process—that is what America is supposed to be about, not only in design and theory, but also in practice as well. It has stood the test of time, albeit with bumps in the road, for two hundred twenty-five years. Whenever one branch of government has fallen short of its duties, there have always been two other branches to counter the shortfall, and so we have thus survived, both as a nation and as a form of representative government. To ensure this continuity, there has also been the "fourth estate," essentially, a free press to keep the people informed of what is taking place with regard to our government, the operative word being "our."

Then, again . . .

Today, we have arrived upon a circumstance where this delicate balance is breaking down with such a velocity, either by incompetence or nefarious intent, which truly boggles the mind. Stymied by partisanship and what I will refer to as "all- too-precious incumbency," Congress is at a standoff between a Republican-led House of Representatives who propose laws and a Democrat-led Senate who refuses to take them under consideration. Then we have an administration which has shown a propensity to rewrite laws (i.e., Affordable Care Act, a.k.a. Obamacare), ignore laws (i.e., Defense of Marriage Act) with which it disagrees, and misappropriate laws (i.e., William Wilberforce Trafficking Victims Protection Reauthorization Act, intended to deal with human trafficking and contains a section that deals with children arriving in the U.S. illegally, unaccompanied by an adult, from Central America) in order to pressure Congress into enacting dubious legislation that will do nothing to ameliorate the border crisis so well underway. We have an attorney general who selectively enforces the laws and then selectively ignores those same laws, based solely on his own political and racial prejudices which apply to the situation. For instance, Attorney General Holder launched a thorough investigation into the Trevon Martin case and has summarily refused to investigate what has become an epidemic "knockout game" in cities across America, which is primarily a black-on-white crime spree. Recently, he has also launched an investigation into an outhouse float in a Nebraska parade which mocked a would-be future Obama presidential library, but refuses to seriously pursue IRS targeting of conservative political groups and the resulting felonious destruction of evidence by those subject to investigation. He has shown a propensity to investigate voting district realignments all over the country, duly enacted through state legislatures, but ignored voter fraud which took place in both the 2008 and 2012 elections, as well as videotaped voter intimidation in Philadelphia by the new Black Panther organization.

On sixteen (as of the last count) occasions thus far, the United States Supreme Court has ruled on several different attempts by the Obama Administration to either rewrite or summarily create laws and improperly appoint officials without

Senate confirmation. Our foreign policy is at best a mish-mash of incongruous and feeble attempts to address increasingly volatile and incendiary situations all over the world. The economy is in a shambles, subject to repeated *ex post facto* revisions of rosy quarterly reports that suggest the opposite, despite the fact that fifty million are on EBT assistance and the unemployed and under-employed rate are approaching 25% when those who have dropped off the statistical counting rosters are included. And that's just the beginning.

Where is the press? Aside from Fox News and only a handful of newspapers around the country, we remain virtually uninformed of what is taking place in the halls of Washington, in cities and towns across America, at our borders, and beyond. What used to be a free press has largely become a propaganda machine for the Obama administration, most notably evidenced when one weighs the amount of coverage of "Bridgegate" as it compares to the amount of coverage given to the IRS scandal, Fast and Furious, Benghazi, *combined.*

In short, there is plenty of blame to go around, no doubt, but we recall what William Shakespeare once wrote in Act I, Scene 2 of *Julius Caesar*, when Cassius says to Brutus:

> "The fault, dear Brutus, is not in our stars,
> But in ourselves, that we are underlings."

Unless and until we ourselves hold our elected officials accountable for both their actions and inactions, nothing, nothing will change, and it is to our own peril that we stay silent, uninformed, and disinterested, thus rendering a disservice to ourselves and our posterity.

Disinformation

9 October 2014

A very close friend of mine, whose name, ethnicity, sexual persuasion, religion, and gender will not be disclosed, is admittedly the polar opposite of me concerning all things political. A lifelong, committed liberal Democrat who is in lockstep agreement with all things left, this friend honestly believes:

> Hillary Clinton genuinely cares about the less fortunate Hillary Clinton is "one of us" whose life mission is to make our lives better and has dedicated her life's work to achieve these ends
>
> Barack Obama improved the United States' reputation and standing in the world and our relationships with foreign countries, when in 2008, he went around the world apologizing for all of the transgressions of George W. Bush and that he deserved the Nobel Prize for doing so.
>
> That Michelle Obama is the most beautiful and graceful first lady who ever occupied the White House and has done more for improving the lives of Americans than anyone else who has ever been first lady
>
> That the Affordable Care Act, also known as Obamacare, will ensure that all people will have unfettered access to health care, which should be an absolute right guaranteed by our government
>
> That anyone who is a member of the Tea Party should be silenced
>
> That the only bias in the news media is Fox News
>
> That George W. Bush, despite having both an BA in History from Yale and an MBA from Harvard, gained both degrees by having his father bribe both of these Ivy League universities and is, in fact, a demented individual with a sub-par IQ
>
> That anyone who favors any Republican running for office hates women, minorities, and children
>
> That anyone who is a member of the NRA or who stands for the preservation of the 2nd Amendment wants child-

ren to have unfettered access to automatic assault
rifles

That Richard M. Nixon, George W. Bush, and Dick Cheney
should have been sentenced to capital punishment for
crimes against humanity

I could go on with a list of what my friend believes to be
absolutely true, but you get the picture. This person has bought
into each and every lie that has been thrust upon him/her by the
likes of MSNBC, the major networks, the Democratic National
Committee, Joy Behar, Rosie O'Donnell, Bill Maher, Stephen
Colbert, Al Sharpton, and Ben Affleck. All of which brings about
the question of "Why?"

Why would this person, who is highly successful in a career
and who has benefitted from a good education, believe all of this
to the extent that he/she does?

Answer: Propaganda.

History tells us that when propaganda is repeatedly thrust
upon the otherwise uninformed—you know, the type that say
they are not interested in politics—eventually, it becomes an
orthodoxy that cannot be questioned. The most notorious
example of this fact is Adolph Hitler, whose Propaganda
Minister Joseph Goebbels manipulated German newspapers,
magazines, film-makers, and radio to spew Nazi lies to an
extent unforeseen before, thus giving credence to the passage in
Hitler's *Mein Kampf* that "people will believe the big lie before
they will believe the small one."

The only difference between Germany in the 1930s and
America today is the message being proselytized. Yet the
means are precisely the same. The establishment news media,
Hollywood, network television, newsprint, and the entertainment
industry were and are very much "in the tank" for Obama and will
just as assuredly be "in the tank" for Hillary Clinton, Elizabeth
Warren, or anyone else who is the Democratic nominee in 2016.
Based upon that fact alone, the GOP would have to nominate the
very reincarnation of Ronald Reagan in order to thwart such a
collective onslaught of left-wing co-conspirators and thereby
have any chance at actually being elected.

In the face of such an onslaught of absolute disinformation,

I can safely assume that my very close friend will not be swayed otherwise, and it is this very fact that somehow bothers me, and should bother all of you, to no end.

Midterms

28 October 2014

With the midterm elections of 2014 a week away and control of the United States Senate in play, much has been made about the prospects of a possible shift in the control of that chamber. A shift of six Democrat-held seats to Republicans would mean that Harry Reid, the stubborn and constipative block to all things legislative coming from the House of Representatives, would lose his position as Senate Majority Leader and thereby transfer his diverticulative functions to 1600 Pennsylvania Avenue, where the President would rule by veto, as opposed to ruling by fiat, as he has done since being elected in 2008.

Could this be a harbinger of more and continued dysfunction in Washington? Admittedly, yes, and yet there are other, more far-reaching implications of a shift in the power structure of the United States Senate.

First, the president would no longer be unconstrained in his Chicago-style manipulation of regulatory control, as he has been with regards to the IRS, the Justice Department, the EPA, and a host of governmental agencies that have become *de facto* extensions of his political machine. Republican control of both legislative chambers would necessarily constrain the continued abuse of power by this president and his operatives (Lois Lerner, anyone?).

Second, the Supreme Court would no longer be the inevitable heir to the Obama/Holder system of justice, a system where "equal justice under law" only applies to those in lock-step agreement with Barack Obama and his extra-Constitutional allies on the political left. A Republican Senate would surely keep the President from appointing judicial activists bent on curtailing free speech and tearing asunder the Bill of Rights that have served this country quite well for more than two centuries. Lastly, a chastened Obama, if such a creature is indeed possible with regards to "His Arrogance," would think twice before continuing his quest to "fundamentally transform the United States of America," a transformation that was neither needed, desired, nor sought by a majority of Americans who were snookered by a complicit media in 2008, a media who, despite obvious political bias leaning left, really only wanted to harvest the news value associated with electing the first African-American to the nation's highest office. This complicit attitude on the part of the media continued in 2012 (Remember Candy Crowley's performance as, ahem, a moderator, ahem, in the decisive debate?). By the way, look for this same media to be "all in" for Hillary in 2016, who will no doubt drool at the prospect of electing the first woman to this same office.

It never ceases to amaze me how many times Democrats will play the "let's not play partisan politics" card whenever they find themselves in the unenviable position of having to defend the indefensible actions of their own party's leadership. Here in Virginia, we hear the same old B.S. from Senator Mark Warner (D-VA) that our nextdoor neighbors to the south hear from Kay Hagan (D-NC) "that it's time to reach across the aisle" despite the fact that both of these senators have voted lock-step with the President and Majority Leader Harry Reid 99% of the time. Surely, those who are in other states where incumbent Democrats are facing re-election are hearing the very same B.S. as we in the Old Dominion and Tar Heel states are hearing (note: *please* don't believe a word of it).

Meanwhile to our immediate north, there are stories that polling machines in divergent parts of Maryland are automatically changing Republican-cast ballots to Democrats in what officials are laughably blaming on "calibration issues," which means that playoff losses by the Orioles and divisional losses by the Ravens aren't the only thing plaguing voters in the Old Line state. This also begs the question, "How is it that such machine malfunctions always, *always* tend to favor Democratic candidates?" Answer? The long line and standing tradition of Democratic political corruption going back to the days of William Marcy Tweed (Tammany Hall) in New York City and, more recently, Mayor Daley in Chicago.

But then again, that's politics.

Election 2014 and
the Decline of the Democratic Party

5 November 2014

While the final results of the 2014 Election are still yet to be determined, there is still one clear message that is inescapable- The Democratic Party is in decline, and this is the direct result of, and attributable to, their own party's pathetic leadership: President Barack Obama, Senator Harry Reid, Congresswoman Nancy Pelosi, and DNC Chairman Debbie Wasserman Schultz. These four individuals have brought asunder their own party, albeit without much, if any, help from their Republican opponents. In the three years since the midterm elections of 2010, the Democrats have lost (and the Republicans have thereby gained) a total of eleven seats in the United States Senate, fifty-five seats in the U.S. House of Representatives, and a net total of two gubernatorial offices, including Democratic bastions of Arkansas, Illinois, Maryland, and Massachusetts, all of which elected Republican governors in 2014. In fact, Republicans were able to win eight of the nine contested gubernatorial elections in 2014, where they were already incumbent.

These results, when considered in the long view, are symptomatic of a Democrat party in decline and bereft of fresh ideas, ideas which can benefit the citizenry which politicians are elected to serve. The Democrat's strategy of dividing people along race, gender, and socioeconomic strata has at long last failed miserably, and all indications are that people have said "enough is enough." Enough of media manipulation, false polling, rigged elections, election fraud, and faulty "calibration issues," all of which always tend to favor Democrats.

Now it is the Republicans who have their work cut out for them heading into the 2016 elections. The GOP has made great strides in attracting Hispanic, African American, and female candidates who can win elections across the country, even in former Confederate states like South Carolina, in blue collar states like West Virginia, and in western states like Utah. They must continue these trends if they wish to expand their voting demographic.

The GOP must discontinue the dubious strategy of reaching across the aisle to recalcitrant Democrats who have absolutely no intention of compromising in any way shape or form. This strategy of appeasement, which goes back to the late Ronald Reagan and Thomas P. "Tip" O'Neill, has always come back to bite Republicans in their collective keisters, and they have lost congressional, senatorial, and even presidential elections *ad nauseam* by trying to cooperate with opponents bent on their destruction.

In short, for the next two years, Republicans must learn how to act like a party of opposition (to the president) and allow the arrogant and intransigent Barack Obama to paint himself into his own corner. Those of you who think that the president will reach across to Republicans in the spirit of cooperation to affect beneficial governance are still slumbering in the dreamland that started with the concept of Barack Obama becoming a "uniter" rather than the divider he has proved himself to be throughout his presidency.

Let the Democrats continue their politics of division, their supposed and fallacious "war on women" strategies, and their demagogy so that Republicans can make a clean sweep of it in 2016 and restore this once-great nation to its rightful position of pre-eminence in a world otherwise bent on ensuring our demise. Then all of us can abide in the promise of that "shining city on a hill" that we were meant to be, rather than the "source of the world's ills" as Obama and his pathetic partisans have suggested we are instead.

Demagoguery

2 April 2015

It's a story that has become all too familiar and has its roots going all the way back to the 1964 Presidential Election, when incumbent Democrat Lyndon Johnson was running against Republican Barry Goldwater. Johnson, who had succeeded his predecessor when John F. Kennedy was assassinated the preceding November, really had this election "in the bag." However, Johnson being Johnson would leave nothing to chance and chose instead to paint Goldwater into a corner with an extremist brush. Those who are of a certain age remember well the television advertisement of a little girl picking daisies, chanting a familiar rhyme, only to be interrupted by a juxtaposed video of a nuclear detonation, suggesting that Goldwater and the Republicans were war mongers who would bring about a nuclear apocalypse if elected, and so began the dubious tradition of Democratic candidates stooping to absolute lows in the quest for electoral victory.

Throughout the 1970s and beyond, Democrats dined on the dish of demagoguery with absolutely no scruples or ethics in their quest to lie, cheat, and thereby steal elections. We can remember 1980 when Jimmy Carter, whose presidency was the epitome of well-meaning incompetence, played the extremist card against Ronald Reagan, suggesting that the former two-term California governor was an amiable dunce and a war monger, neither of which were even close to being factual, as Reagan's personal diaries have otherwise proved he was erudite, intellectual, and quite cerebral in every major decision he made as president. So goes the career of the underestimated, as Reagan pounded Jimmy Carter in both the popular and electoral balloting.

Fast forward to 2012 when Senate Majority Leader Harry Reid, while trying to assist Barack Obama's re-election bid, outrageously and slanderously used his office and in-chamber senate immunity to falsely accuse Republican nominee Mitt Romney of paying no income tax for the preceding dozen years, an absolute and unequivocal lie, perpetuated by an abiding and complicit mainstream media. Romney, by any measure, was and is an honorable man, who nevertheless had to prove that he had in fact paid all of his taxes, and quite a lot, actually. Yet the damage was done, and Reid knew it. When last week he and the White House showed absolutely no remorse for the lie that they had perpetuated (Reid even boasted, "Romney lost, didn't he?" with a smile on his face) in the pursuit of victory, it revealed to the nation a sickening and dastardly ethos that Democrats will do anything, say anything, truth be damned, that winning elections, as opposed to the noblesse oblige of public service and love of country, is what they are all about, which means Hillary Clinton is well-placed and supremely suited to carry the soiled banner of the party she represents, since her own ethical and legal lapses are well-documented and increasingly obvious.

Meanwhile, the all-too-compliant major media, in conjunction with the loony liberals of leftist leprosy, are presently ginning up controversy about Indiana's version of the 1993 Religious Freedom Restoration Act (a federal law signed by President Clinton) by suggesting that it amounts to wanton discrimination against the LGBT community when, in fact, it does not. Republican Governors Pence and Hutchinson from Indiana and Arkansas, respectively, have been cowed into amending and curtailing this legislation which exists in twenty-seven other states, because Republicans know full well that to do otherwise invites the narrative that they are nothing but extremist, bible-thumping bigots. The mass media rubber-stamps this narrative as absolute fact, and a lazy and ill-informed electorate buys into the lie, just as they did in 1964 when they feared nuclear annihilation from a Goldwater presidency.

It will not matter who is the eventual Republican nominee, because whoever it is will thus be labeled as an extremist, regardless of his positions on the issues of today. This is what the left does all too well, but after all, they win, don't they?

The Cancer of Division

23 July 2015

Take heed of the symbol of a dismembered serpent. For those familiar with American history, it is recognized as an emblem associated with the early days of the American Revolution. It represents eleven of the thirteen colonies, omitting Georgia and Delaware, (Massachusetts, Connecticut, Rhode Island, and Connecticut amalgamated into "N.E.," as in New England). The message was as clear then, as it is today. "Join or Die" or, in other words, "United We Stand, Divided We Fall," and just as prescient today, perhaps even more so.

Today, we live in a divided America, perhaps more divided than at any time since the 1860s, when this country was ripped apart by the bloodiest war ever to take place in the Western Hemisphere, the American Civil War. Much of the blame, perhaps all of the blame, for this division rests at the feet of those who we elect to serve in Washington, D.C., particularly with a president who spent both of his campaigns and all of his presidency dividing Americans and pitting them against one another in an ignoble attempt to divide and thus conquer a country whose exceptionalism he derides and whose greatness he denies. Black against white, poor against rich, union against management, gay against straight, women against men, Muslim against Christian, agnostic against religious, pro-abortion against pro-life, immigrant against native-born, and the list goes on and on *ad nauseam*. Barack Obama did not invent these divisions, but instead of ameliorating these divisions, he has instead accelerated them, just as an arsonist would accelerate a small fire into a conflagration with the addition of gasoline. He did so with a purpose of camouflaging his real intent to "fundamentally transform the United States of America," just as he promised on the night of his election in 2008. In actuality, this is code for bringing the greatest country in the history of the word, down into the depths of mediocrity and, ultimately, destruction.

And yet . . .

There is another, less corrosive but equally destructive cancer of division taking place within the Republican Party. For many election cycles going back to 1964, Republicans have gone at one another in the quest to nominate the "perfect candidate" and each time have ended up with the nominee's supporters being elated and the rest of the GOP disgruntled, so disgruntled at times to the extent that these disgruntled Republicans have sat out elections, easily giving the presidency to a united Democrat Party, as best evidenced by the elections of Jimmy Carter, Bill Clinton, and Barack Obama.

Today, it is happening again in the G.O.P. True conservatives, (Ted Cruz, Rick Santorum, Scott Walker), moderates (Jeb Bush, Chris Christie, Lindsay Graham), moderate conservatives (Rand Paul, Rick Perry, Marco Rubio), outsiders (Ben Carson, Carly Fiorina, Donald Trump), and (forgive the term) wannabes (Mike Huckabee, Bobby Jindal, John Kasich, George Pataki) are all having what amounts to a sophomoric food fight with one another in an effort to gain a point or two in polls which are wildly premature. Even the candidates who are/were senators (Cruz, Graham, Paul, Perry, Rubio, Santorum) are having a go with candidates who are/were governors (Bush, Christie, Huckabee, Jindal, Kasich, Pataki, Walker) and those who have never been elected to any office (Carson, Fiorina, Trump), trying to say that their current/former occupation is more suited to being president than the others, and all to the delight and pleasure of Democrats and their oh-so-partisan allies in the media.

Some of these candidates, most notably Ted Cruz, have been magnanimous in reaching out to other candidates, welcoming them into the fray or joining together with them in discussions, as evidenced by the meetings between Cruz and Trump, and the Independence Day get-together with Rubio and Christie at the home of 2012 Nominee Mitt Romney. While these get-togethers are a positive sign, this much remains certain. A divided Republican Party, not to mention a third party run by *any* of them, will ensure that the next president will have a "D" after their name, and as things stand now, that president will be a former first lady and Secretary of State. Worse, these intraparty spats are pitting Republican voters against one another, a trend that is virtually orgasmic to Democrats who will unite behind their nominee regardless.

Since Republicans cannot do anything to heal the divisions that are the perverse progeny of Barack Obama for so long as he remains president, they would be wise instead to resolve to unite as a Republican Party. They should call on *all* of their candidates to stop trashing one another (including Donald Trump, along with his own trashing of the others) and remember "the Gipper's" eleventh commandment: "Thou shalt not insult another Republican." Each of the candidates must resolve to support whoever the nominee is, regardless, because *any* one of them would be a far better president than *any* of the Democrats running today. Instead, they need heap their vitriol on Obama and Hillary and keep pounding away day after day.

To do otherwise is to metastasize the cancer of division—one of their own making—and will ultimately lead them and their country to peril.

Conservative vs Liberal
and what it *Really* Means in 2016

17 August 2015

Whether it is labeled "Conservative" or "Liberal," "Right" or "Left," "Tory" or "Labour," or more ambiguously albeit less accurately, "Republican" or "Democrat," it is shorthand for the eternal political struggle of one philosophy versus the other, as it relates to countries which allow partisan divides. History tells us how these determinations have been fluid during the last three centuries where people have had some level of say, more or less, in how their governments function. Political stances which at one time were labeled "Liberal" are now championed by the "Right" and vice versa and have been since the mid-twentieth century.

Since the 1960s, these philosophies, generally speaking, have been static in that there hasn't been much movement in how we define ourselves politically. The anti-war, anti-establishment, socialist leanings of the 1960s, finding root in the political "Left," still reside in that arena, just as the pro-defense, pro-business, capitalist leanings of the 1960s, finding root in the political "Right," still reside in that arena as well. In short, most who are old enough to have defined themselves as "leftist" in the 1960s (and were honest enough to do so) would still find refuge in the political left today. The reverse is equally as true.

What *has* changed is the degree to which the major political parties have shifted their respective "centers" when it comes to where they lie on the political spectrum. The Democratic Party which exists today is much more "leftist" than it was in the 1960s, while the Republican Party is far less "rightist" today, as compared to where they used to be when Ronald Reagan left office in 1989.

What has *also* changed is how individuals define themselves in terms of political affiliation, with fewer Americans identifying themselves as "Democrat" or "Republican" than their forebears did a generation ago. A higher percentage of people in the United States today classify themselves as "Independent" than ever before, reflecting a growing dismay with political parties generally and have given rise to the "anti-candidate," most notable in the candidacies of Donald Trump, Carly Fiorina, Ben Carson, and to a lesser extent, Ted Cruz, all of whom are basing their campaigns on common themes of being "outsiders" to the establishment politicians centered in Washington, D.C. Such a trend has also impacted voter participation overall with a generally downward slide in voter participation since 1960.

So how does one determine whether they are "conservative" or "liberal" in the lexicon as it is generally used in today's parlance? Generally speaking, it is this:

A "Conservative" generally advocates the rights of the many over the rights of the few, be they social issues, foreign policy issues, immigration issues, legal issues, and economic issues. The Republican candidate who can best tap into these advocacies will be best suited to encourage their party's turnout. In short, this will not be Jeb Bush.

A "Liberal" generally advocates the rights of the few over the rights of the many- be they social issues, foreign policy issues, immigration issues, legal issues, and economic issues. The Democratic candidate who can best tap into these advocacies will be best suited to encourage their party's turnout. In short, this will not be Hillary Clinton.

While Mr. Bush and Ms. Clinton can still win their respective party's nominations, such nominations will no doubt leave their party's rank and file nonplussed and will encourage either a third-party run, low voter turnout, or both, all of which will generally favor the Democratic nominee over the Republican nominee, as no third party candidate will ever get the requisite 270 electoral votes necessary to win.

Having said this, in such a contingency whereby no candidate is able to amass the 270-vote threshold necessary to win the election will throw the election into the House of Representatives for the Presidency and into the Senate for the Vice Presidency, with each state's delegation having one vote apiece, which presumably would elect a Republican, given the current balance of power in those two chambers.

Despite who wins, rest assured that the new president will have an extremely difficult time pulling together a country as divided as is the United States today. With all of the current challenges Americans face in a fast-changing world, it will require a rare breed indeed to successfully lead this country out of quagmire in which we now regrettably find ourselves, all of which can only lead to one question. Just who is crazy enough to want *that* job? To be continued . . .

The "Gotcha" Game—
How the Media Controls Elections

22 September 2015

Question: How do you know when a Republican Candidate has a reasonable chance of winning an election?

Answer: It's simple. When the media starts asking the Republican Candidate "gotcha" questions.

Regrettably, no media outlet, neither print nor broadcast, is above playing the "gotcha" game, not even the supposedly conservative Fox News Network. Going back to the early days of television and the even earlier days of print journalism, the fourth estate swims in its own sweet sauce of bringing down candidates with whom they politically and philosophically disagree. It has gotten worse, much worse, since the election of Ronald Reagan, and with every election since, the inherent bias in the media has become more and more egregious.

It works like this. "Candidate X" declares his candidacy for the Republican nomination for the presidency. Based upon the candidate's timing of the announcement, the candidate has a twenty-four hour window of intense media attention, which the candidate admittedly craves and seeks to milk to the fullest extent that he/she can. Then one of two things happens:

> If the candidate is relatively unknown or does not engender much of a bounce in the polls, the candidate is largely ignored or at best marginalized to the extent that he/she gets no attention unless he/she says something outrageous.

(or)

> If the candidate is relatively well known or engenders a substantial bounce in the polls, the media swarms around the candidate, pounces on him/her, and starts laying interrogative landmines which, if stepped on, begin to destroy the efficacy of his/her campaign.

The process of candidate destruction is very effective and can make or break a candidate long before balloting even begins.

Take for instance the very first question during the main event of the Fox News debate in Cleveland. Brett Baier's question was so obviously pointed at Donald Trump, it was obvious that Fox News was participating in the "Gotcha" Game. Megyn Kelly confirmed this over-the-top bias when she asked Trump about disparaging comments he had previously made about Rosie O'Donnell, which has about as much to do with prescient issues as the color of the tie he was wearing at the time. Fox News, often accused of being conservative, showed its true colors by deciding beforehand which candidates are acceptable to them and which are not. Obviously, Fox News does not like the idea of a Trump nomination.

If that wasn't bad enough, the second debate, hosted by CNN at the Reagan Library, was even more egregious, egregious against Trump, as fully eighteen minutes was devoted to shooting him with all types of interrogative poisoned darts by the CNN moderator and egregious against the entire GOP field, spending much of the balance of time indirectly attacking him or pitting one candidate against another in an effort to make the entire group of candidates look like an eleven-member troupe performing a verbal version of a pie-throwing, slapstick farce.

Admittedly, it's no surprise that CNN would show its all-too-obvious bias against the Republican Party, as they would *never* do such a thing in a Democrat debate.

Notice also, in both of these televised events, the grossly inordinate amount of time spent on some candidates as opposed to the other, comparatively marginalized contestants who barely registered themselves due to the lack of opportunity to speak at all, cases in point Scott Walker, Mike Huckabee, Rand Paul, Ted Cruz, and to a lesser extent, Ben Carson, Marco Rubio, John Kasich, and Chris Christie. All of these candidates were afforded only a fraction of time that was allotted to Trump, Jeb Bush, and, in the second debate on CNN, Carly Fiorina.

This media manipulation is not limited to the televised debates, not by a long shot. Take for instance the question posed by Chris Todd to Ben Carson on NBC's *Meet the Press* on September 20th. He asked Dr. Carson about whether or not he would support the presidential candidacy of a Muslim. This question, completely irrelevant to this campaign for its complete lack of a Muslim candidate, was an obvious attempt by Todd and his network to create a controversy that does not exist and take down the candidacy of an increasingly popular candidate with whom they object, as if to say, "How dare an African American run for office as a Republican?" Does anyone imagine that Hillary Clinton would ever be asked such a question? Now that Carly Fiorina's popularity is surging following her stellar performance in the CNN debate, they will no doubt do the same to her, all for having the temerity of being a woman seeking the Republican nomination, a Republican Party who supposedly hates women. The message is quite clear. Substantially rise in popularity and show some promise as to the possibility of becoming the next president, and the media will absolutely destroy any chance of one's survival. The reason that they don't attack Jeb Bush is because he is the candidate who the media has ordained as acceptable, largely because of the perception, warranted or otherwise, that the country will not elect a third Bush to the Oval office.

The media has largely ignored Scott Walker. Couple this with his lackluster performance in both events, and the resultant drop in funding led to his decision this week to suspend his campaign. Walker effectively took on the unions in Wisconsin, survived two recall elections, and was an early-on and odds-on favorite to be a front-runner. At both debates and on the campaign trail, it was obvious that Walker was given about as much attention as an unoccupied bellboy at a five-star hotel. One down, others to go. Essentially, the mainstream media *wants* either Donald Trump or Jeb Bush to be the eventual nominee, and there is precious little that any other candidate can do to change this paradigm. They want Trump, because of the delicious possibility that he will commit an over-the-top *faux pas* and thus guarantee the election of a Democrat. They want Jeb Bush because of the perception that another Bush is one too many. For Fiorina and Carson, the media will no doubt besiege them in an obvious attempt to drive these two "outsiders" out of the mix. Promising conservatives like Rubio and Cruz will have to scratch tooth and nail to get any attention at all, because they have the chutzpah to offer substantive conservative ideas that fly in the face of Democrat dogma. This dogma, which purportedly advances the idea of a supposed correlation of intelligence and the degree of liberalism so espoused, explains why Ronald Reagan was and is portrayed as "an amiable dunce," despite the fact that it was Reagan who stood down the Soviet Union and why Barack Obama was and is portrayed as a political version of "the second coming," while it is Obama who caved in to Iran, the worst deal ever struck by a US president.

In summary, when journalism, both in print and over the air, sheds the vaunted veneer of objectivity and takes on the trappings of over-the-top advocacy, representative government is then perverted to the point of polemic pointlessness, and the potential then arises that such a form of government shall sadly be sacrificed to the effete egos of sanctimonious media malcontents.

The Perils of Playing Papal Politics

24 September 2015

This week is absolutely abuzz with the visit of Pope Francis to the United States. Pope Francis, the first Catholic prelate from the Western Hemisphere and, for that matter, the first non-European to ever ascend to the throne of Saint Peter, is enjoying a tour-de-force in his first visit to the United States with stops in Washington, Philadelphia, and New York and making his presence well known in the halls of power. His stops will have included visits to the White House, meetings with the president, addressing a joint session of Congress, addressing the General Assembly of the United Nations, all in addition to his many pastoral activities, including celebrating Mass at the Basilica of the National Shrine of the Immaculate Conception, where he has canonized Father Junpero Serra into the sainthood of the Catholic Church, the first time any saint has been canonized by a pope while in the Western Hemisphere, history thus made on a profound scale.

His visit to the United States followed his visit to Cuba and its former dictator, Fidel Castro. Reportedly, the pope had a hand in brokering a deal between his ruling brother, Raul Castro, and Barack Obama, where full diplomatic relations have been restored following fifty-six years of what had become stalemated estrangement between the two countries.

The Roman Catholic Church teaches that, on matters of faith and morals, the Pope is infallible, essentially granting his office absolute and unequivocal authority in matters of Catholic doctrine, based upon his predecessor, Saint Peter, being given this authority by Jesus Christ Himself.

This authority, however, *does not* extend to temporal matters, not in the least. On matters pertaining outside the Church, the Holy See is nothing more than a head of state (the Vatican) and, as such, one world leader amongst several. It is in this realm that his visit to the United States transcends the ecclesiastical and thereby enters into the tempestuous world of politics, where his authority does not present itself, not in any way shape or form.

When the world politic begins to mingle with the world religious and vice versa, trouble can, and often does rear its ugly head. In the case of the pope's visit here, both he and political leaders have regrettably wandered into the perils of playing papal politics, where anything said by the pope becomes co-opted by politicians with far more earthly and clandestine agendas. How ironic it is that many politicians on the left, including the president, will attempt to use his statements about an array of issues ranging from climate change and open borders to wealth redistribution and capital punishment, all to advance their own political narratives, while fully well ignoring his stances on abortion and same-sex marriage. That's called selective endorsement of papal positioning or, if you will, opportunistic grandstanding, for which they should be ashamed of themselves. With all due respect to His Holiness, he himself treads these same treacherous waters when he inserts himself into domestic political discourse and into US foreign policy, as he has evidently done so on several occasions. It is one thing for the Vicar of Christ to spread the good news of the Gospels to all corners of the watching world, but it is quite another to use his offices to declare what is politically moral and what is not politically moral, as when he said "people who manufacture or invest in weapons cannot call themselves Christians" and, in so doing, essentially seeks to ex-communicate those who happen to make or own guns. Such proselytizing is not consistent with his offices, and it is for this reason that what should otherwise be a celebration of his visit to our country is now sullied in the licentious world of political debate. The same can be said of his apparent displeasure with capitalism, despite the undeniable reality that free-market capitalism has done more, far more, than any other system to alleviate poverty and lift up millions from want.

Having said this, Pope Francis himself fully admits that he has not read nor watched the news in more than thirty years except for a brief daily scan of a Roman newspaper, which means essentially that His Holiness is out of touch with contemporary and worldly politics. With deep and abiding respect for his office, he would do quite well to remain outside this arena when it comes to saying what is and is not correct, for it is neither his purview nor his profession to do otherwise.

Socialism

20 October 2015

socialism \ˈsō-shə-li-zəm\ n. 1. a system or condition of society in which the means of production are owned and controlled by the state; 2. a way of organizing a society in which major industries are owned and controlled by the government rather than by individual people and companies; 3. any of various economic and political theories advocating collective or governmental ownership and administration of the means of production and distribution of goods; 4. a system of society or group living in which there is no private property; 5. a stage of society in Marxist theory transitional between capitalism and communism and distinguished by unequal distribution of goods and pay according to work done.[1]

Slice it, dice it, blend it, and mix it any which way you want, but at the end of the day, socialism is not compatible with the American way, nor is it commensurate with the Constitution of the United States. Simply put, socialism is an anathema to what it means to be an American, and anyone, *anyone* who advocates the introduction of socialism into the American way of life is either ignorant as to what socialism is, ill-informed, or bent on the destruction of the United States of America.

Consider the fact that the United States, a nation built on self-sufficiency and capitalism, has achieved by all meaningful measures the highest standard of living in the entire world. Indeed, it was capitalism that created what we now know as the middle class. Yes, there are those who will toss about examples of smaller, *much* smaller Nordic countries like Finland, Norway, Denmark, and Sweden as socialist "utopias," but these countries are racially and culturally homogeneous, with populations equivalent to a few of our largest cities combined.

Comparing these countries to the United States, countries which spend barely a farthing on national defense, is like comparing soldier ants to draught horses, because the United States is in reality augmenting and ensuring *their* own defense with *our* own taxpayer's money and *not* theirs, based upon their membership in NATO, which ceases to exist without the United States paying the tab.

It is amusing, to a point, that Senator Bernie Sanders (I- VT) attempts to redefine socialism as "democratic socialism," amusing because it is an obvious dodge to the fact that what he is advocating is nothing less than socialism, pure and simple. He very clearly indicates that what he wants to do is tax the wealthy at 90%, in other words, for every dollar the wealthy earn, he wants to take ninety cents and use it to fund social programs which he says are necessary to achieve what he deems to be "fairness," essentially confiscating money from those who earn it and distributing the proceeds as he deems fit. He calls this "democratic socialism." A more honest term would be "theft."

The point to which it is not amusing is the fact that there are millions of people, particularly young people, who buy into this "horse hockey." This is particularly true with regard to college students, who are too young or too ignorant or too brainwashed by their aging professors to remember that socialism in Germany during the 1930s and 1940s, China since the 1940s, Russia since the 1910s, combined to result in the deaths of well over 100 million people in the 20th century; and that doesn't include socialism in Vietnam, Cambodia, North Korea, and a host of countries in Africa and Latin America, where socialism resulted in the deaths of many hundreds of thousands as well. Simply stated, socialism kills, eventually, because once the rich have been liquidated financially and otherwise, the populace becomes insatiable for the meager benefits to which they have become accustomed, and the well runs dry. British Prime Minister Margaret Thatcher so famously once said, "The inherent problem with socialism is that, eventually, you run out of other people's money."

In the end, socialism results in an economic system where everyone, except those in power, becomes equally poor, equally deprived, and equally miserable, which might be pleasing to the likes of Bernie Sanders and his Democrat allies, but strikes this writer as nothing more than the recipe for failure and the basis of a lie, a cruel lie which would have people believe that all fortunes were made as the result of someone getting screwed. Socialists and those who advocate socialism want to sell people on the concept that the only way to right that wrong is to forcibly take money from one person and have the government give some of it to another. which once extrapolated, means that innovation, technological advancement, medical and scientific discovery all come to an abrupt halt when the profit motive and the desire to improve one's own lot in life become disincentivized to the point of cultural regression. But don't tell this to a wild-eyed young liberal bent on achieving social and economic justice, lest you be branded as a "hater" insensitive to the needs of others.

'reprinted from Merriam-Webster's Dictionary, an Encyclopedia Britannica Company

Open Season on Conservatives—
The Obama Regime's Refusal to Indict Lois Lerner

27 October 2015

In truth, it wasn't unexpected that Lois Lerner would get away with openly and wantonly targeting conservative-leaning 501(c)(4) organizations applying for tax exemptions running up to the 2012 Election. Ultimately, she did what she was told to do and kept her mouth shut during congressional hearings, and the administration duly kept their promise to her, that if she co-operated with the administration by cloaking their obvious involvement, nothing would happen to her at the end of the day.

Quickly summing up what led to all of this, the IRS targeting of conservative organizations applying for 501(c)(4) tax exemptions was originally and falsely blamed on rogue operatives in the IRS Cincinnati office, which was later traced to the IRS Headquarters in Washington. The former Commissioner of the IRS, Doug Shulman, went to the White House 138 times during his tenure when the targeting was going on, but in Congressional testimony said that he could only recall an Easter egg hunt as the reason for one of these 138 visits, and somehow, he could not remember why he went there on the other 137 occasions. Then two years after Lois Lerner's e-mails were subpoenaed by Congress, these e-mails suddenly vanished into thin air, purportedly due to a hard drive crash, and the subsequent disposal of the computer's hard drive conveniently waylaid and prevented further investigation into e-mails that Lerner had sent to government entities outside the Treasury Department, e-mails which might otherwise have revealed IRS communication to other government entities like OSHA and the FBI, which also launched investigations into businesses run by taxpayers who supported these same conservative organizations. Also noteworthy was the fact that seven other IRS officials being tied to the IRS abuse scandals also somehow had the "misfortune" of hard drive crashes and lost e-mails. All the while, Obama insisted that there was "not a smidgen of corruption" in this arena. Lois Lerner subsequently appeared before Congress twice, pled the fifth on both occasions (this is only done when someone would otherwise open themselves to criminal charges), and ultimately got away with this illegal targeting, because the all-too-corrupt Department of Justice, first under Eric Holder and now under Loretta Lynch, on orders from the President himself, has not and will not pursue a case which, if fully investigated, would show the president's involvement in the aggregated abuse of power.

Well, this wasn't the first time President Obama played fast and loose with the truth (Hillary's e-mail, specifically related to the Benghazi investigation, anyone?), and it won't be the last time either.

Call this a precursor into how the Obama administration will ultimately handle (or rather, not handle) the FBI investigation into Hillary's e-mail scandals. The FBI, investigating multiple felonies which have clearly been committed by Mrs. Clinton (remember David Petraeus?), will eventually seek to hand down indictments of Mrs. Clinton related to a host of violations of federal law, and the Obama administration will, as they have with Ms. Lerner, summarily refuse to press charges.

The mainstream media, in full betrayal of the principals their forefathers set during the Watergate era, will give both Obama and Hillary a free ride on these scandals because they are no longer a free press practicing the safeguards against tyranny as the "fourth estate," but rather have become an advocacy- based cheering section for the Democratic Party. Just as they did everything they could to elect Obama twice, they will do everything they can to elect Hillary in 2016 by painting even the most moderate Republican nominee as a racist, misogynist, right-wing extremist who will drive women seeking abortions back into the dark alleys of coat hangers and death. This is what has become of the free press in America today, ironic in that here we find ourselves living in the "information age."

Yes, it is indeed open season on Republicans and conservatives in particular who are being labeled by the Obama administration as "domestic terrorists" while this is being written. The same thing happened before in the Soviet Union, in Nazi Germany and in Communist China, when political opposition became illegal, and we are ultimately reminded, once again, of what Martin Niemöller (1892-1984) once wrote:

"First, they came for the Socialists, and I did not speak out, because I was not a Socialist. Then they came for the Trade Unionists, and I did not speak out, because I was not a Trade Unionist. Then they came for the Jews, and I did not speak out, because I was not a Jew. Then they came for me, and there was no one left to speak for me."

When the last conservative Republican is left, who will speak for this person, and who at long last will speak for representative democracy and the Constitution of the United States?

Voter Vexation — the Quest for the Perfect Candidate

3 November 2015

My interest in politics began in the fall of 1968 when I was all of ten years old. The Republicans, who briefly flirted with the idea of a last minute, hastily-constructed campaign effort by California Governor Ronald W. Reagan, chose instead another Californian, the former Vice President Richard M. Nixon. Meanwhile, the Democrats, reeling from the decision by incumbent President Lyndon B. Johnson not to seek reelection at the end of March and the June 6th assassination of front-runner Robert F. Kennedy at the Ambassador Hotel in Los Angeles, settled on Hubert H. Humphrey, the Minnesota liberal known to be a friend of big labor and his being the incumbent Vice President. So irritated with this choice of a pro-union liberal, the southern Democrats put their partisan loyalties aside and urged Alabama Governor George C. Wallace to launch a third-party run. Wallace, famous for his resistance to racial integration and his oft-quoted "segregation now, segregation tomorrow, segregation forever" was actually one of the most successful third-party candidates in American history, having carried five southern states, and thus ensuring the greatest political comeback ever with the election of Richard Nixon as thirty-seventh President of the United States. It was Nixon who famously lost to John F. Kennedy in 1960 for the presidential election by less than 100,000 votes and who had announced his retirement from elective politics following his failed bid to unseat the California Governor, Edmund G. "Pat" Brown, Sr. (father of current Governor Jerry Brown) two years later, bitterly saying to the adversarial press, "Think of all you will miss. You won't have Nixon to kick around anymore." (It was the senior Brown who ultimately lost his bid for a third term to a movie-star-turned-politician Ronald Reagan in 1966, largely due to his mishandling of the Watts riots the year before).

That 1968 presidential election had a voter participation percentage of 61%, one of the largest turnouts in U.S. history, and garnered so much attention that the 1969 Super Bowl, in which the Joe Namath-led New York Jets defeated the heavily-favored Baltimore Colts, "themed" its halftime show on voter participation *three months following* the presidential election.

One of the things I learned as a ten-year-old, whose two major passions were, in order, the Baltimore Colts and presidential politics, was that it is the imperfect candidate who can win elections if a) the candidate's party rallies around its nominee (Nixon), and b) the other candidate's party is divided (Humphrey and Wallace). Nixon, who my own parents derisively referred to as "Tricky Dick," won the election and handily so, because he faced a decidedly-divided Democrat Party.

Fast forward to this November of 2015, a full year before the 2016 presidential election. While Democrats have pretty much united around Hillary Clinton and, setting aside a most improbable possibility, given the all-so-corrupt and partisan Justice Department under Barack Obama, that she might otherwise face indictments for having committed multiple felonies related to her e-mail obfuscation while compromising national security relating thereto, the Republicans are in a comparative free-for-all with fifteen *still* in the running for the G.O.P. nomination.

One need only read through Facebook commentaries to see that most Republican and conservative voters are saying in effect, "I'll vote for 'x' and maybe 'y' but certainly not for 'z', no way." The aforementioned variables can and do interchangeably apply to Jeb Bush, Ben Carson, Chris Christie, Ted Cruz, Carly Fiorina, John Kasich, Marco Rubio, and Donald Trump (given that Mike Huckabee, Rand Paul, Jim Gilmore, Lindsay Graham, Bobby Jindal, George Pataki, and Rick Santorum are effectively though not technically out of the race). This on its surface suggests a historically competitive race for the Republican nomination, but in reality must be a veritable "wet dream" for Hillary Clinton, who can sit back and watch the leading eight spend money trying to one-up each other in the feeding frenzy that has become all too evident as never before.

In truth, there is only one way Republican voters can defeat Hillary Clinton next fall in an election that should otherwise be theirs to lose. They must swallow their pride and commit themselves to support, campaign, and vote for whoever becomes the eventual Republican nominee, regardless of who that person is and regardless of that candidate's imperfections. To do less will effectively bring about a third term for Barack Obama, which is making Hillary Clinton and her united Democratic Party drool at the prospect of winning an election which, on its surface, they should not come close to winning, but is nevertheless theirs for the taking if Republicans don't grow up and face the music of their own making.

Chapter 11

Election 2016 and the Presidential Debates

The "Poll" Vault—A Preview of Thursday Night's Debate

4 August 2015

Fifteen months from now, Americans will be casting ballots to determine on a state-by-state basis which set of their parties' electors will select the next resident of the United States. In essence, we don't have a popular election; we have fifty-one separate state elections, which actually and eventually take place in the first week of December when Electoral College votes are cast, based upon the popular vote in each of the several states and the District of Columbia.

On Thursday night, the sixth of August, the top ten candidates vying for the Republican nomination, based upon an average of five national polls, will be featured in a prime time debate on Fox News, a debate to be moderated by Chris Wallace, Bret Baier and Megyn Kelly. Earlier that evening the remaining seven candidates will have (forgive the term) a junior varsity debate amongst the candidates who failed to make the top ten cut.

While it might not be "fair" to split them up this way, with seventeen candidates running (as of this writing) for the nomination, it's most likely that this is the only way to manage such a sizable cast of combatants. The die is presumably cast with Chris Christie, John Kasich, Rick Santorum, Rick Perry, and Carly Fiorina on the bubble to secure the ninth and tenth spots, giving them the right to join Donald Trump, Jeb Bush, Scott Walker, Ben Carson, Marco Rubio, Ted Cruz, Mike Huckabee, and Rand Paul at 9:00 EDT. The remaining candidates, Rick Perry, Bobby Jindal, George Pataki, Lindsey Graham, and latecomer Jim Gilmore will have to hash it all out four hours before this prime time "smackdown," with two of four struggling to secure those all-important ninth and tenth spots.

All eyes will be on the 9:00 debate, primarily motivated by curiosity to see which of "the Donald's" will show up. Will it be the "in-your-face" Trump who can seemingly take on anyone in a heated *tete-a-tete*, or the "refined and restrained" Trump who can lay back and be "above it all," while the rest of the field gets into the muckety-muck? Don't look for Jeb Bush or Scott Walker or Ben Carson to taunt him; after all, these three candidates are hardly the taunting type and won't take the risk to fall down further in the polls. Marco Rubio most likely won't; it's not his all-too-refined style to do so. Ted Cruz could possibly land a couple of blows, as could Mike Huckabee or Rand Paul, if they are willing to take the risk of doing so. Chris Christie and John Kasich, should they get in, could also wave a Republican red cape in the Donald's face. Regardless, at this early (and I do mean *early*) stage, Thursday's debate is Trump's to lose and, should he avoid a gaff or not lose his cool, he'll walk away the winner.

The United States is indeed unique in the way we select a President, perhaps because it is, after all, the world's most important job. Like everything else American, most notably holidays for example, we have a tendency to overdo things and do them prematurely, which is why essential polling fifteen months before an election seems as absurd as Halloween decorations appearing on August store shelves and Christmas decorations appearing on October shelves weeks before Halloween. We are at long last a nation of excess, and we seem, politically speaking, to be suffering under the weight of our own excess.

So, to all of the candidates who have "poll-vaulted" their way into this, the first of some seventeen such debates (between candidates of both parties, prior to their respective nominating conventions), may the best of them win squarely and fairly, assuming such a feat is possible.

The "Poll" Vault (Part II)—Picking Up the Pieces of the First Debates

7 August 2015

It was Donald Trump's debate to lose, and he lost the first Republican debate in a big way both tactically and effectively. Right at the onset, when moderator Brett Baier asked if there was anyone who would not pledge to "support the eventual nominee, no matter who that person ends up being, nor rule out a third-party run," Donald Trump raised his hand, much to the dismay of the audience gathered in Cleveland. When Baier asked him to confirm this with the understanding that a "third party run would effectively elect the Democratic nominee" in 2016, Trump indicated that he knew full well what he was doing, essentially stating that he would only pledge to support the Republican nominee if he himself were that nominee. There was more, much more. Throughout the debate, he was surly and condescending and carried a facial expression which suggested his utter contempt and complete distaste for the debate and its moderators as well. In doing so, "the Donald" may have effectively delegitimized himself as a prospective Republican candidate and, more importantly, has exposed the veneer of a would-be candidate who has no depth to his flashy political persona. Based on this, unless he can pull off a miracle, his candidacy may not last to the New Hampshire Primary and the Iowa Caucus early next year, because as a Republican, it appears that he may be all but finished.

So who were the winners?

First, some kudos must go to the Fox News moderators who posed very difficult and pointed questions to each of the contenders, specifically challenging each of them to address their own shortcomings to policies and their respective past statements. In essence, nobody got off easy in either debate. Hillary Clinton can thank her lucky stars she did not have to face these five moderators, as they would have likely ripped her façade to shreds.

Overall, none of the remaining candidates (other than Trump) "blew it" per se, but there were some clear winners, most notably

Carly Fiorina in the first debate, whose overall performance was most likely the best all evening. The rest of the candidates in that first debate did okay, but did nothing to really bring their polling numbers up the way Ms. Fiorina almost certainly will. She was crisp, cool, and cerebral in her statements and seeming flawless in her delivery, without any hint of hesitation or unease. There is no doubt she will climb into the top tier prior to next month's debate. As a whole, the remaining candidates in that first debate showed that they were competent, but that's all.

In the second debate, the clear winners were Marco Rubio, whose eye contact and charisma only added to the substance of what he said, Ted Cruz, whose considered statements rang true with honesty and conviction, and Mike Huckabee, whose clarity and specific vision revealed his grasp of the issues discussed. Ben Carson started off poorly, but improved his performance when the debate continued and had a very warm and personable closing statement that will only serve to endear him to a far greater degree than when he entered the arena. Jeb Bush and Scott Walker had plausible performances, but only managed to do just enough to maintain the number of their supporters without adding any by essentially playing it safe. An exciting exchange took place between Rand Paul and Chris Christie when dealing with the issue of collecting telephone metadata, and each surrendered no ground, but Christie won that exchange by only the slimmest of margins. Ironically it won't help Christie's standing, but in the final analysis, it did seem to weaken Paul's position in the field. John Kasich, having a distinct "home field advantage" in the Quicken Loans Arena, did better than expected, but not enough to drastically improve his standing in a crowded field.

All in all, it was an eventful and potentially consequential evening, in that the front runner has stumbled in a big way. Look for Trump's numbers to fall, and the beneficiaries of this fall will most likely be Rubio, Cruz, Huckabee, Carson, and Fiorina, who will be in a better position to take on Jeb Bush and Scott Walker for the right to oppose Hillary or, if not, Joe Biden in the general election of 2016.

The Trump Card — A Preview of the Second GOP Debate

14 September 2015

On Wednesday evening, September 16th, at the Ronald Reagan Presidential Library in Simi Valley, California, CNN will be hosting the second GOP Presidential Debate. Participating in the main event will be, alphabetically, Jeb Bush, Ben Carson, Chris Christie, Ted Cruz, Carly Fiorina, Mike Huckabee, John Kasich, Rand Paul, Marco Rubio, Donald Trump, and Scott Walker. The night's opener will consist of the rest of the remaining field: Lindsey Graham, Bobby Jindal, George Pataki, and Rick Santorum, as Jim Gilmore failed to qualify for the preliminary round, and Rick Perry dropped from the race early last week.

Carly Fiorina's stellar performance in the last debate's opener led to her anticipated advancement to the varsity round. Barring any surprise in Wednesday's preliminary round or an unexpected and utter collapse by one of the candidates in the night's main event, those participating in the first round are not likely to follow Fiorina's footsteps to the upper level. By the time October's third debate rolls around, a shortfall of campaign funding will have likely winnowed the entire field by a couple more candidates at least, and our guess is that only ten candidates will remain in the GOP field by year's end. Looming large in the main event will be the following:

Donald Trump. Now that "the Donald" has signed the pledge to support the eventual GOP nominee and thereby forego an independent run should he not win the eventual GOP nod, will he show more or less bravado in his performance, or will he (excuse the analogy) "step in it," so to speak, and reverse his rise in the polls? More to the point, will any of the aforementioned contingencies matter?

Jeb Bush. Given the degree to which his poll numbers are shrinking, the former Florida Governor is just about a half dozen yawns from being obliterated by the flashy frontrunner. Will Bush risk credibility and become more feisty towards Trump, or will he come across as the policy wonk and take on further attributes of a wannabe who in the final analysis never was, despite being the early-odds favorite of the political class?

Carly Fiorina. Will the lone lady in a crowded field continue to impress with her steady and cerebral candor and enable her poll numbers to rival that of Dr. Carson? Will she now go for broke and take on "the Donald" before a nationally televised audience? Ben Carson. Will he continue to be the suave and debonair gentleman in the room by charming viewers with his calming and measured demeanor, or will he cast off his courtly manner and thereby provoke "the Donald" into a faux pas of consequential proportions?

Then again, there are the others in the mix. Will Chris Christie have another dust up with Rand Paul, as they did in the last debate, and will one knock the other off of the top tier? Will Cruz, Huckabee, Kasich, or Rubio turn in a much-needed strong debate performance to substantively change their standing in the polls, and will they be afforded the opportunity to do so by the CNN panel of questioners? Will Scott Walker resuscitate his campaign from what seemingly seems to be his journey into the land of irrelevance? Lastly, will there be anywhere near as large an audience watching this debate as there was in the last debate. Here is a prediction: the larger the audience, the more consequential the effect on the respective candidacies, for better or for worse. Regardless, another deck of cards is about to be dealt, and we'll see if a whole new, ahem, *Trump card,* ahem, will be played.

Trump Card II — The Free-For-All at the Second GOP Debate

17 September 2015

In our youth, we played a version of football that we called "Smear the Queer." which in other areas of the country was called "Get the Goat," "Maul the Man," or other such monikers. The football was thrown high in the air and whoever caught it became the target of everyone else, who would jump on the ball carrier until he coughed it up, and then the next kid with the ball became the target, etc., etc., etc. Essentially, it was a kid's game which melded football with a juvenile version of a "Free for All." Last night at the Ronald Reagan Presidential Library in Simi Valley, California, CNN hosted the political equivalent of our childhood game with a twist; the "ball" didn't change hands, for the most part, and everyone including the moderators piled on Donald Trump. This was by design. Almost half of the questions in both the preliminary and main events were aimed at "the Donald," whether directly or indirectly. When the moderators were not targeting Trump per se, they were setting the candidates against one another, and even then, many of these matchups eventually became focused on the GOP frontrunner. To the shame of CNN, not a single question asked any of the candidates what they would do differently than Barack Obama, Hillary Clinton, nor any of the Democrats, none.

As for "the Donald" himself, he did a plausible job in fending off the attacks, such as they were. As was suspected, he appeared to have come into the debate unprepared to delve into the specifics of how he intends to tackle the larger issues confronting the country and instead put forth broad generalities and thematic grandiosities along the familiar and off-stated lines of his campaign, essentially sizzle without much substance. It is uncertain as to whether or not his performance will matter much, especially to his loyal following. Our guess is, however, that last night's debate performance may do little to add to this following. As was the case in the first GOP debate last month, it was Carly Fiorina who prevailed with the best overall performance during the evening's two-heat debate. She only made one tiny mistake (and this is a stretch) the entire night when she failed to say her name during the initial introductions, the only candidate to do so. After that, when she spoke, she was absolutely on fire. Whether it was responding to Trump's comments in a previous interview concerning her looks, assessing her own record of accomplishments in the private sector, outlining specifics on how best to handle threats from overseas and specifics as to how she intends to build up military and naval forces, and how she views the Iran deal and organ harvesting at Planned Parenthood, she was direct, pointed, and thoroughly substantive in her responses. In a word, she seemed more than anyone else "ready" to assume the presidency right then and there and handle the job with much aplomb and self-confidence. As a result, look for Carly to substantially rise in the polling prior to next month's third GOP debate.

Marco Rubio, for his own part, turned in a fine performance revealing the depth of his understanding, particularly in the areas of foreign policy and national security, of the issues at hand. He came across as a serious, focused, and vigorous candidate, and his smooth delivery reminded us of the man whose plane they all stood in front of at the Reagan Library. His numbers too may rise as a result.

Jeb Bush, who came into the debate a half dozen yawns from being obliterated by Trump, turned in a solid performance, tactfully taking on "the Donald" and showing that he does indeed have some degree of fire in his belly to assert himself and show a not-so-programmed persona as he had previously shown in the first debate. While he nobly took up for his wife concerning the comments Trump had previously made as to how being married to a Latino affected his view of immigration policy, Bush's call for a face-to-face apology came across as shrill and school-boyish. He did, however, a fine job defending Trump's attacks against his brother, reminding everyone that George Bush managed to keep us safe in the seven years that followed the attacks on 9-11.

Chris Christie also turned in a strong performance and at one point took over managing the debate where CNN so egregiously failed when he chided Trump and Fiorina about their mini-spat on who had accomplished more (or less) in the business world instead of focusing on the plight of America's middle class, reminding them that the television audience doesn't care about their respective resumes.

Going into the debate, Ben Carson was riding a surge of popularity, and while his performance last night was satisfactory, it was less than inspired and may well mark the apex of his candidacy. His charm and easy demeanor remained intact, but the less-than-substantive policy positions seemed as hollow as those of Trump.

Where they were able to get a word in edgewise, the remaining candidates Ted Cruz, Mike Huckabee, John Kasich, Rand Paul, and Scott Walker did well enough not to commit any *faux pas*, and of this group, it was Walker who showed the most and much-needed improvement, while Ted Cruz and Mike Huckabee offered the best content amongst these five candidates. Sadly, their numbers probably won't move much, likely due to lack of attention on the part of the media more than anything else. Interestingly, the otherwise very likable John Kasich reminded us of Ed Sullivan in his seemingly spastic physical gyrations and tics, something his debate coaches need to work on, if fixing these are even possible.

Insofar as the initial round, featuring Lindsey Graham, Bobby Jindal, George Pataki, and Rick Santorum, was concerned, two things stood out. First, none of these candidates has a snowball's chance in the tropics of becoming the eventual nominee. Second, while fewer contestants have a greater opportunity to engage one another, as was the case last night, it does not necessarily mean that such engagement lifts the chances of those so engaged. Our guess is that these four will have effectively ended their campaigns by year's end.

Given the usual liberal bias that is recognized to be a part of CNN, the moderators did better than expected in their questioning, but the *modus operandi* of trying to pit candidates against each other and against Donald Trump in particular makes us wonder if they would do the same were they moderating a Democratic debate instead.

One thing did come to mind as we watched both rounds. Given the "free-for-all" nature of this debate and the mismanagement on the part of the moderators to control its delivery, there isn't a single one of them who would be a worse president than any of the candidates running for the Democrat nomination, and that bespeaks of the seemingly certain fact that it is the Republicans' election to lose in 2016, rather than the Democrats' one to win.

Leftward Ho in Las Vegas—
The Democrats' Debate Preview

13 October 2015

Tonight's debate featuring five or six contenders for the Democrats' presidential nomination (we predict that the vice president won't show, despite the additional podium being added at the last minute) is to be hosted by CNN, the same CNN who hosted their own generated pie-throwing contest for the Republicans last month. It will feature, alphabetically, Lincoln Chafee, Hillary Clinton, Martin O'Malley, Bernie Sanders, Jim Webb, and, possibly but not probably, Joe Biden.

This debate offers nowhere near the intrigue that the last two Republican debates offered, primarily because there are currently only two real contenders for the nomination: Hillary Clinton and Bernie Sanders, with Joe Biden waiting in the wings for just the right moment to launch his own campaign. Just why Chafee, O'Malley, and Webb are even showing up is a mystery indeed, for if their respective polling numbers do not drastically improve, their candidacies will end by year's end, if not beforehand.

The logistics surrounding this debate are very different from that of the Republicans, primarily due to the very strictly limited number of debates being offered by the Democratic Party itself. The DNC Chairwoman, Debbie Wasserman-Schultz, engineered this limited number of debates by design, as she seeks to protect the party's frontrunner and at-one-time presumptive nominee, Hillary Clinton, from any possible misstep on the debate stage. Reduce the debates, and you geometrically and diametrically reduce the propensity for gaffes, according to this leap in liberal logic.

The most exciting two minutes of this debate will take place at the onset when the candidates are introduced, specifically because of that sixth podium and whether or not it will be manned by the vice president (we predict it won't be). After that, the debate will be a total bore. CNN, who oh-so-blatantly wants Hillary to be Barack Obama's successor, will toss very soft questions to the former first lady designed to make her look oh-so-presidential and then ask the other candidates questions which will, a) make Hillary look good, b) make it almost impossible for the other candidates to attack Hillary, and c) make Republicans look monstrous by comparison. So there will be many questions about the fictitious "GOP war on women," the fictitious "GOP war on immigrants," and the fictitious "GOP war on minorities," and very few questions concerning e-mail servers, socialism, and Obama's failed foreign policy if at all, any.

Aside from whether or not Joe will "show," the big news for the evening will be the questions that are *not* asked. By candidate, alphabetically, these questions are as follows:

> Lincoln Chafee. "One of the principal reasons you cited when your campaign was launched is that you wanted the Unites States to 'go metric.' Do you believe that this issue is as important as the other issues facing this country, and if so, why?"
>
> Hillary Clinton. "With all of your changing and evolving responses to inquiries regarding your e-mails, deleted or retained on your own private server, which clearly violate the law, why should the American people trust you, either on a professional or ethical basis, to lead our country, given all of the challenges facing the United States in 2017 and beyond?"
>
> Martin O'Malley. "You once said that climate change and global warming were the primary reasons for the rise of ISIL/ISIS. Do you still believe this, and if so, can you explain the connection between climate change and radical Islam?"
>
> Bernie Sanders. "You have advocated a tremendous increase in taxes on the wealthy, as well as a tremendous increase in corporate taxes, as a means to make college tuition-free for students. Given the fact that U.S. corporations already pay the highest income taxes in the industrialized world, how will increasing these taxes encourage job creation for all of these college students entering the work force?"
>
> Jim Webb. "Amongst the current slate of Democrats running for the nomination, you are alone in advocating

for a stronger defense and a more assertive foreign policy. Specifically, where do you differ from the Obama administration with regard to the administration's Middle East policy, the Iran 'deal,' and the war on terror, and what changes would you make in these specific areas?"

Joe Biden (assuming he shows). "Do you believe that President Obama's foreign policy, specifically related to Vladimir Putin, the Middle East, Iran, and ISIL/ISIS, has been a success, and if so, why? If not, where would you change direction in U.S. foreign policy from that of President Obama's?"

These are the types of questions that a responsible, impartial media would ask candidates running for the most important job in the entire world, but CNN is anything but impartial or responsible, because they are advocates instead, and representative democracy is not served as a result of such advocacy. All that's "left" therefore, figuratively, literally, politically, is how far leftward these Democrat candidates can leap in the luxurious lap of Las Vegas.

Left Behind in Las Vegas — The Democrats' Debate that Wasn't

14 October 2015

There's an old adage that is often said about gambling in Las Vegas: "At the end of the day, 'the house' always wins," which means that while a few can leave the casino wealthier, it is the casino itself which comes out ahead.

Last night at the Democrats' first debate, it was indeed "the house" that won, "the house" being the debate that was managed by DNC Chairwoman Debbie Wasserman-Schultz, CNN Anchor and Clinton Global Initiative Member/Contributor (not kidding) Anderson Cooper, and the candidate herself, Hillary Clinton.

So managed and coordinated was this debate, it seemed that the four candidates supposedly opposing Hillary Clinton, Lincoln Chafee, Martin O'Malley, Bernie Sanders, and Jim Webb, were under direct orders from "the house" not to lay a single, solitary glove on Hillary Clinton. The presumption that the Democrats are engaged in a contest for the presidential nomination is actually a farce, which was exposed for the entire world (who bothered to watch) to see once and for all.

While Hillary was able to land some punches on her would-be opponents, it was blatantly obvious that there was not a single challenge to anything she said, nor any position (in many cases, opposite from one another) she has ever taken in the past, by any of the other four so-called contestants. Never was this more obvious when none other than Bernie Sanders, the self-described socialist running for the Democrat nomination and who actually leads Clinton in New Hampshire, came to Hillary's defense concerning her e-mail scandals, when he said "America is sick of hearing about your damned e-mails," with Hillary nodding and smiling in agreement even before Sanders had even finished his sentence, suggesting that this moment had been rehearsed and scripted prior to the debate.

As predicted, the entire debate came down to three themes:

1. The debate was engineered by CNN and the other four candidates to make Hillary look good.

2. The debate was moderated by CNN far differently than the way this network moderated the Republican debate, as the questions in last night's debate were issue-oriented as opposed to the questions in the Republican debate, which were designed to encourage the Republicans to attack each other instead.

3. The debate was engineered to give Hillary the lion's share of focus that night and all in a scripted theme of party unity, unity behind Hillary and unity in the absolute avoidance of criticism against her and Barack Obama as well.

Jim Webb, the "lone adult" on the stage, was repeatedly cut off from answering the few questions directed at him. No wonder. He is the type of Democrat that harkens back to the days of Harry Truman and John F. Kennedy, anti-Communists who advocated a strong military and a robust international presence, the type of Democrat who hasn't run for president in a half century. Alone in his recognition of the greatest threats to American security, it was obvious that Senator Webb is well outside the mainstream of today's Democratic Party, a party whose distinction from socialism is almost invisible.

Martin O'Malley, the feckless, albeit loquacious speechmaker whose biggest credentials are his steadfast opposition to gun ownership, got into a brief dustup with Sanders on that issue, based on an odd separation of rural (Sanders) versus urban (O'Malley) views toward gun ownership. What was obvious were his adoring glances towards Hillary and her calculating ("Hmmm, he would make an excellent ambassador to Ireland.") eyes appraising him as a supportive member of her team.

Lincoln Chafee was the clownish presence on the stage, whose biggest accomplishment, as he stated three times, was avoidance of scandal during the terms of office he has held (it's easy to avoid scandal when you accomplish absolutely nothing). The biggest laugh he provided was when he blamed one of his votes in the senate on his new arrival immediately following his father's death. Now there's a man we can all believe in, right?

Bernie Sanders came across as an angry revolutionary in the style of the old communist radical, even advocating "revolution" on three separate occasions. His themes, "the rich are evil," "the corporations are evil," "the banks are evil," "Wall Street is evil," were all joined together in his plan to take all of that wealth and use it to pay for universal health care, prescriptions, and college tuition for all, including illegal immigrants, advocating a complete socialist transformation of the United States away from the very thing that made it the economic powerhouse of the free world. Yet when it came down to Comrade Bernie's opportunity to knock Hillary out of the ring by going after her on the e-mail scandals, he caved. Not only was he a conscientious objector during Vietnam, he was also a conscientious objector to attacking the Democrat frontrunner as well.

For Hillary, it was her chance to shine amongst the lessers surrounding her, and throughout the night she glowed in the admiration bestowed upon her, as though she were saying, "Mirror, mirror, on the wall." When pressed by Cooper on the e-mails, she ended the questioning with a oh-so-prepared and scripted, "I want to talk about the issues and what the Republicans are doing to this country," fulfilling expectations that the entire evening was designed to make the Republicans look like monsters: "The Republican War on Women," "The Republican War on Immigrants," "The Republican War on Religious and Racial Minorities," and her own admission that she is the "outsider" by virtue of her sex, and that it is she who is best qualified to bring change to Washington because, at the end of the day, she is a woman.

On a question as to whether "Black Lives Matter" or "All Lives Matter," each of these candidates opted for the former, going out of their way as if to say, "Black lives matter more, and here's why . . . " Ahh, there's nothing like the race card being played by five elderly white politicians against a Republican field which includes one African-American, two Hispanics, and a woman to boot.

What also became quite clear during the debate is that none of these candidates would make any changes to Obama's failed foreign policy if ultimately elected, which should provide a "wake-up" call to anyone who has grown skeptical of Obama's "leadership from behind." In fact, save for Webb, the candidates were in unison when they indicated that they would pursue a foreign policy that not only embraces Obama's foreign policy, but goes far beyond it.

It is also oft-stated that "what happens in Vegas, stays in Vegas," but sadly for the American people, this will not be the case regarding last night's debate, regardless of whether or not Vice President Joe Biden decides to "ante in."

"Bouldered" in Colorado—
CNBC Fails to Moderate GOP Debate

29 October 2015

CNBC, the financial and economic news division of NBC, promised to host a substantive debate on economic, fiscal, and financial issues last night at the University of Colorado in Boulder, but they failed miserably due to their own innate and over-the-top bias against all things Republican.

So egregious in the condescension, arrogance, and hostility toward the candidates last night that even the audience—a Colorado audience, mind you—booed the moderators five times, based upon the out-of-line questioning put forth by Carl Quintanilla, Becky Quick, and John Harwood. The fact that these licentiously liberal lapdogs of the Hillary 2016 Campaign Committee actually made the Republican candidates look good by comparison was the ironic turn of events that not even NBC could have imagined in their wildest nightmares.

We have come to expect and, for that matter, rely upon the fact that the mainstream media by all accounts has an inherent bias in favor of the Democrats, as this has clearly been the case going back to the election of Franklin D. Roosevelt in 1932. Yet, even with that expectation in mind and the extremely liberal slant that is the hallmark of NBC News, television journalism hit an all-time low last night when the so-called moderators who were anything but moderate went after each and every candidate on stage with hostility, contempt, and absolute aggression. That partisan attack-dog mentality has never been displayed to a greater degree than it was in the two hours that comprised what was supposed to be a debate on fiscal policy. In short, the National Broadcasting Company should truly be ashamed for even claiming to be a news organization, much less moderating a GOP Debate, where their absolute contempt for Republicans was so blatantly obvious.

Hand it to the Republican candidates themselves who, in the midst of such wanton hostility, managed to avoid the degree of mudslinging that was the milieu of the debate hosted by CNN some weeks ago. For the first time, with some minor exceptions, the candidates rose above the puerile performance of their questioners and managed to provide some semblance of substance in the wake of such boorish behavior on the part of these partisan panelists, who in turn demeaned their own profession, not to mention the network with whom they are employed.

Marco Rubio, Ted Cruz, and Chris Christie in particular turned in the best performances of the night, especially when the three of them took note of the bias and disdain with which questions were posed, questions that would never have been posed to Democrats by this, nor any, network. These three candidates were the big winners of the night, with Mike Huckabee and Carly Fiorina running a close second. The remaining candidates, Donald Trump, Ben Carson, John Kasich, and Rand Paul, did manage to hold their ground and managed to escape the night without costing their candidacies much in terms of polling numbers. Jeb Bush, however, did manage to stumble when out of the blue he decided to turn on fellow Floridian Marco Rubio, who handled the assault with much aplomb and made Bush look weak and desperate by comparison. Aside from this instance and a brief counterpunch by Trump against Kasich, the Republican candidates by and large laid off one another, much to the chagrin of their inept interrogators, who tried their level best to make the Republicans attack each other instead. These ten, along with the four J.V. candidates, Lindsey Graham, Bobby Jindal, George Pataki, and Rick Santorum, did manage to prove themselves to be of more substance, with much more competence to lead than any of the remaining three Democrat candidates vying for their own party's nomination.

These candidates will meet again in two weeks when the Fox Business News network will host the next GOP debate on November 10th with Neil Cavuto and Maria Bartiromo, who are set to host the varsity edition that night. Perhaps in the end, they will resuscitate the concept of what is supposed to be the fourth estate of a free press in the wreckage of what took place in Boulder. Truth be told, all they have to do is sit down at the table to improve upon what was seen last night on CNBC.

Brewing in the Milwaukee Debate—
Fox Business News and the GOP Twelve Pack

11 November 2015

And then there were twelve.

It had to happen eventually. A somewhat-culled herd of Republican wannabes, assembling for an actual debate, a debate without the media bias that had become the rule rather the exception, where real issues were bandied about sans personal and ad hominem attacks on one another. Kudos go to Fox Business News and the moderators thus assigned for producing a truly fair and balanced debate, where, get this, the candidates were at long last allowed to *be* the story rather than the moderators themselves. Voters, especially Republican voters, who did not have an opportunity to see this debate were the only *real* losers, because all twelve of the GOP contenders received ample opportunity to explain their policies in a constructive and substantive format, one which was as informative as it was enlightening, and the candidates delivered.

Not really missing from this debate were candidates George Pataki, Jim Gilmore, and Lindsey Graham, not really, because none of those three have any chance to register any real support in any of the primaries or caucuses scheduled for early next year. The "junior varsity" edition of last night's debate featured Chris Christie, Mike Huckabee, Bobby Jindal, and Rick Santorum. While clearly it was Christie who won this preliminary round, fending off broadsides from Jindal and aiming his sites at Democrat frontrunner Hillary Clinton instead, all four of these contestants made a good showing of it, thanks in part to the quality of questions posed to them, save for the "Which Democrat do you admire most?" question which seemed to be rather silly, as compared to the remainder of the questions posed to them. Wisely, each of the four chose to ignore that question and discuss their own political agendas instead. How such a silly question was asked in the first place remains a mystery, because the rest of the questioning was on-point and quite relevant.

In the night's main event, featuring Jeb Bush, Ben Carson, Ted Cruz, Carly Fiorina, John Kasich, Rand Paul, Marco Rubio, and Donald Trump, all of the candidates performed well enough not to lose any support, although clearly it was Rubio, Cruz, and Fiorina providing the very best performances, with frontrunners Carson and Trump rounding out the top five. Jeb Bush showed much improvement but, given the fact that debates are clearly not his forte, he did not have any "moment" that will substantially improve his standing in the polls. Rand Paul had a good night, even tossing it around with Rubio over whether or not substantially increasing military expenditures was in and of itself "truly conservative." However, Paul's comparatively isolationist policies will inevitably prove to keep him from gaining the nomination of a Republican party, most of whose voters desire a much more robust presence confronting ISIS and radical Islam, not to mention a stronger and better-funded defense footprint. If there had to be someone bringing up the rear in the main event, it was clearly Kasich, whose position on bank bailouts was murky at best and whose position on illegal immigration was more in line with Democrats than Republicans.

With the possible exception of how Maria Bartiromo's question concerning Hillary Clinton was framed, touting Clinton's "resume" and thus eliciting some degree of laughter from Marco Rubio to whom the question was posed, the panel at the varsity event also deserved much praise for both the quality of questions being asked as well as their allowing the candidates to dive deeply into their own policy platforms and not pitting them against one another, as happened in the previous GOP debates.

All in all, it was a veritable GOP "twelve-pack," offering substantial and thoughtful discourse that brewed in the Milwaukee Theatre last night, and any impartial observer would have to favorably compare this dozen against the three Democrats running for their party's nomination. As Donald Trump indicated, *any* of the tax policies that were presented last night, diverse as they are, were substantially better than the ones being advocated by the opposition and better than the status quo. Now that Fox Business News has set the standard for how debates should be moderated going forward, as even rival network CNN has noted, we look for and hope for similar moderation in the debates to come, with the American people being the real beneficiaries in the end.

Settling Scores in Las Vegas —
The Final Republican Presidential Debate of 2015

16 December 2015

In the final Republican debate of 2015 hosted by CNN at the Venetian Hotel in Las Vegas, it was evident all thirteen remaining candidates came prepared to substantively discuss the issues of national security and the issues surrounding foreign policy with respect to ISIS. As expected, the CNN moderators Wolf Blitzer, Dana Bash, and Hugh Hewitt did their level best to pit the candidates against one another and make the Republican frontrunner, Donald Trump, look like a fool. They were successful with regards to the former, but in the end fell flat with regards to the latter.

That said, it wasn't as though "the Donald" was sailing through the debate, as the former favorite and once-presumptive nominee, Jeb Bush, finally showed that yes, indeed, he *does* possess the intestinal fortitude to be combative in a debate. He squarely landed some punches on Mr. Trump and did so quite effectively up to the point where Trump reminded him that recent polling indicated the vast difference in their respective numbers, Trump 42%, Bush 3%, and said that Bush was "progressing" towards eventually being shoved off of the primary debate stage altogether, effectively ending Bush's assaults on Trump. Trump's best moment occurred when he settled, once and for all, the questions concerning whether he would run as a third-party candidate. In short, he said he won't, much to the chagrin of the liberally biased *Washington Post*, which had previously floated a bogus story about Trump running as a third party candidate, otherwise assuring Hillary Clinton of a victory in November. Trump said he would abide by the Republican Party's eventual nomination and do everything in his power to defeat Hillary Clinton in the general election. By doing this, he also allayed the irrational, albeit frequently stated, fears that he was secretly attempting to help Clinton win the election by trying to derail the Republican Party.

Recognizing that Ted Cruz and Marco Rubio were very much in a heated running for second place, the moderators accomplished their goal of setting the two against each other. Both handled themselves with much aplomb, despite the substantive and intensely debated positions they hold with regard to dealing with immigration and Syrian President Bashir Assad, points on which they differ. With help from Rand Paul, whose own views are somewhat closer to Cruz's than they are to Rubio's, Senator Cruz very narrowly won the *tete-a-tete* on points. Despite this, both Cruz and Rubio came across very presidential and solidified their chances in the upcoming primaries and caucuses to come in second place.

Chris Christie also had a solid performance, perhaps the best of the evening with regard to sounding resolute and presidential, while Ben Carson showed the favorable results of "boning up" on the issues when compared to his previous performances. While the debate performance may help Christie when it comes to the upcoming New Hampshire primary, it is doubtful that Dr. Carson will fare as well in that state, nor in Iowa, as a result of his sinking numbers.

With regard to the remaining varsity debaters, Carly Fiorina, John Kasich, and Rand Paul, their respective overall performances, like Bush's, were adequate but not strong enough to change their comparatively lower polling numbers. These four and the junior varsity debaters, Lindsey Graham, Mike Huckabee, George Pataki, and Rich Santorum, will not likely last following the New Hampshire primary and the Iowa caucus, which will basically leave Trump, Rubio, Cruz, Christie, and possibly Carson the only viable candidates left in the run-up to "Super Tuesday" on the first day of March, 2016.

Setting aside Lindsey Graham's Obama-like love of all things Muslim, not to mention his rolling eyes and all-too-condescending grimaces during the first round, as well as his emotional outburst in defense of former President George W. Bush, the junior-varsity debaters handled themselves well, but not well enough to change the fact that none of these contenders will be in the running at all, which begs the question as to why they remain in the race.

Going into year's end, it appears that the nomination is very much Trump's to lose and, save a major turn of events, he looks to be the likely and eventual Republican nominee. With a united Republican Party, essential to defeating Mrs. Clinton, his chances of winning the election remain as good as they ever have been. That aside, it also appears that Ted Cruz, Marco Rubio, Chris Christie, and possibly Ben Carson could be just as successful, if, again, if Republicans fall into line behind their nominee, regardless of who that happens to be. Hillary Clinton can only win if some disenchanted Republicans decide to sit this one out, upon which is exactly what the mainstream media hangs their hopes.

Obama's State of the (dis-)Union Speech and Thursday's GOP Debate

13 January 2016

Last night, President Barack Obama delivered what hopefully will be his final State of the Union speech before a joint session of Congress. The "lecturer-in-chief" did his level best to embellish what history, true history, will view as a failed presidency, a presidency that will have been remembered as an existential exercise in narcissism and self-aggrandizement taken to pathological extreme. To listen to the president is to come to one of two conclusions. Either a) he exists in a fantastic world completely devoid of any sense of reality, or b) he is a pathological prevaricator who knows no equal, with the possible exception of the former first lady who seeks to succeed him.

His list of "accomplishments," such as they are, read like a platform put forth by the Democratic National Committee rather than a Constitutionally-mandated report on the state of the American union, and his bloviating was only outdone by his condescension to the American people and the representatives and senators thus assembled. Predictably, the partisan nodding and nattering nabobs enthusiastically jumped to their feet, enthusiastically cheering their champion of chicanery, which seemed at times reminiscent of the speeches delivered by the North Korean Supreme Leader, Kim Jong Un, considering the knee-jerk ovations provided by his cabinet and his party's legislative delegation. Truly, any informed and level-headed observer would find this performance as effective at producing emesis as a good belt of syrup of ipecac, but, alas, we digress.

Thursday night, in Charleston, South Carolina, ten of the eleven remaining Republican candidates will square off in the last debate prior to the Iowa caucus and New Hampshire primary. Senator Rand Paul, miffed that he was delegated to the Junior Varsity event, chose not to participate with the other J.V. players, Carly Fiorina, Mike Huckabee, and Rick Santorum. On balance, this is certainly bad form not to show up. It also may be indicative that his campaign, like others, will soon be suspended for lack of support.

The main event, scheduled for 9:00 p.m. EST on the Fox Business Network, will feature, in the order of their seeding, Donald Trump, Ted Cruz, Marco Rubio, Ben Carson, Chris Christie, Jeb Bush, and John Kasich. Look for the possibility of a dust-up between Marco Rubio and Ted Cruz, while Jeb Bush and John Kasich will continue to attack Donald Trump in a last-ditch effort to gain the credibility that so far has proved elusive. Just as Trump predicted in the last debate, Jeb Bush has been relegated to the end of the stage. A poor showing for him in the Iowa caucus and New Hampshire primary will most certainly be the straw that breaks the back of his campaign, and the same will go for Kasich and the remainder of the GOP contestants in the earlier event, Fiorina, Huckabee, and Santorum.

That leaves, for all intents and purposes, five *real* contenders: Trump, Cruz, Rubio, Carson, and Christie who have much to gain and everything to lose in tonight's main event.

Trump needs to rise above the fray and certify his credentials that he can lead the party to victory, despite what the establishment Republicans and talking heads in the media would have the rest of us believe.

Cruz has the toughest job of all; he has to disencumber the notion that his Canadian birth to an American mother disqualifies him as a "natural born" citizen and candidate for president, all the while doing so with charm and charisma, the two things that so far have seemed to be his personal drawbacks, despite the fact that he is the most consistently conservative and intellectually savvy candidate running.

Rubio, who needs more than two-and-a-half-inch heels to rise to the occasion, needs to utilize his glib delivery and statesmanlike oratory to underwrite his credentials as someone who can take on Hillary Clinton without fear or a propensity to be shut down, if such a debate were to occur next autumn. In short, he cannot be the timid Mitt Romney of the last election, because there will surely be another Candy Crowley ready to pounce on the GOP nominee if they get close to landing a punch on Hillary.

Carson needs to show that he is continuing his mastery of the issues, something that was sorely lacking in his first few performances. He also needs to show a bit more aggressiveness, so that the voters can believe he has a chance to defeat Hillary in an election. Despite his many fine qualities, this is NOT the year for a gentle spokesman, and Dr. Carson needs to realize this sooner rather than later.

Christie, on the other hand, is the quintessential opposite of Dr. Carson, as he has the fight necessary to put Mrs. Clinton on the proverbial mat. What Christie needs to do is to dissuade the notion that he is too moderate to gain the support of conservatives in a way that Mitt Romney, John McCain, Bob Dole, and Gerald Ford could not, costing them elections in 2012, 2008, 1996, and 1976, respectively. For all intents and purposes, Jeb Bush and John Kasich are through, along with the J.V. squad, if either fails to win, place, or show in Iowa and New Hampshire.

That said, Thursday's debate will be far more interesting, far more informative, and far more substantive (thanks to the questioners being Neil Cavuto and Maria Bartiromo) than the performance of the president last night. No doubt, the ratings will prove this to be the case, which at days end are really what these debates are all about.

Palmetto Posturing—
Recapping the 2016 Charleston GOP Debate

15 January 2016

. . . and then there were ten . . . ten remaining Republican contestants, each longing for a good showing in next month's Iowa caucus and New Hampshire primary.

In the final run-up to those opening contests, ten of the eleven remaining candidates for the GOP presidential nomination participated in Thursday night's debate in North Charleston, South Carolina. Included in the comparatively raucous crowd was South Carolina Governor Nikki Haley, fresh off of her response to the State of the Union, where she attempted to tacitly assail frontrunner Donald Trump for his stance on temporarily banning Muslim immigration, and the erstwhile-trailing candidate Lindsey Graham, who this very morning endorsed Jeb Bush (no shock, there), who is the ultimate mainstream, moderate go-along-with, get-along-with Washington insider and who never had *any* chance of either winning the nomination or being elected in the first place.

For his own part, Trump needed to tamp down the potential effects of Governor Haley's comments regarding the "angry voices who would seek to ban immigration." He also very much needed to rise above the fray and certify his credentials that he can lead the party to victory, despite what the establishment Republicans and talking heads in the media would have the rest of us believe. On those scores, "the Donald" managed to make a good show of it by "owning" the "anger" to which Governor Haley had alluded. His finest moment, however, occurred when he chastised Ted Cruz for his commentary regarding Trump's "New York values," reminding the Texas senator of the greatness of New Yorkers' response in the aftermath of the 9/11 attacks on the World Trade Center.

Going into the debate, Ted Cruz had the toughest job of all, to disencumber the notion that his Canadian birth to an American mother disqualifies him as a "natural born" citizen and candidate for president, all the while doing so with charm and charisma, the two things that so far have seemed to be his personal drawbacks, despite the fact that he is the most consistently conservative and intellectually savvy candidate running. He addressed the former well enough, but fell a bit short of cementing his legitimacy as a viable candidate, even though the fact that the circumstances of his birth indeed qualifies him as a "natural born" candidate. He also provided some good one-liners, but ultimately lost his dust-up with Marco Rubio regarding Rubio's charges that Cruz has repeatedly flip-flopped on immigration.

Marco Rubio himself needed to utilize his glib delivery and statesmanlike oratory to underwrite his credentials as someone who can take on Hillary Clinton without fear or a propensity to be shut down if such a debate were to occur next autumn. In short, he delivered splendidly, quashing any doubts that he has the skills to effectively and aggressively take on both Hillary and Obama. Not one of the contenders can frame an argument or deliver it more convincingly than Marco Rubio, as he has consistently shown in the course of these debates.

Dr. Ben Carson needed to show that he is continuing to master the issues, something that was sorely lacking in his first few performances. He also needed to show a bit more aggressiveness, so that the voters can believe he has a chance to defeat Hillary in an election. As to the former, he has caught up with the rest of the field in his understanding of the issues and was quite masterful in delineating his platform regarding the same. Sadly, as to the latter, he is just not combative enough to take down Hillary Clinton in the way that she would need to be taken down in a debate because, in this election year, a nice guy like Carson would come up short in this regard.

Chris Christie, on the other hand, is the quintessential opposite of Dr. Carson, as he has the fight necessary to put Mrs. Clinton on the proverbial mat. What Christie needed to do last night was to dissuade the notion that he is too moderate to gain the support of conservatives in a way that Mitt Romney, John McCain, Bob Dole, and Gerald Ford could not, costing them elections in 2012, 2008, 1996, and 1976, respectively. There is no doubt as to Christie's dedication to the mission at hand, that is, to defeat Hillary Clinton in November. Yet it can also be said that the Republican rank and file still has some doubts as to his stances on abortion, gun rights, and immigration.

Jeb Bush and John Kasich turned in their best debate performances to date, as did Carly Fiorina, Rick Santorum, and Mike Huckabee in the preliminary event. For all intents and purposes though, Jeb Bush and John Kasich are through, along with the J.V. squad, if either of these five fails to win, place, or show in Iowa and New Hampshire. Rand Paul, who chose to abstain from attending the preliminary event, did not do himself any favors in his absence, despite the ten-second chant "We want Rand" by a dozen of his supporters when moderator Neil Cavuto was asking a question toward the end of the evening.

There has been much talk as to how Americans have shifted their views on the most important issue of this 2016 presidential campaign, a shift from the economy to ISIS/Islamic terrorism. While very much true, the central issue confronting Republican voters is analyzing who is best suited to defeat Hillary Clinton in the fall election and will doubtlessly be zeroing in on that particular question when they go to the polls in Iowa, New Hampshire, and the "Super Tuesday" elections and caucuses on March 1st. Unless the polling is very, very wrong, this race has largely come down to a three-man contest between Donald Trump, Ted Cruz, and Marco Rubio. The only thing left is the actual polling to take place in those states; in the final analysis, regardless of posturing, those are the polls that really count.

Iowa in Absentia—
Megyn Kelly's "Minus-1 Debate"

28 January 2016

Reveling in her star role in the making and management of the Iowa Republican Presidential Debate, Fox News's *diva prima donna*, Megyn Kelly, star of the nightly Fox News show "The Kelly File," eclipsed her two co-moderators, Chris Wallace and Bret Baier, and jumped from her assigned role as co-moderator to acting the part of a candidate and active participant herself by engaging in argument with candidates Marco Rubio and Ted Cruz during last night's event.

For those who witnessed this spectacle in Des Moines last night, never have they seen anything like this performance by Ms. Kelly, who acted as though she were a judge presiding over a show called the "GOP Gotcha Game," as she went beyond her role as questioner and assumed the role of prosecuting attorney, all in a determined effort to make fun of frontrunner Donald Trump's absence, take down the other two frontrunners, Ted Cruz and Marco Rubio, and prop up the Fox News preferred candidate, Jeb Bush.

When a reporter becomes the story to the extent that a fair and balanced debate is in question, then a debate has been replaced by nothing less than a feature show starring a reporter whose looks have largely, in essence, become a substitute for fair and balanced journalism. Given her tremendous following, thanks in large part to what many perceive as her overall attractiveness and her over-the-top persona which has propelled Ms. Kelly's weeknight show high in the ratings, she has taken her lofty position and used it to assume an active role in presidential politics by picking for herself the winners and losers in the GOP nomination of 2016.

It is true enough that leading candidate Donald Trump has only magnified Kelly's role in this regard by first demanding she be pulled from the moderating panel and then abstaining from participating in the debate itself when this demand was rebuffed by Fox News director, Roger Ailes. This led to the misguided perception that he was "afraid" to answer questions posed by

Kelly when, in actuality, much more was at play here. It is no secret that Fox News has played an active role in seeking Trump's marginalization, first by downplaying his candidacy and then by actively criticizing his stances on immigration, his often boorish behavior towards his GOP opponents, and his advocacy of a temporary ban on Muslim immigration. However, behind the scenes, there is much more at play in this *tete-a-tete* between Trump and Fox News, given the fact that News Corp's (the owner of Fox News) Executive Chairman Rupert Murdoch just happens to also be co-chairman of the Partnership for a New American Economy (PNAE), a lobbying firm which advocates *open borders*.

As for the "debate" itself, Trump's absence did manage to open up a venue for the "candidate wannabes," Jeb Bush, Rand Paul, Ben Carson, and John Kasich, to turn in what can arguably be said as their greatest performances to date. In their respective dust-ups with Megyn Kelly, Marco Rubio managed to fare better than Ted Cruz, both of whom were asked questions about their stances on immigration, coupled with videos of each of them addressing the issue several years before, a first for a presidential debate (surely, it would be a cold day in hell before *any* network, *including* Fox News, would give such treatment to Hillary Clinton in a debate). It is also suspect that the questions posed to Jeb Bush were comparatively grapefruit-sized "softballs," which the former Florida governor managed to hit out of the park. New Jersey Governor Chris Christie had a good night as well, especially when he said, "Let's cut out the Washington 'bull' and fix these problems instead."

Despite what all of the pundits are saying concerning Donald Trump's absence from Megyn Kelly's "Minus 1 Debate," it will be left to the Iowa voters to determine whether or not "the Donald" made the right decision in sitting this one out. He's not the first to do so. Ronald Reagan decided not to participate in the Iowa Debate back in 1980, and he ended up trouncing Jimmy Carter in a landslide the following November. Certainly, Trump is no Reagan, but alas, it has become obvious that he is also no fool for Megyn Kelly and Fox News either.

Let the voting commence!

Cruz-n' on the Right, Cliff-hangin' on the Left — The Iowa Caucuses of 2016

2 February 2016

Back in the day when the Baltimore Colts prepared to take the field, the team's three captains would each be given a chance to address the team just before exiting the locker room. The defensive team's captain and the special team's captain would each implore their respective squad's members to "give it their best," etc., etc. Then, after all of the "we gonnas" were all said and done, the offensive team's captain who from 1957-1972 was all-time great Johnny Unitas always, *always* said the same thing each and every time, "Talk's cheap. Let's go play."

Insofar as Iowa goes, the time for cheap talk was finally over, and Senator Ted Cruz won the day handily, defeating frontrunner Donald Trump by a solid four-point margin in the nation's first official nominating contest. Cruz won the contest in the Hawkeye State the old fashioned way with a solid ground game and an in-person, tour-de-force statewide canvassing throughout Iowa's ninety-nine counties. It just goes to show that hard work and diligence does indeed pay off, pre-election polling and punditry be damned. Cruz managed to weave together a winning tapestry of evangelicals, dyed-in-the-wool conservatives, and Republican stalwarts to fashion a hard-fought and hard-won victory, one sorely needed as he heads into first, the New Hampshire primary, where he is not expected to win, and then the South Carolina primary, where he could very well parlay the Iowa win into his first primary victory.

Donald Trump and Marco Rubio also turned in solid results, with Trump edging out Marco Rubio by a single percentage point. Admittedly, Trump lacked the ground game that was key to Cruz's victory, and much of his own support came from first-time voters who flocked to "the Donald" out of their disgust with the "same old, same old" from Washington politicians. There was much posturing, particularly by Fox News, as to whether or not Trump's skipping the Iowa debate had anything to do with his second-place finish. Yet that is at best nothing more than conjecture, because he just did not have an in-state organization and ground game that came anywhere near what Cruz had put into place. Meanwhile, Marco Rubio stunned the nation with a very solid third-place showing, beating the odds as well as the pre-election polls and nearly surpassing Trump in the end. Rubio rode the wave of a last-minute surge and goes into New Hampshire as the odds-on rising star in that state's primary, who for the time being is Trump's to lose, given "the Donald's" polling numbers in the Granite State. If Rubio manages a second-place finish in New Hampshire, he will have surpassed Chris Christie and the other "mainstream candidates" vying for solid "also-rans" in the nation's first primary. Additionally, if Rubio does manage a second- or a third-place finish, it will prove to be the swan song for the remaining candidates Christie, along with Ben Carson, John Kasich, Carly Fiorina, Jeb Bush, Rand Paul, Rick Santorum, and Jim Gilmore, who will join Mike Huckabee, Lindsey Graham, George Pataki, Bobby Jindal, Rick Perry, and Scott Walker in suspending their campaigns.

Speaking of Carson, there were some reports of some of Cruz's surrogates, including his co-campaign manager, Rep. Steve King, sending out a false narrative that Dr. Carson had suspended his campaign in a deceptive effort to woo Carson's evangelical delegates to the Cruz camp. Carson himself managed to gain just under ten percent in the Iowa caucus and thereby achieved a fourth place finish. Even if Dr. Carson's allegations prove to be true, there wouldn't have been enough "pilfered" votes to propel him into the top three finishers, nor would it have driven Cruz into a second-place finish.

Over on the Democrat side, *three tenths of one percent*– a difference of *four* delegates—is the razor-thin margin that Hillary Clinton maintains over Bernie Sanders, as of this writing, in a race still too close to call. It is significant that in at least six of the precincts, a coin-toss was needed to produce an eventual outcome and delegate determination, and as fate would inexorably and inexplicably have it, Hillary "won" all six of the coin-tosses. Had they gone Sanders' way, it would be Sanders who would have been leading Hillary by two delegates. Sanders, who is expected to win by a wide margin in New Hampshire, is nevertheless able to claim a moral victory, considering he was down fifty points in Iowa's polling less than a year ago. Hapless

Martin O'Malley, who barely registered in Iowa, had no choice but to suspend his campaign well before the night's caucuses were over.

By this time next month, the quest for the Republican nomination will be essentially a three-man race between Cruz, Rubio, and Trump or, at most, a four-man race between these three and one more. The only question will be as to who, if any, will be that fourth. Carson or Christie are the only possibilities, and these are remote at best.

Now that the Democrats are *officially* down to two choices, as they have essentially always been, their nomination remains as murky as ever. If Hillary Clinton prevails in South Carolina and Nevada and runs the table on "Super Tuesday," she will essentially have gained the Democrat nomination. Should Bernie Sanders prevail, then look for Joe Biden and/or Elizabeth Warren to make a late bid for a nomination, even if it means doing so at a brokered convention, that is, unless the Democrats enter the fantasy land that would foresee a self-described and elderly socialist becoming the next president of the United States.

... And that's Politics for You, Caucus Consternation and All That's to Follow

4 February 2016

With the Iowa caucuses behind us (well, *almost* behind us) and the New Hampshire primary looming next week, the herd of candidates is starting to be culled with more undoubtedly on the way ensuing after this coming contest.

Following the Iowa caucus, Mike Huckabee, Rand Paul, and Rick Santorum suspended their campaigns, leaving GOP frontrunners (listed alphabetically) Ted Cruz, Marco Rubio, and Donald Trump leading the remaining pack, which includes (again, alphabetically) Jeb Bush, Ben Carson, Chris Christie, Carly Fiorina, John Kasich, and the Republican version of Don Quixote, Jim Gilmore, still attempting to win, place, or show in the Granite State.

Speaking of Don Quixote, on the Democrat side, hapless Martin O'Malley, the former Mayor of Baltimore and Governor of Maryland, also ran up his own white flag of surrender, suspending his campaign while the Iowa caucus was still *in progress*, an unusual step considering the fact that O'Malley did so without releasing his would-be delegates to *either* of his own opponents, Hillary Clinton and Bernie Sanders. O'Malley was from the start of his campaign a mystery unto himself, never registering any notice, never engendering any interest, and his presence in the Democrat debates was at best an exercise in futility and inconsequence.

With *the Des Moines Register* calling for a complete audit of the Democrat caucus, it seems that the shenanigans of that party's caucus even managed to surpass the kerfuffle of the Republican kluster-phuck. At least six Democrat precincts settled their respective impasses with a coin toss, all of which fell to the favor of Hillary Clinton—practically impossible as odds of coin tosses go—there was even more ambiguity regarding how the delegates were allotted in the first place, because the rules in the Iowa Democrat Party eschew the counting of actual popular vote totals. Given the fact that Clinton claimed victory the evening before the tallies were released the following afternoon, it seemed that the Iowa Democrats fixed the outcome and that Hillary Clinton knew the "fix was in."

Meanwhile, the GOP had their own issues, with the Ted Cruz campaign tweeting to all of their 1,500 precinct captains a pejorative claim that Dr. Ben Carson was suspending his campaign in an effort to pilfer his own votes to Cruz. Attempting to blame the confusion on CNN, Ted Cruz apologized to Carson the next day, but this did nothing to calm the fears that Cruz "won" the caucus, based on a lie that Carson was out. While it is *possible* that the resulting votes propelled Cruz past Donald Trump (assuming that merely an average of four votes in each of the 1,500 precincts went to Cruz that might otherwise have gone to Carson), Dr. Carson would still have come in fourth place behind Cruz, Trump, and Rubio. Yet it *may* well have denied "the Donald" a victory in the contest, but that is something that may never be known definitively in any event. While second-place finisher Trump, third-place finisher Rubio, and fourth-place finisher Carson can grumble all they want about the dirtiness of Cruz's victory, inane calls for a caucus "redo" are not going to happen, primarily due to the costs associated with a repeated caucus and the fact that in the end it would only amount to the shift of one single delegate awarded for each of Cruz (-1), Trump (+1), and Rubio (+1).

Should the remaining Republican contestants Bush, Carson, Christie, Fiorina, and Kasich, fail to win, place, or show in the New Hampshire primary, their campaigns will essentially be finished, leaving the South Carolina, Nevada, and "Super Tuesday" contests to be settled among the top three, Cruz, Trump, and Rubio, as Gilmore doesn't stand a chance of accomplishing anything other than appearing to be the south end of a northbound elephant, should he decide to stay in the race.

Meanwhile, Bernie Sanders is expected to win the New Hampshire primary with great ease, but for all intents and purposes, that will mark the high tide of his campaign, setting aside *even worse* revelations about Hillary's illegal e-mail operations, because Comrade Sanders has no chance of winning primaries in the South.

However, *if* that unlikely win by Sanders should come to pass and/or it is followed by an unlikely, albeit *deserved* indictment of Hillary Clinton, there is a sitting Vice President (Biden) and a Massachusetts senator (Elizabeth Warren) ready to snatch the nomination away from Sanders, and this will surely set DNC Chairwoman Debbie Wasserman-Schultz's curly hair afire.

Governors Grasping in the Granite State—
The New Hampshire GOP Debate

7 February 2016

In the final debate before the nation's first primary election, three of the nation's current and former governors, Jeb Bush of Florida, Chris Christie of New Jersey, John Kasich of Ohio, grasped onto their respectively tenuous footings in the race for the GOP presidential nomination. In a *seemingly* coordinated effort, each of these governors set his sights on taking down a distinct and different one of the frontrunners, Marco Rubio, Donald Trump, and Ted Cruz.

First of all, it was Chris Christie pursuing an aggressive line of attack against Marco Rubio, essentially lambasting the Florida senator on his three vulnerabilities: lack of legislative accomplishments and attendance in the U. S Senate, lack of depth in his own political posturing beyond what Christie claimed were "twenty-five second soundbites," and Rubio's infamous abandonment of the "gang of eight" immigration reform bill, which Rubio had initiated with Senator Chuck Schumer (D-NY). Christie was extremely effective at shaking up the junior senator from the Sunshine State and pushed Rubio into a four-time repetition of the same and almost identically-worded statements regarding whether or not Barack Obama knows exactly what he is doing in his overall failings of domestic and foreign policy. Rubio's repeated phrasing seemed to prove Christie's charges of programmed soundbites replacing substantive stances by Rubio.

Secondly, as has often been the case, it was Jeb Bush aiming his slings and arrows at Donald Trump, taking aim at "the Donald's" stand on eminent domain, oddly enough because, by and large, the concept of eminent domain is primarily a local and state issue, where private property interests come into conflict with municipal and statewide interests, based upon a vague concept of "the public good." Bush seemed to get the better of Trump, but only just slightly, as the line of attack about eminent domain was far from the top of the policy issues of 2016.

Lastly, and much more subtly, it was John Kasich who contrasted his approach to conservatism against the conservatism of Ted Cruz. Kasich, a champion of "compassionate conservatism" preaching the virtues of leaving no one behind, including those on the street, portrayed a type of conservatism that seemed in bold contrast to the "dyed-in-the-wool" conservatism that is the *sine qua non* of Ted Cruz's candidacy.

For his own part, Senator Cruz initially fumbled on a question as to whether or not he would reinstitute advance interrogation techniques such as water-boarding, giving first, a "have it both ways" jumbled response on the issue and then framing the issue in a lawyerly (as opposed to a political) manner. In doing so, he left the door wide open for Donald Trump to seize the moment and stress that, when dealing with an enemy who would employ medieval tactics including the beheading of innocents in this day and age, he would advocate even more stringent means of interrogation.

Cruz also took the heat from Dr. Ben Carson concerning the way Cruz's operatives used a bogus report from CNN that suggested that Carson had ended his campaign during the initial hours of the Iowa caucus in an effort to persuade Carson's delegates to support Cruz. In doing so, Carson elicited *yet another* apology from Cruz, which seemed too little, too late.

Overall, the debate was clumsily managed at the outset, with the introduction of each of the contestants completely out of sync with their respective stage entrances, and even Martha Raddatz began the questioning, only to stop herself when she was informed by Christie that John Kasich hadn't yet entered the stage.

While it is still uncertain as to whether or not the debate had a substantial effect upon Tuesday's voting in New Hampshire, what remains certain is the fact that there are in reality only four Republican tickets out of New Hampshire and into the South Carolina, Nevada, and Super Tuesday contests. While Trump and Cruz have their "reservations" *confirmed* and Rubio's all but certain, the fourth ticket may well depend on money rather than standing in the final analysis, giving a *slight* edge to Jeb Bush. Essentially, if *any* of the governors fail to win, place, or show in New Hampshire, they are all "done," leaving the fourth ticket to Dr. Carson.

Fairly or unfairly, Carly Fiorina's exclusion from the debate will have effectively ended her pursuit of the nomination, that is, unless the former CEO of Hewlett Packard can somehow pull off a miracle in an increasingly malicious milieu, where such miracles may prove to be impossible at long last.

"TRiUMPh" in New Hampshire—
The Death of Conventional Wisdom

10 February 2016

Once upon a time, they (being the pundits, the politicos, the experts) said it couldn't be done. "There's no way a brash and brazen 'reality show' celebrity can win an election against 'tried and true' mainstream Republicans with long-standing pedigrees, no way," they said. "There's no way a 'seventy-something year old socialist can threaten an inevitable political force like Hillary Clinton, no way."

Well, it happened.

By respective margins of more than fifty thousand votes apiece, Republican Donald Trump and Democrat Bernie Sanders soundly defeated their opponents and won the New Hampshire presidential primary elections of 2016.

So convincing were their margins of victory that *all* of the pundits, *all* of the politicos, and *all* of the so-called experts who thought that they knew *everything* that was needed to be known about politics received a message, loud and clear, that they don't know "flip" about politics at the end of the day.

Trump, who bested his nearest rival with a percentage that more than doubled John Kasich, who had devoted himself to a strategy that heavily invested both time and treasure into winning the New Hampshire primary, beat Kasich *and* the rest of the "mainstream" Republicans quite handily. Trump has also retaken the lead in the quest for the Republican nomination going into the Nevada, South Carolina, and Super Tuesday contests, which will ultimately decide who will be the GOP nominee. Coming in third behind Trump and Kasich, Ted Cruz, who was not expected to do well in New Hampshire and did not expend much comparative effort into winning the Granite State, *still* bested Jeb Bush and Marco Rubio and defied the conventional wisdom that said, "an evangelical cannot do well" in a comparatively secular state like New Hampshire. The remaining candidates, Chris Christie, Ben Carson, and Carly Fiorina, did so poorly that the future of their own campaigns largely remains in doubt.

Over on the Democrats' side, Bernie Sanders (I-VT) used a combination of his state's proximity to New Hampshire, a groundswell of enthusiasm on the part of young voters, and a ponderous gap (93% to 5%) in comparatively perceived honesty and trustworthiness, to trounce the once-inevitable Hillary Clinton. He did so by more than a three-to-two margin of twenty-two percentage points. Clinton, who had hoped to attain a single-digit margin in defeat, had these same hopes crushed in the snowdrifts of a New Hampshire winter. Moreover, Sanders, who lacks both the political machinery and control of the mainstream media that is Hillary Clinton's, is now looking at a possibility, however remote, to continue his campaign into the Democrats' national convention this summer, turning conventional wisdom on its ear. If Hillary cannot turn around a three-pronged triad of perils associated with her handling of e-mails, the selling of favors vis-a-vis the Clinton foundation, and her own angry and caustic persona, her eventual nomination is anything "short" of the lock that it once was.

Essentially, the Republican tickets out of New Hampshire are four: Trump, Cruz, Rubio, and perhaps Bush, because despite his impressive second-place showing, John Kasich can only last at the expense of Jeb Bush, who has much more money and resources than has the Ohio governor. Rubio himself must either win or place in South Carolina and Nevada, or he is through as a candidate for the top spot.

As both of these contests, Democratic and Republican, head toward much warmer climates, the vicious and frosty attacks that America saw in New Hampshire will only heat up and become more incendiary in the six weeks to follow.

Get ready and take out the sunblock.

Part IV

A Murky Future

Chapter 12

The Future of Politics

In re Killing the Beast

23 June 2014

Revelations that the IRS has supposedly lost Lois Lerner's e-mails and that her hard drive allegedly crashed and then was disposed of (along with seven others who were also subject to Congressional inquiry), not to mention that these instances occurred one year before Congress was notified last week, will prove to be the smoking gun of corruption that is the *sine qua non* of the Obama presidency, far and away the most corrupt administration in U.S. History. Obama succeeded where Nixon failed in using the IRS to target his political opponents (remember the second article of Nixon's impeachment, which he avoided by way of resigning his office, accusing his administration of **attempting** to use the IRS in this manner, which the IRS rebuffed at the time), and it is clear that Lois Lerner notified other agencies outside the Treasury Department of confidential taxpayer information which launched separate inquisitions by OSHA, the FBI, and others on private citizens, and this much is what we know so far.

The time has come for Congress, vis-a-vis Speaker John Boehner, to appoint a special select committee on IRS abuse and a Special Prosecutor to subpoena her and others to testify regarding these abuses. That much is certain.

Having said this, and very much aside this particular scandal, the time has come for the complete elimination of the Federal Income Tax as we know it, to abolish the Internal Revenue Service completely, and effectively repeal the 16th Amendment to the United States Constitution. This will require, in order:

1. A Bill from the Republican-led House of Representatives to abolish the Internal Revenue Service in the Spring of 2015
2. A Republican-controlled Senate to approve the bill and send it to the president for signature on January 20, 2017
3. A Republican president to sign the bill on January 21, 2017

The Federal Income Tax Code, comprising all of 9,831 *sections*, has become so inherently corrupt, so onerous, and so selective in its power to tax some and exempt others that the only real beneficiaries of these complex regulations are CPAs, tax attorneys, and employees of the Internal Revenue Service, along with the lobbyists who fund the campaigns of politicians to add to it every year.

This must end.

Since it is universally accepted that this country prefers to have a progressive tax system, whereby the affluent pay more taxes than either the middle class who pay a substantial part of their income in taxes and the poor who pay no income taxes, there is a very simple way to fund the federal government, and that is to replace, not augment, but REPLACE the Federal Income Tax with a Consumption Tax (i.e., Sales Tax) on all products and services purchased. Since wealthy people spend more than middle class and the poor, taxing all consumption would necessarily mean that the rich would continue to pay more taxes because they spend more money, and the same would apply to businesses as well. Hence, no more complicated tax code, no more exemptions on anything, no more write-offs, no more corruption, and, by God, no more abuse by government employees at the direction of their president to use their power to harass political opponents.

Now it is clearly understood that such a measure would meet the ire of the CPA Lobby, the Tax Attorneys Lobby, and all such lobbyists who make their living by further complicating an already unworkable tax system. Let these lobbyists partner with their Democratic allies in the House and Senate to try and defeat this initiative in the wake of the IRS Abuses taking place. *Please* let the Republican Party, the same Republican Party that brought about the abolition of slavery 150 years ago, have the wisdom and the courage to say "no" to these special interests and become the Republican Party who will abolish the 16th Amendment to the Constitution and scrap the tax code in its beastly entirety. Nothing else would assure their winning the U.S. Senate in 2014 and the White House in 2016 more (what's in it for them). Nothing else would jumpstart the economy more (what's in it for us, with larger paychecks in the form of take-home pay). Nothing else would ensure that the Obama IRS abuses never ever happen again.

Taxation

17 April 2015

In *Julius Caesar,* Act I, Scene 1, William Shakespeare begins with, "Beware the Ides of March," but it is the "ides" of April which terrorize and traumatize taxpayers across the country.

April 15th, the day Federal Tax Returns are due, is a day in which no tax-paying citizen can cherish. We should know. All told, I paid just under $39,000 in income and income-based taxes, and I only earn in the five figures, which means that, taken together, Federal, Social Security, State, Medicare, etc., almost 49% of what I earned got gobbled up by the government at one level or another, and that does not include the sales taxes we pay when we purchase anything, or the real estate taxes on my home, or the personal property taxes on my automobile. Is that fair? If you say yes, then you are either an idiotic socialist who believes I did not earn that money despite the fact that I have been working my ponderously fat keister off since I was a teenager, or you believe that I am merely a slave to the government and not an individual who is guaranteed the pursuit of happiness, as stated in the Declaration of Independence.

Okay, enough of my personal rant, except to say that we as a nation are over-taxed, *waaaaaaay* over-taxed. When one considers the tens of thousands of pages of tax code that exists here in the United States, such an enormous kluster-phuck of confiscatory and, in some cases, exculpatory tax code is by definition inherently corrupt. Were it not so complex, it would not be corrupt either.

The various lobbies, in particular the CPA lobby, the ABA lobby, the tax attorney lobby, are what is getting in the way of tax reform. Why? They want it to be as complex, corrupt, and kluster-phucked as possible because the more complex, corrupt, and kluster-phucked it is, the more business they can generate as a result of it being so.

The very fact that the average American needs professional help in preparing his/her tax return bears witness to this inherent corruption. It should be as easy as reporting one's income, reporting one's withheld taxes, indicating the tax actually owed from a table, and either sending or receiving a check to make up the difference, all on the back of a postcard, *but* that would endanger the livelihoods of CPAs and attorneys (particularly tax attorneys), and their continued greasing of the hands of politicians in Washington will ensure evermore complication and kluster-phuck with every passing tax year, that is, unless *real* change is made.

Then again, there is the IRS targeting of conservative organizations applying for 501(c)(4) tax exemptions, originally and falsely blamed on rogue operatives in the IRA Cincinnati office, which have now been traced to the IRS Headquarters in Washington. The former Commissioner of the IRS, Doug Shulman, went to the White House 138 times during his tenure, when the targeting was going on, but in Congressional testimony said that he could only recall an Easter egg hunt as the reason for one of these visits and could not remember why he went there on the other 137 occasions. Then two years after Lois Lerner's e-mails were subpoenaed by Congress, these e-mails suddenly have vanished into thin air due to a hard-drive crash and the subsequent disposal of the computer's hard drive conveniently waylaying and preventing investigation into e-mails Lerner had sent to government entities outside the Treasury Department, e-mails which might otherwise have revealed IRS communication to other government entities like OSHA and the FBI, which also launched investigations into businesses run by taxpayers who supported these same conservative organizations. Also noteworthy was the fact that seven other IRS officials, being tied to the IRS abuse scandals, also somehow had the 'misfortune" of hard drive crashes and lost e-mails. All the while, Obama insists that there is "not smidgen of corruption" in this arena. Well, this wouldn't be the first time President Obama has played fast and loose with the truth, and it won't be the last either.

So what to do? Eliminate all income taxes. Eliminate all estate taxes (which fall particularly hard on family businesses and family farms). Eliminate entirely the corporate tax, which at its current level is the world's highest (which is why so much of our wealth is disappearing overseas). Eliminate all forms of taxes as they exist today and replace them all with consumption taxes. The rich will pay more taxes because the rich buy more products and services and tax consumption at every level so that there is no exemption and no way of getting around the consumption taxes. If the rich choose to try to circumvent this consumption tax by purchasing their products overseas, they can also pay the import duties when they bring these goods back to the United States. This would by design ensure that everyone, *everyone* pays "their fair share" and would also ensure that a progressive tax system (meaning the rich pay more) applies to everyone with no exceptions, no loopholes, no deductions, and at long last no tax return preparation, and *no IRS* (as we know it today).

The candidate and the party who espouse this will have my vote in 2016, and I hope that such a candidate and party will have your vote, too.

Pondering the Impossible (thank God for *that*) . . .
If I were President . . .

9 June 2015

Many of my liberal friends would produce a considerable amount of emesis, were yours truly ever elected President of the United States; change that, many of my conservative *and* liberal friends would . . . change that, again . . . *all of my friends* would produce a considerable amount of emesis, were yours truly ever elected President of the United States.

Because it will never happen; relax, sports fans.

But *what if,* what *would* I do during my term of office? Hmmm . . . well . . .

First, I would send to Congress a bill that would in effect outlaw lobbying of all public officials who have been elected to federal office. It's very difficult to clean up a brothel if you don't rid the establishment of the whores as well as their johns. And the time has come to put public service back into public service.

Second, I would send a bill to Congress that would limit service in the U.S. House of Representatives to three consecutive terms, limit service in the U.S. Senate to two consecutive terms, and limit appointments to the U.S. Supreme Court to twenty years. This would put an end to the "same old, same old."

Third, I would send a bill to Congress effectively ending all foreign aid and investment to any country which does not guarantee freedom of religion, universal suffrage, and due process of law. You want our money, then adopt our freedoms, period.

Fourth, I would send a bill to Congress effectively ending all aid and financial support to the United Nations OR limit such aid and support to a dollar amount equal to the average aid and support given to the UN by all of the remaining countries who are members of the UN. We shouldn't be paying the lion's share of a club that treats us as though we were nonmembers.

Fifth, I would send a bill to Congress effectively announcing a comprehensive trade embargo on the nations of Iran, North Korea, Syria, and any other nation who violates the international nuclear proliferation accords and cease and desist from financially aiding and investing in any nation who would continue to trade with these countries. You are either with us or against us, and we put money where our interests are well served, period. Sixth, I would send a bill to Congress effectively ending all individual, corporate, and estate taxes entirely and replace this with a consumption tax at all levels of commerce instead. Attached to this bill would be funding for the tax attorneys and certified public accounts who would find themselves out of work as a result of this legislation, because to have a system requiring their assistance is in and of itself inherently corrupt.

Seventh, I would send a bill to Congress eliminating the Departments of Commerce, Education, Energy, Health and Human Services, Veterans Affairs, Agriculture, Interior, Labor, Housing and Urban Development, Transportation, and Homeland Security, as well as the EPA. As part of this legislation, I would turn all of these departmental functions over to the several states and, if not practicable, over to the remaining departments of Defense, State, Treasury, and Justice. A vastly smaller and manageable federal government is far more efficient and far less costly than the obesity of government that exists today.

Eighth, I would send a bill to Congress effectively putting the elimination of ISIS and Radical Islamic extremism into the well qualified hands of the Department of Defense, with an admonition they can and must do whatever it takes to rid the entire world of this menace. I would also give them one year to complete this mission or find other work to do if they cannot. If one is going to get rid of a "cancer," we should start by removing the "cancerous cells," and we need to leave this up to the experts who know far more about military strategy than the rest of us.

Ninth, I would send a bill to Congress that would, first, build an impenetrable wall along our southern border from the Pacific Ocean to the Gulf of Mexico; second, put an embargo against all immigration for a period of no less than five years and require anyone who has entered this country illegally to either, a) apply for U.S. citizenship (which would entail taking mandatory classes in and passing English literacy tests as well as tests in the U.S. Constitution, government, and citizenship) or b) be declared ineligible for employment in any trade or career. Those not wishing to do so would be deported to the countries of their origin. My Sicilian grandfather arrived here with twenty-five cents in his pocket and a third-grade education. He learned to speak seven languages and had to pass a citizenship test in order to remain here. If he could do this, then anyone else should be able to do what this legislation proposes. Tenth, once all of the above are enacted into law and put into place, I would send a bill to Congress requesting that they impeach their president because, after getting all the above accomplished, I would be so tired and exhausted that I would not be able to effectively function as President of the United States, any longer.

So there you have it: my ten-point program for my supposed presidential term, beginning in the year 2021 if a Democrat is elected or beginning in the year 2025 if a Republican is elected, does a good job, and is re-elected. Why the hell not? After all, I am only about a hundred million dollars or so away from launching my candidacy!

In re — The Proper Role of the Republican Party

21 July 2015

In all of the kerfuffle of the ill-considered way that Donald Trump assailed John McCain this past week, what has been lost is the great divide within the Republican Party, a divide which has cost them five presidential elections in the last forty years (1976, 1992, 1996, 2008, and 2012) and control of both houses of Congress during much of this time. Unlike the Democrats who are always, ALWAYS united during presidential elections, Republicans have not been so united since the re-election of Ronald Reagan in 1988, and that election was the first time Democrats confronted a truly unified Republican Party since Dwight Eisenhower ran for re-election in 1956.

In looking at the divide within the GOP, a broad generalization would find that this divide exists between the GOP moderates (a.k.a. the Establishment Republicans), as personified by Nelson Rockefeller, Richard Nixon , Gerald Ford, George H.W. Bush, Bob Dole, John McCain, Mitt Romney, John Boehner, Mitch McConnell, etc., and GOP conservatives, as personified by Barry Goldwater, Ronald Reagan, Newt Gingrich, Trey Gowdy, Jason Chavitz, etc. (For the purposes of this discussion we have omitted the sixteen current candidates running for the 2016 Republican Nomination).

While Democrats have a predisposition to rally around their party's nominee, be they moderately liberal or extremely liberal, Republicans have an unfortunate tendency to hold out for the "right" candidate, meaning that moderate Republicans refuse to support conservative Republicans and conservative Republicans refuse to support moderate Republicans, all of which more than delights their Democratic adversaries, as well as the *de facto* running mates of Democratic nominees, also commonly known as the mainstream media.

Conservative Republicans find this tendency most distasteful for the simple reason that it allows Democrats and their allies in the mainstream media to fracture what would otherwise be a united Republican front. It also allows the Democrats and their mainstream media allies to paint *all* Republicans as right wing extremists, regardless of whether they are moderate or conservative. One look at the past ten presidential elections and all ten of the Republican nominees were labeled as "extreme" even though, in reality, only one of them has been a true conservative (Reagan) and the other has been a semi-conservative (George W. Bush). What is the message? Regardless of who the Republicans nominate in 2016, that person will quickly find himself/herself so labeled as a right-wing extremist, regardless of their position on any issue, for the simple reason that it will be a signal to all of the identity constituencies, blacks, Latinos, gays, pro-abortionists, union members, and those on the dole, to queue up and vote for the same Democratic politicians who have managed to keep them in the fold and in the harness since the 1940s. It's not that conservative Republicans in particular have ignored any of these specific constituencies, but rather they have in fact offered non-governmental alternatives to those governmental solutions, which the Democrats are so famous for offering.

The folly of moderate Republicans is that they have an unfortunate tendency to imitate, if not duplicate, the programs and platforms of the Democrat Party, which begs the question "why have two parties if they are the same?"

This is precisely what far too many Republicans, especially establishment Republicans, have failed to grasp, especially when they find that the keys to the White House are in possession of their Democratic opponents. In their efforts to be comparatively bipartisan, the "go-along, get-along" cabal of establishment Republicans have ceded far too much ground in the overarching political debate, even before the "battle" is joined. If the Republican Party is ever going to "get back in the game," as it were, they must differentiate themselves from the Democrats and stop trying to imitate, much less duplicate, the Democrat Party's platform positions. Otherwise, all one is left with effectively is a one-party state not unlike that which exists in Russia.

It is indeed unfortunate that the resultant graying of lines between supposed conservatives and liberals have left this country a bickering, albeit sickening, mass of gelatin between two parties that in the final analysis are almost identical in their pursuit of ever-expansive government and political stasis. What this country needs really is a true election between two distinct political philosophies, i.e., a contest, say, between a Bernie Sanders and a Ted Cruz, so that this country at long last can settle the abiding issue of what type of country it wants to be, a socialist country which provides all things to all people like the ones we would find in Europe, or a free-market economic powerhouse that would elevate all people to their fullest potential with the inherent virtues of self-sufficiency, individual liberty, and the unfettered pursuit of happiness and prosperity that once made this country the envy of the world.

Yet if this election turns out to be, as the pundits would have us believe, a contest between Hillary and Jeb, the can will once again be kicked down the proverbial path of pathetic posturing that sees the greatness of this country slip further and further into the dustbin of history. So while we argue as to whether or not "the Donald" owes an apology for his inartfully stated characterization of Senator McCain, let us resolve to keep our eyes on the prize of national renewal and the destiny of this nation that in the last seven years has lost its way.

In re Term Limits — An Idea Whose Time Has Come

19 August 2015

Would-be and wanna-be constitutional "experts" will take issue with this, but the time for the imposition of term limits has come and is most likely long overdue. Not since the twenty-second amendment was enacted into law in 1951 has the United States Constitution addressed the issue of term limits, and this amendment only addressed the presidency, limiting a president to two four-year terms. Nothing has been done to limit the terms of U.S. senators, representatives, or for that matter, Supreme Court justices. Doing so would require constitutional amendments, and given the seemingly addictive nature of holding congressional office, such action would most likely have to be initiated through state conventions, *thirty-seven* of them to be precise. After all, what self-respecting congressman or senator would *ever* support anything that would limit his/her tenure in office?

The "Whorehouse on the Hill" (a.k.a. the U.S. Capitol) whose members on both sides are, okay, we'll call it what it is, *bribed* by well-connected "johns" (a.k.a. lobbyists) to do their bidding, are merely plying their trade in the halls of the Capitol and in their own offices. *That* is the narcotic that keeps these political prostitutes from wanting to relinquish their office. As much as we would all love to believe this bunch is motivated purely by public service, only the naïve would truly believe this. As evidenced by their own recent rulings, it is not unthinkable that such malfeasance has even made its way into the sacred halls of the U.S. Supreme Court, and given its proximity to Capitol Hill, this is not surprising because any city's red-light district always has more than one house of ill-fame located within its confines. Sorry to say, but the only *real* difference between this area of D.C. and the red-light district in any large city is the architecture.

So, without further ado, let us put forth the following four points as an idea for discussion and consideration:

1. House of Representatives – Members should be limited to three two-year terms and then ineligible

for returning to the House for six years thereafter.

2. Senate—Members should be limited to two six-year terms and then ineligible for returning to the Senate for sixteen years thereafter.

3. Supreme Court Justices—Members should be limited to a single twenty-year term and then ineligible to return for life.

4. Lobbying of any elected/appointed official, where an exchange of money or financial benefit is involved, should be henceforth deemed illegal and punishable by imprisonment of no less than ten years for both the lobbyist *and* the elected/appointed official.

Such action would maintain the constitutionally intended balance of power between the three branches of government and would go far to clean up the cesspool that is our nation's capital. Those aspiring to office would then be more likely to serve the nation's interest, rather than lining the pockets of their pinstriped suits. Most importantly, we would be closer to that cherished idea of government of, by, and for the people.

Any objections? Then write your congressman, as we are certain he/she will have plenty of objections, much to our own chagrin and demise.

Chapter 13

The Future of America

Race to the End or the End to Race—
From O.J. to Trayvon and Where We Must Go

12 July 2013

Like most of us who were born at a time when the playing field was not level among the races, I have witnessed the transformation of a society that has sought to eliminate discrimination in matters as divergent as education, hiring, lunch counters, and housing, and no one in their right mind can draw any comparison between the United States that existed in 1958 (the year I was born) and the United States in 2013, when it comes to how we as a society view the factor of race in our public and, to an extent, our private discourse.

Take yourselves back to the O.J. Simpson murder trial. When asked as to whether or not O.J. Simpson was guilty of murdering Nicole Brown Simpson and Ronald Goldman, the answer very much depended upon the race of the person being asked. Generally speaking (and, yes, there are always exceptions), if the person being asked was white, the answer was "yes, he did it," and if the person being asked was black, the answer was "no, he was framed." Despite overwhelming evidence that would have convicted Simpson of the murder, were it not for his lawyer, Johnnie Cochran's playing the so-called "race card" in his final appeals to the jury, Simpson would have spent the rest of his life in prison for a premeditated murder that no one else could have possibly committed. Yet the verdict did not seem to matter as much as the feelings of people who considered the eventual outcome of that verdict, and the opinion of O.J.'s guilt or innocence still very much breaks along racial lines all of these years later.

Fast forward to 2012. Trayvon Martin got into a scuffle with George Zimmerman in Sanford, Florida. During the scuffle in which Zimmerman's nose was broken and his head lacerated, Zimmerman shot Martin in what he claimed to be self-defense. There was not enough evidence at the time for Zimmerman to be charged with homicide. Enter Al Sharpton and Jesse Jackson, who have made careers of race-baiting, the Mayor of Sanford, and then no less than the Obama/Holder Justice Department, and the result of their collective influence resulted in Zimmerman's indictment on second-degree murder charges, charges that would not have been brought if the two men involved were of the same race. Add in the media circus (just as it was added into the Simpson murder trial), and you have the perfect recipe for the same stirred-up emotions that defy reason, which took place in the aftermath of the acquittal of the LA police, charged with the beating of Rodney King so many years ago.

At the time this is being written, the jury's verdict is yet to be decided in the Zimmerman trial. Never mind the fact that Mr. Zimmerman is part white, part Hispanic and, as I have been told, part black as well (he claims to be one eighth black). He is *perceived* to be white, and unfortunately this adds to the hubris surrounding this trial. Once again, the view of guilt or innocence depends largely upon the person being asked, just as it was during the O.J. Simpson trial. If one is white, the tendency is to believe that this is a case of self-defense. If one is black, the tendency is to believe that Trayvon Martin was the targeted victim of racist "wanna-be cop," despite no testimony or evidence that remotely suggests that George Zimmerman is a racist.

Whatever the verdict is, whether Mr. Zimmerman is found guilty of either second-degree murder or manslaughter or an outright acquittal, this trial won't end for him, his family, Trayvon Martin's family, or even for us. That is because the verdict and all of the attendant implications of the verdict will no doubt hang with all of us for the foreseeable future. At the end of the day, the race to the end, that end being the color- blind society that most all of us truly seek, will not end until we reach an end to race, in terms of the way each of us, white, black, Asian, Hispanic, views ourselves and our neighbors.

Until and unless that day comes, we're all screwed.

Questions to Ask Yourself

10 March 2014

Perhaps the best thing one can do to help one's self identify who one is politically speaking is to self-examine what one truly believes without the partisan posturing and media manipulation that we have all been subjected to for decades innumerable. Here is a simple self-test to assist in this self-examination. Be honest with yourself and don't equivocate, and where you truly stand will be reflected in the answers you have chosen.

1. Do you believe that the United States is or should be exceptional and that the American people believe that our place in the world is one of good or evil?

2. Do you believe that our government should be the servant of the people or that people should be the servants of government?

3. Do you believe that the rights with which we are endowed are granted by government, or do you believe the power of government is power granted by the people?

4. Do you believe that the most important job assigned to the president of the United States is to preserve, protect, and defend the Constitution of the United States, or do you believe the most important job of the president is to ensure social justice by any means he/she deems as necessary to achieve those ends?

5. Do you believe in a true balance of powers existing between the legislative, executive, and judicial branches of government, or do you believe that the president can determine when his/her authority can override such balance of powers?

6. Do you believe in the sovereignty of the United States of America, or do you believe that the United States should be subjected to the sovereignty of international law and/or the United Nations?

7. Do you believe that the United States is a nation of laws which must be upheld in all cases, or do you believe that the president should be able to decide whether to enforce or not to enforce specific laws?

8. Do you believe that all individuals are entitled to receive equal justice under law, or do you believe that exceptions should be made to ameliorate past injustices with regards to race, creed, sex, gender identity, sexual orientation, and the like?

9. Do you believe that human needs such as housing, food, healthcare, and human wants such as internet service, transportation, and telephone communications are the responsibility of individuals, or do you believe that these things should be provided to us and guaranteed to us by the government?

10. Do you believe that those elected to office are entitled to act in what they believe will serve their own purposes, or do you believe that those elected to office should serve the will of the people in all cases?

Why We Need a *True* Independence Day

2 July 2015

July 4th, 2015 will mark the 239th anniversary of the signing of the Declaration of Independence in Philadelphia. To commemorate America's birthday, there will be the customary parades and fireworks displays and barbeques and picnics all across the land, just as there should be. Americans, the TRUE Americans who are not swept up in the anti-Americanism that seems to be the *cause celebre du jour* that has taken hold of many on the left, will no doubt celebrate America's birthday and all for which it has stood and still stands today.

This is the Independence Day which most of us revere and of which most of us are familiar.

However, there is a grievous need for another type of Independence Day, a *true* Independence Day, the type of Independence Day which will reaffirm all that has made us independent and thereby has guaranteed the freedoms that we all too often take for granted. In essence, we need an Independence Day which will revive the slumbering spirit of independence before we finally lose this spirit.

This spirit of independence has little to do with governmental largesse. In fact, it is this same sense of governmental largesse that has come to threaten our very freedoms and sense of independence as we know it.

This spirit of independence is thwarted by the demands for welfare and the transition to a welfare state. This spirit of independence evaporates with every new user added to the growing rolls of public assistance, EBT, extended unemployment benefits, pre-retirement social security distributions attributable to growing and specious disability payments, aid for dependent mothers, and other such programs, all of which have grown exponentially in the last decade. For every person thus put on the public dole, there is one less person who is independent and one more person who, albeit unintentionally, weakens our nation.

This spirit of independence is threatened by the growing clarion calls for universal (meaning government-provided) cradle-to-grave health care, as though good health were something that should be not only guaranteed as a right, but provided for by right when such an ideology does more than anything else to increase the burden on healthcare providers and take ever more earnings from those who still work for a living, by transferring their wealth to those who refuse to work for a living.

This spirit of independence is under attack by those who favor open borders and to those who believe that suffrage (the right to vote) should be extended to non-citizens who will increase dependency on social programs, the cost of which is already spinning well out of control. The costs of uncontrolled and illegal immigration, when measured in terms of the crimes being perpetrated by many entering illegally through our porous southern borders, are enormous and exponentially growing year by year.

This spirit of independence is assaulted by those who believe that post-high school education should be "free," meaning that it should be paid for by increased corporate taxation, despite the very fact that the United States already has the very highest corporate tax rate in the entire world. The strains that this ideology places upon those who pay their own tuition and those who must borrow money to pay for their own tuition does more than anything else to astronomically increase the cost of education to ridiculously high levels. These costs are increasing at such an a alarming rate that we are quickly approaching the day that we will see the margins of diminishing returns apply to the demand for college education; in essence, a college education will be deemed not worthy of the costs of acquiring a college education.

It has been said that a nation in which people depend upon government for everything is a nation of servants, that to depend upon government for everything will produce a system where the people are subject to the loss of personal freedom; in essence, we become enslaved to our masters in government who would seek to control all aspects of our lives in exchange for the largesse they provide.

This dependence is most certainly *not* that upon which our forefathers risked their lives, their property, and their sacred honor, as stated in the Declaration of Independence. They did not fight a war with Great Britain to create a nation of "suckling pigs" permanently attached to the teats of a massive "sow" that is government largesse. No, these patriots were the very expression of self-sufficiency and independence that once made this nation the greatest in the world. Yet now, those very things that made us so strong and independent are threatened to the point of extinction by the ever-increasing dependence on the state for everything we want and determine to be our entitlement.

On this, the 239th anniversary of American independence, let us resolve to reincarnate a spirit of *true* independence. Let us endeavor to revive the spirit of self-sufficiency and reacquire the can-do determination to make for ourselves a more perfect union without having to depend upon someone else to do this for us. Let us, as a nation, once again project a righteous indignation to persevere on, without having to depend upon a state that would seek to further enslave and constrain our desire to pursue our birthright for this day and for all time.

God bless you and the United States of America *forever*.

-FINIS-

Acknowledgements

I would be remiss if I were to fail to acknowledge some individuals, who made possible the publication of All That Rendered Trump (and what led up to his election).

First, there is my wife, Mary Ella, who first suggested that I begin a blogsite in September of 2015. Since that time, http://www.drewnickell.com and its 400+ essays have been read by tens of thousands in over 112 countries across six continents, has attracted more than 9,700 subscribers since its inception, and was the basis for the re-publication of this book. From the beginning of our relationship in the summer of 2014, she has been a constant and candid source of feedback and has encouraged me in all aspects of these endeavors.

Second, there is my mentor, Nora Wahl Firestone, who has opened numerous doors for me, both personally and professionally, and who steered my work towards its original publication by her honesty, counsel and tireless coaching. Without Nora's guidance, there simply would have been no book bearing my name, and there would have been no opportunity to act as her designated guest host on her own weekly Nora Firestone Show on WKQA-AM in Hampton Roads, Virginia.

Lastly, I would like to acknowledge the support of my publisher, Lynn Yvonne Moon of Indignor House who did so much to make the publication of this book happen. From the start of our friendship, Lynn has always encouraged me to pursue the possible at times when I had erroneously and otherwise thought the opposite.

To all these fine folks, I thank you from the bottom of my heart.

Drew Nickell, July 2020